Adobe® Photoshop®
LIGHTROOM® 3
Streamlining Your Digital Photography Process

NAT COALSON

WILEY

Wiley Publishing, Inc.

Adobe® Photoshop® Lightroom® 3: Streamlining your Digital Photography Process

Published by

Wiley Publishing, Inc.
10475 Crosspoint Boulevard
Indianapolis, IN 46256
www.wiley.com

Copyright © 2010 by Wiley Publishing, Inc., Indianapolis, Indiana

Published simultaneously in Canada

ISBN: 978-0-470-60705-3

Manufactured in the United States of America

10 9 8 7 6 5 4 3 2 1

For general information on our other products and services or to obtain technical support, please contact our Customer Care Department within the U.S. at (877) 762-2974, outside the U.S. at (317) 572-3993 or fax (317) 572-4002.

Wiley also publishes its books in a variety of electronic formats. Some content that appears in print may not be available in electronic books.

Library of Congress Control Number: 2010920664

Credits

Acquisitions Editor
Courtney Allen

Project Editor
Mimi Brodt

Technical Editor
Monte Trumbull

Copy Editor
Mimi Brodt

Editorial Manager
Robyn Siesky

Business Manager
Amy Knies

Senior Marketing Manager
Sandy Smith

Vice President and Executive Group Publisher
Richard Swadley

Vice President and Publisher
Barry Pruett

Book Designer
Nat Coalson

Media Development Project Manager
Laura Moss

Media Development Assistant Project Manager
Jenny Swisher

All photographs © Nathaniel D. Coalson

For my students and clients,
who have taught me so much

About the author

Nathaniel (Nat) Coalson is a travel photographer, instructor and writer based in Denver, Colorado. He has worked in the graphic arts since 1987. In addition to photography, Nat has worked professionally in graphic design, prepress, printing and Web development. His work has been exhibited extensively, received national awards and is held in numerous collections. Nat is an experienced instructor who provides training in photography, printing and digital imaging for private and corporate clients.

For more information and to see Nat's work visit www.NatCoalson.com.

CHAPTER ONE: GETTING STARTED

Preface

I've worked my entire adult life in digital imaging, from managing high-volume production departments to running my own photography and printing businesses. And for many years, I've been teaching photographers how to be self-sufficient when it comes to working with their digital images.

Having used all major image editing software released over the past twenty years, I now choose to use Lightroom because it allows me to work quickly, helps me deal with large numbers of images and lets me get back to enjoying the creative aspects of photography.

From my experience, I know how hard it can be to learn new ways of doing things–especially computer stuff. Unfortunately for a lot of photographers, struggling with digital processing can take the fun out of photography. Trying to figure out the intricacies of file formats, resolution, color management, etc., and even simply where to put all the files can be daunting tasks. Worse yet, sometimes it's hard just to know the right steps to get the best quality from a single photo!

It's my mission to ease your pain; to show you that you really can be in control of your entire imaging process, and help you develop a personalized workflow that fits your style and needs. My students frequently tell me how liberating this is: to comfortably handle all the files coming off the camera and residing on hard disks, to work methodically through a known sequence of steps and to produce finished pictures that you're proud to show other people. This is at the heart of the photographer's experience, and I want you to know this sense of confidence and capability.

I've taught large groups and individual photographers alike. Over the years I've learned where people get stuck. I understand the pitfalls new users face when first starting to use Lightroom as well as the concerns of more experienced users looking for ways to tweak their workflow for better performance. I want to help you overcome these challenges.

My goal for this book is to teach you to effectively use Lightroom 3 as quickly and easily as possible. My writing has been heavily influenced by my experiences working with clients and students, and I've approached the content of this book as I would tutor someone in a one-on-one training session. The order in which concepts are presented and the emphasis I give to certain aspects of the workflow are unique among books of its kind.

We'll start by reviewing some important, basic principles, such as working with Lightroom catalogs, the Lightroom workflow, color management, and an introduction to Lightroom 3's updated tools and screen interface. From there, we jump right in to importing images into Lightroom. This is followed by a step-by-step editing tutorial that will make your work much easier. Then we move on to in-depth explanations of how to perfect each photo for tone, color, contrast, sharpness and much more. After a detailed look at exporting images out of Lightroom, the next three chapters deal with presenting your work to others with prints, Web sites and slideshows. Finally, we'll wrap up with an in-depth look at advanced techniques for integrating Lightroom with other software.

The material presented in this book is appropriate for digital photographers working in all disciplines, at all skill levels. The information and tutorials are applicable to every kind of photography: from weddings and portraits to fine art landscape work, everyone can learn to streamline their digital photography process using Lightroom 3.

NAT COALSON
CONIFER, COLORADO
MAY 2010

Acknowledgements

The people listed below each played a significant role in the production of this book and I am very thankful for their support.

Monte Trumbull

Mimi Brodt

Courtney Allen

Tom Hogarty

Charles A. "CAZ" Zimmerman

CHAPTER 1

GETTING STARTED

1

Welcome to Lightroom 3

Welcome to Lightroom 3! I'm pleased to be your guide as we explore this powerful, exciting new photography software. If you've never used Lightroom before, you're in for a treat. For many photographers, using Lightroom has brought much of the joy back to the process of working with photos on the computer.

NEW FEATURE OVERVIEW

Those folks upgrading from previous versions of Lightroom will find a number of major improvements to functionality, plus some really useful new tools. Here's a brief overview of some of the new and improved features in Lightroom 3:

- Significant performance increases; faster operation, better quality

- Dramatically streamlined Import process

- Support for video and CMYK files

- Greatly improved sharpening and noise reduction

- Lens corrections and lens profiles to fix distortion, chromatic aberration, etc.

- Customizable watermarking

- Tighter integration with photo sharing Web sites like Flickr

- Totally customizable print layouts for any number of photos

- Options to export Slideshows as HD video with sound

- Lightroom can now do catalog backups when exiting the program

… and this is just scratching the surface! With all it offers, Lightroom 3 is an essential upgrade for all photographers using Lightroom.

How to use this book

This book was written for digital photographers capturing and processing lots of images. As a metadata editing platform, Lightroom represents a major change in how we work with our photos. The main purpose of this book is to give you the Lightroom skills to process your images more quickly and with greater confidence while achieving the highest quality results possible. Your expertise will lead to expanded creative freedom and the satisfaction of seeing your inner visions become real.

1

This book is not meant to be *read* as much as it is meant to be *used,* presumably while at your computer. Though the workflow is mostly presented in sequence, it's also helpful to jump from one topic to another as needs dictate. You can use the material to learn Lightroom from the ground up, or refer back to something later.

If you're new to digital photography, or have never used Lightroom, you will benefit from working through this book in a linear fashion. When you have a basic familiarity with the software and workflow, you can later refresh your knowledge by going straight to the section or page containing the shortcuts, tips and techniques appropriate for the task at hand. Before long, you'll know Lightroom inside and out—and that's when the real fun begins!

The content of this book assumes you have at least basic- to intermediate-level computer skills, are comfortable managing files on hard drives and removable media, and understand common computer operations such as copy/paste and manipulating dialog boxes.

I also assume you have a fundamental working knowledge of your camera and that you are capturing in raw format (or ready to start right away).

If you take away one thing from reading this book, I hope it's the full comprehension of what you are capable of doing in Lightroom. Understanding the depth of Lightroom's nuances takes time, but is well worth it. This software can truly change your photography for the better.

Shortcuts: Mac and Windows

A keyboard sequence that eliminates steps and makes performing a task faster. The Mac shortcut is listed first, followed by the Windows shortcut.

The shortcuts in this book are based on Lightroom 3, though most of them also work in earlier versions, and most will continue to work in future versions. Some of these shortcuts are not included in Lightroom Help or other documentation. This increases the possibility they may change from one version release to another. In a printed book, I can't guarantee that the accuracy of the published shortcuts will last forever. There's a list of some of the most useful shortcuts at the end of the book; you can stay current with the latest shortcut revisions online; Google "Lightroom 3 shortcuts" for Web sites offering the most current information.

Keyboard variations

On Mac, the "Apple" key and ⌘ (Command, or cmd) are the same. On Windows, Control and Ctrl are the same. (In some cases, the Control key is also used on Mac.) Option on Mac is the same as Alt on Windows.

1

Tip

Suggestions for speeding up the workflow, methods of processing or the best ways to approach a problem. Though some of the Tips are more important than others, they are all suggested reading.

Warning

Strong cautions against doing something a certain way, or explanations of tricky aspects of the workflow to watch out for.

Getting more help

There might be cases where (gasp!) you need more help than what's provided in this book. Below are some other good sources of instruction and information on Lightroom.

Lightroom Help

From within Lightroom, you can access Adobe's online help system, which is quite thorough on many topics. It's in the same place on Mac and Windows, under the Help menu➔Lightroom Help (F1).

Other Web sites

http://www.adobe.com/support/photoshoplightroom/
http://www.lightroomforums.net/
http://blogs.adobe.com/lightroomjournal/
http://lightroom-news.com/
http://www.lightroomqueen.com/

Social media

You'll find all kinds of useful Lightroom resources on Facebook and Twitter. These sites are also good places to ask questions.

My training services

For many years I've trained photographers at all levels, on many photography related topics from composition, to digital workflow, to printing. I offer classes and workshops throughout the year, many focused specifically on Lightroom, and also provide private instruction and consulting, in-person or over the phone. If you're stuck anywhere in the process of learning Lightroom or photography, I'll be happy to help! Feel free to email me at nat@natcoalson.com.

Also, in 2010 I will begin offering live webinars to teach Lightroom online. For more information visit www.LightroomWebinars.com.

Get the book spiral bound

It would be nice if we were able to release this book in spiral-bound form, but it's just not logistically feasible with a publication like this. So I recommend that you take the book to your nearest office supply store or copy shop, have them chop the spine off, and put on a plastic coil binding. This will allow the book to lay flat while you're working through the material.

Now, let's get started!

Hardware configuration

Following are the minimum requirements for a computer to run Lightroom 3:

Macintosh
- Intel based processor

- Mac OS X v10.5 or 10.6

- 2GB of RAM

- 1GB of available hard-disk space

- 1,024x768 display

- CD-ROM drive

Windows
- Intel® Pentium® 4 processor or equivalent

- Microsoft® Windows® 7, Windows Vista® Home Premium, Business, Ultimate, or Enterprise (certified for 32-bit and 64-bit editions), or Windows XP with Service Pack 3

- 2GB of RAM

- 1GB of available hard-disk space

- 1,024x768 display

- CD-ROM drive

If course, the minimum requirements are far from the ideal setup. To get the best performance from Lightroom, you should install it on a computer with a fast processor, as much memory as possible (including video memory), lots of available disk space and a modern operating system.

1

Installing Lightroom for the first time

Whether you're using a Mac or Windows machine, and you've downloaded the Lightroom installer from the Web or are installing from a packaged disc, the installation process is essentially the same. We'll assume you were able to successfully complete the installation (and optional registration) by following the instructions provided in the installer. If you weren't able to install Lightroom, you will need to consult Adobe's documentation.

Upgrading Lightroom from a previous version

Upgrading from previous versions of Lightroom can be significantly more complicated than doing a fresh installation for the first time. Before you jump right in to upgrading, there are a few important things to understand.

First and most critical, every major upgrade to the Lightroom program (and some minor ones) also require a *catalog upgrade.* During this process, your catalog from the old version is copied to a new file. The structure of the copied catalog is modified to support Lightroom's new features. We'll talk more about Lightroom catalogs momentarily; for now, just be aware that you'll need to allow Lightroom to upgrade your catalog to the version 3 format; see Figure 1–1.

Your old catalog will not be modified; in fact, this is where many people get confused. If you still have the earlier version of Lightroom on your computer, you could still run that older

Figure 1-1

program, using your old catalog. If you're not careful about this, you could end up working in several different catalogs without knowing it. You might also upgrade your old catalog multiple times, with each upgrade producing another copy of your old catalog.

For this reason, I strongly recommend that after you've successfully installed Lightroom 3, upgraded your catalog, and confirmed everything looks like it's running OK, you should uninstall the previous version of Lightroom and remove your old catalogs from your hard drives. (If this makes you nervous, just be sure to make backups first.)

About Lightroom catalogs

As mentioned previously, Lightroom uses database files, called *catalogs,* to manage your files and store the work you do on them. Any time you're working in Lightroom, you're working within a catalog.

Image files must be *imported* into a Lightroom catalog before you can work with them, during which Lightroom creates *records* of the photos within the catalog. (Importing photos is covered in Chapter 2.)

It might help to think of a Lightroom catalog like a department store catalog: it contains all the information *about* the items but *not the items themselves.* Maintaining these symbolic links between a Lightroom catalog and the actual files on disk is essential.

Lightroom catalogs are stored on the computer's hard drive as sqLite files with the extension .lrcat. Lightroom also uses other special files to work with your photos, which are located in the same folder as the catalog; see Figure 1–2.

	Lightroom 3 Catalog Previews.lrdata	Today	84 KB	Adobe Lightroom Data
	Lightroom 3 Catalog.lrcat	Today	844 KB	Adobe Lightroom Library
	Lightroom 3 Catalog.lrcat-journal	Today	60 KB	Document
	Lightroom 3 Catalog.lrcat.lock	Today	4 KB	Document

Figure 1-2

Let's take a look at how the Lightroom program works with its catalogs and your image files on disk.

The default catalog's location on disk

When the Lightroom application is first installed, it creates a new (empty) catalog file in these default locations:

- **Mac OS X:** User/Pictures/Lightroom 3 Catalog/Lightroom 3 Catalog.lrcat

- **Windows XP:** User\My Documents\My Pictures\Lightroom 3 Catalog\ Lightroom 3 Catalog.lrcat

- **Windows Vista and 7:** User\Pictures\Lightroom\Lightroom 3 Catalog\ Lightroom 3 Catalog.lrcat

If you've never moved the default catalog, or haven't created a new one, you will be working within the default catalog.

However, you can make additional catalogs, and store them on any hard drive, even one that's different from where your image files reside. The name and

1

location of catalog files have no direct effect on Lightroom's operation, so you can name your catalog whatever you like, and put it wherever you choose. (I keep my master catalog on the same external hard drive with the image files; it makes sense to keep the catalog file with the image files it relates to. This makes backups easier, as well as migrating to larger drives when necessary.)

Use Preferences or hold the Option or Alt key when launching Lightroom
You can set the preference for the default catalog in Lightroom Preferences. Or, press Option/Alt when launching Lightroom to see the Open Catalog… dialog box, in which you can load the default catalog, select another catalog or make a new one.

Catalog corruption
If you don't have a lot of experience using databases—especially for image editing and management—it may come as a shock if a problem with the Lightroom catalog makes your photos inaccessible. It is entirely possible that a Lightroom catalog could become corrupted and not be able to be opened or worked with in any way. **But in the vast majority of cases, a problem with the Lightroom catalog does not necessarily indicate a problem with the image files.** (Of course, in some cases an image file could itself be corrupt.)

⌘+Shift+O
or Ctrl+O
Open a different
catalog

USING MULTIPLE CATALOGS

You can use one or many catalogs to manage your photo library, though as of this writing the Lightroom application can only have one catalog open at a time. For example, some photographers might use different catalogs for work and personal photos, or a unique catalog for each specific client. Also, using temporary "working catalogs" you can maximize the potential of your workflow. One example of how using multiple catalogs can greatly enable your workflow is when traveling, and using Lightroom on a laptop, then returning home to your main computer. These scenarios are discussed in Chapter 9.

However, regardless of the numerous catalogs you may employ for specific purposes, for most photographers, using a single, "master" catalog for your complete library of photos is usually the best solution.

A Lightroom catalog can only contain one instance of a given image file, based entirely on the file name. And though a single image can be imported into any number of catalogs, this is something you need to do deliberately and carefully. Working on the same file—or worse yet, copies of the same file—in different catalogs can lead to real trouble.

Use meaningful names for catalogs

If you use multiple catalogs, name each one for its specific purpose and keep the names simple and functional. For example, if you're shooting a wedding, name the catalog for the client; if you're on a trip, name it for the trip, etc. **If you use just one catalog, sticking with the default name is fine!**

Find catalogs and eliminate unused ones

To find all the Lightroom catalogs on your computer, search in Finder or Explorer for folders and files containing the file extension .lrcat.

Double-click a catalog anywhere in the file system

Opening a Lightroom catalog in Finder or Explorer will launch the Lightroom application and load that catalog. Extending this method, you could place an alias or shortcut on your desktop to ensure you load the correct catalog when Lightroom starts.

Move data between catalogs

If you need to combine data from multiple catalogs, use the *Export from Catalog* and *Import from Catalog* menu commands. See Chapter 9 for more about this.

Always know the name and location of the catalog you're using

Many photographers have had big problems unknowingly using more than one catalog! As you can imagine, this can result in significant confusion and frustration. The easiest way to ensure that you're in the catalog that you intend is to check the name of the catalog, which is located in the window title bar in Lightroom's standard window mode; see Figure 1–3. You can also view the name and location of the current catalog in the Catalog Settings dialog box (accessed from the Lightroom menu on Mac OS X or the Edit menu on Windows); see Figure 1–4.

Lightroom 3 Catalog.lrcat - Adobe Photoshop Lightroom - Library

Figure 1-3

⌘+Option+,
or Ctrl+Alt+,
Open the
Catalog Settings
dialog box

CATALOG SETTINGS

Each Lightroom catalog has its own internal configuration for General, File Handling and Metadata options. Unlike the main Lightroom Preferences, which apply globally throughout the application and remain the same while

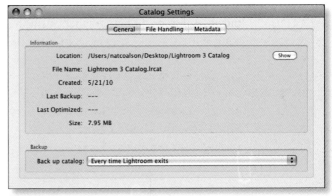

Figure 1-4

1

working in different catalogs, Catalog Settings only apply to the current catalog. Access Catalog Settings under the Lightroom menu for Mac and the Edit menu on Windows.

CATALOG BACKUPS

It's essential that you practice good backup habits when working with your Lightroom catalogs and the image files. If you back up frequently, you really won't have much to worry about. A recent backup (or several backups) removes much of the pain of something going wrong.

Lightroom provides its own backup functionality, determined in the Catalog Settings. Beginning in Lightroom 3, the catalog can now be backed up when you quit the program. The frequency of backups is determined by the Catalog Settings (under the Lightroom menu on Mac and the Edit menu on Windows). Note that with this feature, it's only the catalog that's backed up, not image files or previews.

I recommend that you back up your catalog after every major work session. To that end, I have my Catalog Settings set to "Every time Lightroom exits". You can always skip a backup if you want.

Carefully choose the location where you save your Lightroom catalog backups, on a hard drive other than where the main catalog is stored. You only need to keep your most recent two or three catalog backups (periodically clean out your backup folder).

Backups are discussed further in Chapter 2.

Lightroom previews

During an Import, and at other times while working in Lightroom, Lightroom reads the pixel data from image files and creates image *previews*, which are then also referenced by the catalog. The previews are temporary JPG files *rendered* in several sizes. Lightroom renders new previews whenever necessary while you're working on photos.

Lightroom's image preview files are stored **outside the catalog** in a separate package (refer back to Figure 1–1). When you're working on a photo in Lightroom, its previews are continually updated **but the actual image file on disk is never altered.**

A quick overview of Lightroom's previews (which are notably improved in version 3):

a. **Minimal**: used for displaying thumbnails (the smallest previews).

b. **Standard**: used for larger, single-image previews in the main preview area.

1

c. **1:1:** the largest previews in Lightroom, 1:1 refers to one screen pixel per one image pixel. You'll often be looking at 1:1 previews as you zoom in to look more closely at a photo.

Previews can be purged, deleted and re-rendered at any time, as long as Lightroom can find the original files on disk. Lightroom can't build new previews from missing files, or files stored on offline volumes. Previews are explained in context at various places throughout this book.

Maximizing Lightroom performance

Lightroom 3's processing routines have been re-engineered to provide faster response and better quality than in earlier versions. There are a few things you can to to ensure Lightroom is running at peak performance:

1. Keep ample free space on your system hard drive (where the Lightroom application is installed) and the drive that holds the Lightroom database and preview files. This is true for all photo-editing and imaging applications—you don't want to be working from a drive with limited free space, as data corruption may occur.

2. Load your machine with as much RAM as it will hold (or that you can afford). Lightroom likes to have lots of memory available.

3. If you have 4 GB of RAM or more, and your operating system supports 64-bit processing, make sure you're running Lightroom in 64-bit mode. If you're not sure what this means, you can find more information about it in the Adobe documentation.

4. Take control of your previews. Each time you make an adjustment to a photo, Lightroom has to render new previews. The speed it can do this depends on your computer hardware and the size of the original files you're working with. Remember that Lightroom maintains three separate previews for each image: thumbnail, standard size and 1:1. Lightroom will generate any previews it needs on-the-fly, sometimes this means you'll see a delay as Lightroom builds a preview. If Lightroom already has all the necessary previews rendered, moving between images should be quick. Using the commands on the Library→Previews menu or the contextual menu (discussed in Chapter 3), you can instruct Lightroom to discard and re-render the previews whenever you choose.

1

5. In Catalog Settings➔File Handling (see Figure 1–5), you can set the size of your standard preview, based on your screen size and how fast you want the preview redrawing to be. No need to use larger standard previews than what your display system is capable of handling.

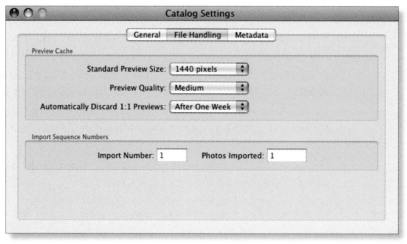

Figure 1-5

⌘+, or Ctrl+, Open Lightroom Preferences

6. Increase the setting for your Camera Raw cache, in Preferences➔File Handling (see Figure 1–6). I usually work with this set to between 3.0 GB and 8.0 GB.

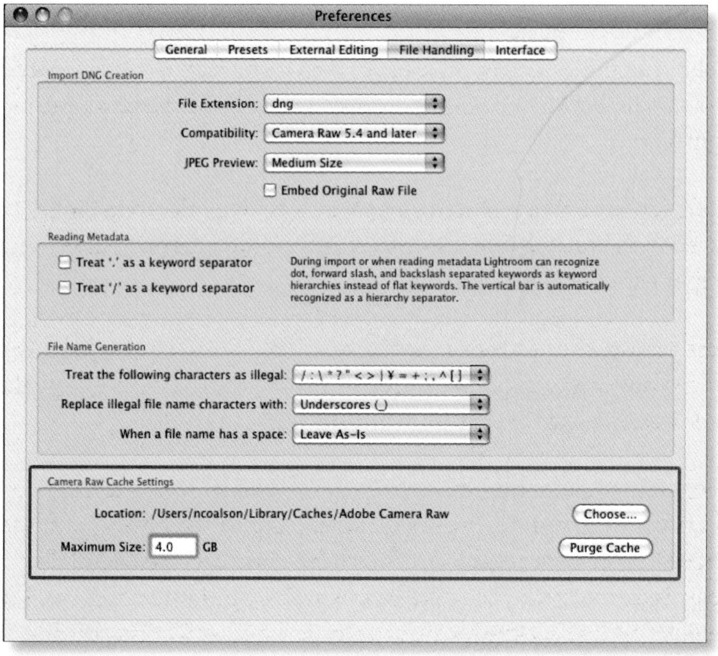

Figure 1-6

7. Optimize your database periodically—maybe every eight to ten days of work—using the command on File menu; see Figure 1–7.

Figure 1-7

8. When working in Lightroom, try not to select folders/subfolders with large numbers of images when you don't need to, because Lightroom will re-read all the files in the chosen source, attempting to get information about all previews and metadata. For example, if you click the All Photographs source from the Catalog panel, and you have many thousands of photos in the catalog, reading all those files can take a while. Click on a folder that contains only the images you want to work with. (Using Collections; see Chapter 3; is a more efficient way to organize your edited photos.)

Avoid force-quitting Lightroom whenever possible

If you experience what appears to be a crash in Lightroom, especially if you can still move the cursor, give it a few minutes to see if the application and/or operating system recover from the condition. Force-quitting Lightroom at any time and for any reason dramatically increases the likelihood of data corruption. Of course, sometimes force-quitting can't be helped… keep good backups!

What to do after a crash

If Lightroom unexpectedly quits on you, or you have to force quit or restart your machine, you need to proceed with care the next time you launch Lightroom.

While Lightroom has a catalog open, a "lock" file (shown in Figure 1–1) is placed in the catalog folder to ensure other programs on your computer can't tamper with the Lightroom data.

After a crash, the previous lock file may remain, and you may also see a Journal file. **Do not delete these files!** Lightroom will them to help restore the previous work session when the program is restarted.

Also, in these situations, there is the possibility of catalog corruption. If Lightroom tells you the catalog is corrupt and needs to be repaired, let it proceed. After a successful repair, optimize and back up the catalog. If the repair is unsuccessful, or the catalog is acting quirky, you may need to restore a previous catalog backup to use as your new master working catalog.

The Lightroom application window

When you launch Lightroom, the main window opens with the same settings and image selections that were in use when you last quit the program; see Figure 1–8. Lightroom's main application window is set up differently than any other program. Below is an overview of the screen layout, tools and controls. More detail about the specific operation of these interface controls is found in the context of the chapters that follow.

⌘+Q or Ctrl+Q
Closing the main Lightroom window quits the application

Figure 1-8

SCREEN MODES

F
Cycle through the three screen modes

⌘+Shift+F or Ctrl+Shift+F
Enter Full Screen mode and hide all panels. Pressing this shortcut again will enter Standard screen mode

The main Lightroom application window has three screen modes:

1. **Standard:** a floating, resizable window. May or may not fill your entire screen. Resize the window by clicking and dragging its sides or corners. Move the window by clicking and dragging the title bar at the top.

2. **Full Screen with Menubar:** fills your screen with the Lightroom application window. This window is not resizable.

3. **Full Screen:** like #2, but the main menu bar at the top of the screen is hidden. (This is my preferred screen mode.) As needed, put your mouse cursor at the top of the screen to access the menu bar. When you're finished, move away from the menu bar and it becomes hidden again.

L
Cycle through
the three Lights
Out modes

LIGHTS OUT

Lights Out dims or hides all the interface elements, showing only the photographs (see Figure 1–9). If no photographs are selected, all the thumbnails will remain visible in Lights Out. If one or more photos are selected, those will remain visible while the unselected photos will be hidden. There are three Lights Out modes:

- **Lights On:** this is the default state, where all interface elements and photographs are shown at full strength.

- **Lights Dim:** the interface is dimmed (by a percentage you can set in Lightroom Preferences).

- **Lights Out:** all interface elements are hidden (by a solid color, also specified in Preferences).

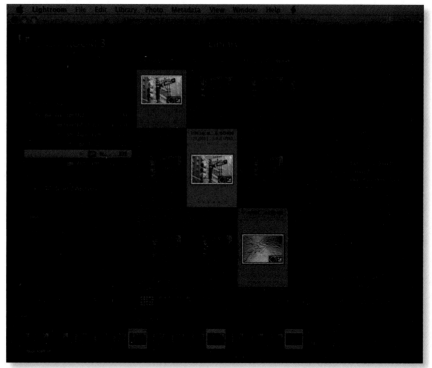

Figure 1-9

THE SECONDARY WINDOW

Lightroom offers support for dual monitors and, even with only one display, you can use the second window in a variety of ways. The second window (see Figure 1–10, next page) is a pared-down version of the main Library window and has its own layout and controls. (You can also play slideshows in the second window; see Chapter 8.)

1

Figure 1-11

Figure 1-10

Open the second window by clicking the button on the upper left side of the Filmstrip; see Figure 1–11.

Modules

All work in Lightroom is done in one of five *modules*. The modules provide tools and commands specific to each phase of the workflow. The modules can be accessed using the *Module Picker* (to the right of the top panel; see Figure 1–12) or by using various keyboard shortcuts.

G
Load the Library module in Grid view

Figure 1-12

E
Load the Library module in Loupe view

Library

This is where you organize, sort and manage your images. A limited subset of processing controls is also included (Quick Develop). See Chapter 3 for more information about Library.

D
Load the Develop module in Loupe view

Develop

Here you can process your photos to perfection. Cropping and straightening, tone and color adjustments, noise reduction, sharpening, creative effects… the list goes on and on. The Develop module is the core of Lightroom's image processing power; see Chapter 4.

⌘+Option+3 or Ctrl+Alt+3
Load the Slideshow module

Slideshow

In the Slideshow module you can design presentations for playback within Lightroom or exporting as video, PDF or JPG files. See Chapter 8 for information about working in Slideshow.

1

**⌘+Option+4
or Ctrl+Alt+4
or
⌘+P/Ctrl+P**
Load the Print
module

**⌘+Option+5
or Ctrl+Alt+5**
Load the Web
module

**⌘+Option+Left
and Right
Arrow or
Ctrl+Alt+Left
and Right
Arrow**
Go Back and
Forward in your
Lightroom work
session

Print

Lightroom's Print module gives you a variety of tools to create custom layouts and make prints. See Chapter 6.

Web

In Lightroom's Web module, generating Web galleries in HTML or Flash format is quick and easy. See Chapter 7.

Switching between modules

There are times when Lightroom's performance slows or seems to stall. Often this happens when switching between modules or tools. In most cases, it's best to wait (stop clicking!!) and let Lightroom finish the current process. You will often find that, even when Lightroom appears to have crashed, if you give it a few moments, the program will recover, finish processing and resume normal operation.

Main preview area

In Library and Develop, photos are shown in the center of the Lightroom window; see Figure 1–13. In the presentation modules, this area is used to preview the current layout. The size of the preview area is variable, based on the visibility and sizes of the panels.

Figure 1-13

1

Tab
Hides/show
the side panels

Shift Tab
Hides/show
all panels

F5
Hide/show the
top panel

Main preview background options

Right-click or Ctrl+click in the main preview background to change color and texture options; see Figure 1–14.

Panels

Around the main preview area, the Lightroom application window is divided into four *panels*. Lightroom's panels contain the majority of controls you will use to process your photos. Note that panels can't be "undocked", moved or floated in the main window; they are always in the same position. However, they can be hidden and resized as described below.

Figure 1-14

The contents of the left and right panels change within each module. Generally, left panels are used for organizing, batch processing and accessing presets and templates, while right panels contain tools used for applying specific settings to photos or output layouts. The top panel (Module Picker) and bottom panel (Filmstrip) remain consistent throughout all the modules.

TOP PANEL

The top panel contains the Module Picker (right) and the Identity Plate (left). During processing, Lightroom's progress indicators are also displayed in the Identity Plate area.

Identity Plates

At the far left of the top panel is the main Identity Plate (see Figure 1–15). You can customize it with your own text or graphic files. The main Identity Plate can be used in slideshows, Web galleries and print layouts, and in those modules you can also create additional Identity Plates.

Figure 1-15

Lightroom menu→Identity Plate Setup or Edit...→Identity Plate Setup

To customize and save Identity Plate presets. See Chapters 3 and 6 for more about using Identity Plates.

The Activity Viewer and Multithreading

When Lightroom is working on a process, the main Identity Plate is replaced with the Activity Viewer, which shows one or more progress bars (see Figure 1–16).

Lightroom is *multithreaded,* which means it can multitask: several operations can be performed at the same time. If more than one process is going, multiple progress bars are shown.

Figure 1-16

Stopping a process

To stop a process, click the small X at the right side of the progress bar.

Move on to other tasks

There is usually no need to wait for a process to complete before moving on to another task. For example, if you are in the middle of an import, you can still work on images already in the Library. If you're exporting a Web gallery, a batch of images, etc., the same applies.

F6
Hide/show
the Filmstrip

FILMSTRIP (BOTTOM PANEL)

The bottom panel, called the *Filmstrip,* shows thumbnails for the images in the current source (see Figure 1–17). The Filmstrip remains the same throughout all the modules. You can change the order of photos in the Filmstrip and the display of the thumbnails. There's more about this in Chapter 3.

Figure 1-17

1

LEFT PANELS

The contents of the left panels very from one module to another. Generally, the left panels provide access to files and templates within the selected module. Refer to Figure 1–17.

The Navigator Panel

F7
Hide/show the left panel group

⌘+Ctrl+0, 1, 2, 3 etc. or Ctrl+Shift+0, 1, 2, 3 etc.
Open/close panels in the left group

The Navigator (see Figure 1–18) is in the first position of the left panel group in the Library and Develop modules (it's called Preview in the output modules, where it functions a bit differently). The Navigator shows a preview of the selected photo, or the active photo if multiple photos are selected. The Navigator panel can be used to select *zoom ratios,* or levels of magnification. Selecting a zoom ratio in the Navigator enlarges the photo preview to that size.

But the Navigator offers more than just another preview. For instance, in Library, moving your mouse over folders or collections will show the first image in that source in the Navigator. And in Develop, Navigator shows previews of presets. Just roll your mouse cursor over the presets in the list, and Navigator will show you what that preset looks like applied to the selected image.

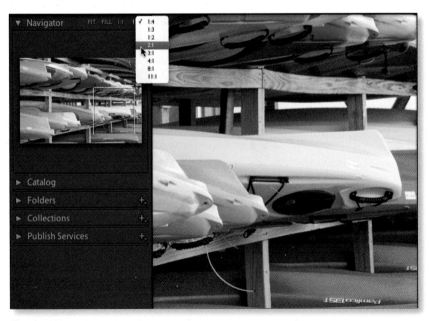

Figure 1-18

Zoom Ratios

Unlike other programs that specify magnification level with a percentage, Lightroom's zoom levels are based on the ratio of image pixels to screen pixels. 1:2 is one screen pixel to two image pixels. 4:1 is four screen pixels to one image pixel, and so on.

The preset zoom ratios are:

- **Fit:** fits the entire photo into the image display area.

- **Fill:** fills the preview area top-to-bottom with the image. The sides of images using landscape orientation may not be visible.

- **1:1:** one image pixel for one screen pixel.

- **User-selected setting:** the fourth zoom ratio shown uses the last custom zoom ratio you selected. Clicking this ratio will also display a popup menu for you to choose the custom zoom ratio.

Move around an enlarged preview with the Navigator.
When zoomed in to a photo, drag the white box in the Navigator preview to change the area shown in the main preview; see Figure 1–18.

RIGHT PANELS

In Library and Develop, the right panels include tools for modifying the photo(s). In the output modules, the right panels contain controls for changing layout settings.

F8
Hide/show the right panel group

Hiding and showing panel groups
The combined assemblages of the left and right module panels are typically referred to as *panel groups.* To hide a panel group, click its outer edge. Click again to show it. Or, when a panel group is hidden, you can temporarily show it by hovering your mouse cursor over the collapsed panel at the outer edge of the window. This is called Auto Hide/Show, and can be enabled or disabled. Auto Hide/Show allows you to temporarily access the panel group to make whatever changes are necessary, and when you move the cursor away, the panel group is hidden again. Right-click or Ctrl+click a panel edge to set options for Auto Hide/Show and syncing between opposite panels.

⌘+0, 1, 2, 3 etc.
or Ctrl+0, 1, 2,
3 etc.
Open/close
panels in the
right group

The state of hidden and visible panels persist for each module until you change them.

Show the panels you use; hide the others
I usually work with different panel groups hidden in each module. For example, in Library, I prefer to keep the right panel hidden and the left panel showing. This is because the left panel provides access to files in Folders and Collections, which I use a lot. I less frequently use the Library right panel to make metadata edits to files (mostly keywords). Conversely, in the Develop module, I usually work with the left panel hidden and the right panel showing, because the tools I use most often are in the right panel. (I may temporarily auto-show the left panel to apply Develop presets.)

Change panel size

Panels can be resized by dragging their edges. Wider panels shows longer file and template names and provides greater sensitivity for adjustment sliders. Narrower panels make more room for photos in the preview area.

Figure 1-19

To change the width of a panel group, position your mouse cursor over the inside edge of any panel; the mouse cursor changes to a double arrow; see Figure 1–19. Click and drag to resize the panel. Note that all panels have a minimum and maximum width. (These can be changed using third-party solutions such as Jeffrey Friedl's Configuration Manager; visit http://regex.info/blog/lightroom-goodies)

Change the size of Filmstrip thumbnails

Drag the bottom panel edge to resize it; this changes the size of the thumbnails in the Filmstrip; See Figure 1–20.

Figure 1-20

Expand and collapse individual panels

In addition to hiding and showing the entire left and right panel groups, individual panels can be expanded and contracted (see Figure 1–21). Click anywhere in the top bar of each panel to hide or show its contents (it's not necessary to click directly on the triangle).

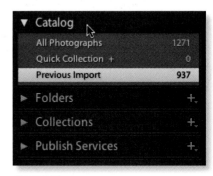

Figure 1-21

Expand All and Collapse All

Right-click or Ctrl+click on the panel header and select Expand All or Collapse All to open or close all the panels in the group.

Keep unused panels closed

Get in the habit of removing all unnecessary information from your working environment.

ADD AND REMOVE INDIVIDUAL PANELS

The individual panels in the left and right panel groups can be removed and restored from the main panel track as you see fit. Right-click or Ctrl+click on a panel header, then make selections from the contextual menu to show or hide individual panels or select Hide All/Show All; see Figure 1–22.

Note: the Navigator/Preview and Histogram panels cannot be removed.

SOLO MODE

When you enable *Solo Mode,* opening one panel closes all the others. This is my preferred way of working, except in the Library left panels, where it's often advantageous to have Folders and Collections open at the same time.

Right-click or Ctrl+click on any of the panel headers; select the option from the popup menu to enable Solo Mode.

Option+click or Alt+click on any panel header to open that panel and simultaneously toggle Solo Mode.

Shift+click on a panel header to open it *without* closing the previous one.

SCROLLING PANEL TRACKS

When multiple left and right panels are open, it's likely their contents will be too long for all the panels to show on the screen. In this event, scroll bars appear to allow you to move up and down within the panel track; see Figure 1–23. Click and drag the bar to scroll, or use your mouse wheel.

Figure 1-22

Figure 1-23

1

PANEL END MARKS

The *panel end mark* ornaments at the bottoms of the left and right panel groups (see Figure 1–24) are designed to let you know there are no more panels below. You can change the graphic used for the panel end marks, you can add your own, or you can remove them completely. Once you get used to the panels, these end marks become unnecessary. I prefer to leave them hidden to reduce screen clutter.

Right-click or Ctrl+click on or around the end mark and select a panel end mark from the list.

Add your own panel end marks

From the panel contextual menu, select Go to Panel End Marks Folder. You can find custom panel end marks on the Web, or create your own in Photoshop. Put the image files in the folder and restart Lightroom; your custom files will show in the list.

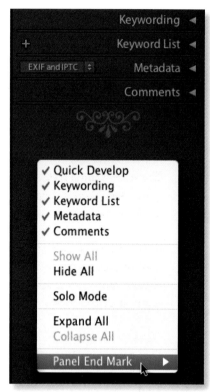

Figure 1-24

Panel input controls

Within the panels, Lightroom provides several types of software controls to edit and process your photos. Most can be manipulated using either your mouse or the keyboard. Some require you to select from a menu; others let you type directly into text boxes.

Triangle buttons

Throughout Lightroom's panels there are very small and easily overlooked black triangle-shaped buttons; see Figure 1–25. These open and close a subsection of the panel, revealing or hiding more controls.

Figure 1-25

Look closely

Many of Lightroom's interface widgets are very small and—using various shades of gray, black and white—can be easily missed. Get in the habit of looking very closely at the Lightroom interface to discover the full set of controls.

Arrow buttons

These are found on the Quick Develop panel (see Figure 1–26). While most of Lightroom's settings are absolute (applying a specific value), the arrow button controls are relative—they are applied on top of whatever settings are

Figure 1-26

already present. The single arrow buttons apply changes in smaller increments than the double arrows. See Chapter 3 for more about Quick Develop.

Sliders

Particularly in Develop, the sliders (see Figure 1–27) are the most common method of making adjustments to photos. Lightroom's sliders can be adjusted in several ways:

- Drag the slider with your cursor.

- "Scrub" the slider's numeric value left and right using the mouse.

- Position your cursor anywhere over the slider and then use the up and down arrow keys to increase or decrease the value.

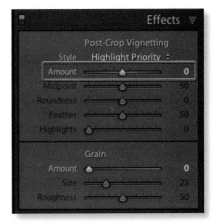

Figure 1-27

- Double-click the field and type in a numeric value.

- Double-click a slider to Reset it to its default value.

Press Return or Enter after typing

Always be sure to press Enter or Return when you're done typing text into a field anywhere in Lightroom. This reduces the chance of accidentally typing something into a text box when you're trying to use a shortcut.

1

Esc

If you change your mind typing into a text or dialog box, or to deactivate a tool, press Esc to cancel.

Option or Alt

In many areas of Lightroom's interface, holding the Option or Alt key reveals additional functions, such as hidden controls, buttons and options. For example, the Quick Develop panel in Library shows additional controls when Option or Alt is held down. The Sharpening panel in Develop has uses for Option/Alt. And, holding Option/Alt changes the Export button to Export Catalog. Memorize the most important places the Option/Alt key is useful, then as you're working, periodically press the key and watch how it changes the options on the screen. Many more functions become readily available.

Hide-and-seek interface widgets

Throughout Lightroom there are controls that will only show if they are relevant to the selected photo or photos. In cases where these controls don't apply, they are hidden from view.

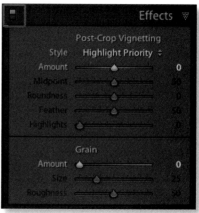

Panel switches

Most panels that provide controls for image adjustments (and Filmstrip filters) provide a small "switch" that allows you to disable/enable the adjustments for that panel. Like a light switch, up is "on" and down is "off". See Figure 1–28.

Figure 1-28

Look for these switches in numerous places throughout Lightroom's interface. In some cases, they may be oriented left/right. In all cases, they perform the same function: enabling and disabling the effects of that panel or control.

T
Hide/show
the Toolbar

Toolbars

Each module has its own *Toolbar* containing various tools for that module; see Figure 1–29. The Toolbar is shown at the bottom of the main preview area and can

Figure 1-29

be hidden and shown. (Most of the tools and functions on the Toolbar can also be performed using shortcuts; once these are committed to memory, it's possible to work most of the time with the Toolbar not showing.)

Change what shows in the Toolbar

At the right side of the Toolbar is a button that activates a menu that you can use to customize the contents of the Toolbar specific to each module; see Figure 1–29.

Lightroom Preferences

Many of Lightroom's interface options can also be customized in the Lightroom Preferences (under the Lightroom menu on Mac and the Edit menu on Windows.)

Tooltips

Place your cursor over part of the interface and let it remain for a few seconds (without moving or clicking) to see a popup *tooltip* telling you what that control does. If there is a keyboard shortcut for the tool or command, it will also be shown in the tooltip. See Figure 1–30.

Figure 1-30

Lightroom menus and commands

Lightroom's main menu bar changes from one module to the next. In this way, Lightroom is like five programs in one. To memorize all the commands available in Lightroom requires using and remembering all the different menus in each module. However, the main menus and commands persist between modules.

As you're learning to master Lightroom, frequently look at the menus, commands and shortcuts available in each module. This will not only give you a better grasp of the full functionality available in Lightroom, it will speed your work as you memorize the locations and shortcuts for specific commands.

⌘+/ or Ctrl+/
See a list of shortcuts for the current module

COMMANDS AND SHORTCUTS

All the commands available in Lightroom can be found on menus throughout the program interface. But often, using a menu is not the fastest method: Lightroom is replete with shortcuts; keyboard and otherwise. It's designed to let you work quickly and smoothly—kind of like "stream-of-consciousness" editing. Once you get the hang of it, the software steps aside to allow your photographs and editing work to come to the forefront of the process.

As with Lightroom's menus, each module has its own shortcuts, and some shortcuts in different modules share the same key.

1

Shortcuts are shown next to the corresponding commands in menus (see Figure 1–31).

Many shortcuts are toggles
In Lightroom, many of the keyboard shortcuts turn tools on and off or make items active/inactive. This is a *toggle* control.

Right-click or Ctrl+click
Open contextual menus throughout Lightroom

CONTEXTUAL MENUS
Lightroom is full of contextual menus (see Figure 1–32); using them is essential to speeding up your work. A contextual menu's contents are determined by the context in which you clicked. Depending on where you click, contextual menus appear showing the commands most useful and appropriate for the object clicked.

Though this book provides many keyboard shortcuts, I use contextual menus as much or more than the keyboard. I always work with a Wacom tablet and stylus and a right-click or Ctrl+click is often faster than switching to the keyboard.

Color management in Lightroom
For your photos to look their best, implementing *color management* is a critical aspect of getting from capture to print. Color management refers to an integrated system of computer hardware and software working together to translate color from one device to another in a controlled way. The color management system (CMS) is built into your computer's operating system; on Mac it's ColorSync and on Windows Vista and 7 it's WCS (ICM on older versions of Windows).

The CMS handles color management at the system level and is responsible for

Figure 1-31

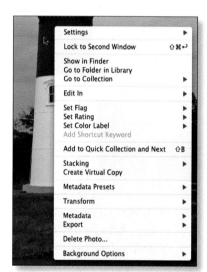

Figure 1-32

translating digital color values to and from digital files and output devices. Software applications, such as Lightroom, can be programmed to take advantage of the CMS, or not. (Some programs, including many Web browsers, do not use color management at all. This explains why the colors in a photo can look different depending on the program used to view it.)

Lightroom is color-managed internally; there are no options to configure. If you're using a properly calibrated and profiled display, you can trust that the colors you see on-screen are accurate. Lightroom will respect and preserve embedded profiles in image files, and uses a 16-bit, proprietary color space for internal processing.

COLOR SPACES

A *color space* is a three-dimensional mathematical model describing the range of colors possible in an image file or on an imaging device, such as a monitor or printer; see Figure 1–33. Using the RGB color model, there are several color spaces in widespread use today. The most common RGB color spaces used in digital photography are:

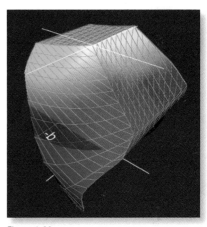

Figure 1-33

- SRGB

- Adobe RGB (1998)

- ProPhoto

Gamut: the range of colors available

Different devices (monitors, printers etc.) interpret color numbers in different ways, because of differences in the type of device and their primaries (their main colors: red/green/blue, or cyan/magenta/yellow/black, etc.) No device can reproduce all colors and all devices reproduce color differently. The range of colors that a device can reproduce (or that a digital file contains) is called the color *gamut*. A large gamut contains many colors and a small gamut has relatively few colors available. A color gamut is described by an ICC profile; see below.

Of the three main color spaces, SRGB has a relatively small gamut, Adobe RGB is considered to have a relatively large gamut, and ProPhoto has the largest gamut and is capable of containing the most possible colors.

Color spaces and their uses are discussed in more detail in Chapter 5.

ICC PROFILES

An *ICC profile* is a small computer file that describes the color space of an image or imaging device. A color–managed workflow uses profiles for each file and device in the imaging pipeline. Profiles are stored in specific places within your operating system so they are made available to any program using the CMS. The CMS uses the profile to handle the translation of numeric color values between devices. Profiles may end in the extensions .icc or .icm (International Color Consortium, or Image Color Management, respectively).

AdobeRGB1998.icc

In many image file formats, the profile for the image's color space can be *embedded* in the file. The embedded profile tells the color management system the parameters for translating the photo's colors to different devices—printer, monitor, etc.

Previously processed image files on your hard drive, such as PSD and TIF, may or may not have embedded color profiles depending on how they were previously saved, and whether or not their file formats support embedded profiles. Camera raw and DNG files can not contain embedded ICC profiles (however, DNGs can contain a camera profile, discussed in Chapter 4). JPG files captured from your camera will have the profile embedded for the color space set on your camera (typically SRGB or Adobe RGB).

Lightroom will respect any profile embedded in imported image files, and for files with no embedded profile, SRGB is used.

Source and destination

The CMS processes the color values in the *source* profile to create the optimum values for the *destination*. For example, when printing, an image file in the Adobe RGB color space would be the source and an Epson printer profile would be the destination.

CALIBRATING AND PROFILING YOUR DISPLAY

The most important factor in achieving accurate color for your digital photographs is working on a calibrated and profiled display. Calibrating your display corrects its output settings, and profiling makes an ICC profile for use by the CMS.

Calibrating and profiling your display must be done with a combination of dedicated hardware and software. Software alone, such as Adobe Gamma, is not sufficient; you must use a measurement device to perform accurate calibration. I recommend the X-Rite i1 (Eye One) or Color Munki systems for this.

The Lightroom Workflow

Even with all the variables involved, it is possible to characterize a standard workflow for digital photography. This is the skeleton framework—you can customize this to the needs for your photography as you see fit. In any case, the basic steps of the workflow remain the same:

1. Capture the digital photos with your camera

2. Download the photos onto your computer hard drive and Import into Lightroom

3. Organize your photos and set aside the best ones

4. Develop the selected images

5. Export files from Lightroom for specific purposes

6. Output your photos as prints, Web sites and/or slideshows

Of course, each of these steps is actually comprised of multiple tasks that vary depending on circumstances. These tasks—and time saving shortcuts and techniques—are explained in detail in the following chapters.

If you perform each phase of the workflow similarly every time, you will soon be able to think several steps ahead. This facilitates better decision-making and dramatically speeds up your work.

Process in Lightroom, not in-camera

Though many current camera models offer varying levels of processing within the camera itself (brightness, contrast, color and sharpness controls, black and white conversion, etc.) it's almost always best to do the image processing on your Lightroom, not in the camera.

THE IMPORTANCE OF BEING ORGANIZED

In digital photography, effectively managing your image files is crucial. Regardless of how many photos you have now, it's very likely that over the coming years your photo library will grow to many hundreds of thousands—even millions—of images. If you're not already using a good organizational system, now is the time to start. Hard drive storage, folder organization and file naming strategies are discussed in detail at the end of Chapter 2.

1

Original, Master and derivative files

For each digital photograph you make, you will likely produce several (if not many) image files on disk, each serving a different purpose. The number of versions you can produce from a single image is unlimited, but efficiency favors conservatism here.

- *Original:* In Lightroom, the original is a file on disk, for example, the raw capture in camera raw and/or DNG format. Originals can be in any file format Lightroom supports. Archive these files and protect them long-term; these are like original slides in boxes. If the worst should happen, and all else is lost, you need to be able to go back to these.

- *Master:* the file that contains all the final processing and from which any other copies are made. In the end, the master is even more important than the Original, because it contains all the painstaking work you did to finish the image. In many cases, the original will also be the master; for example, if you completed all necessary processing just using your raw capture, it can serve as the master. Otherwise, masters are often layered TIF or Photoshop files.

- *Derivative:* files saved from the Master and modified for specific purposes such as printing or Internet distribution. These are usually TIF or JPG files for printing and for the Web. Derivative files are often temporary and trashed when their task is done.

When to export

Sometimes you may want to work on your images in other software after you've gone as far as you can processing them in Lightroom. Think carefully about your plans for the photo and the workflow steps required. You can export new master files to work with in other, specialized software. See Chapter 8 for more about Exporting.

THE IMPORTANCE OF DNG

DNG stands for Digital NeGative, an open source raw format developed and standardized by Adobe. Whereas proprietary camera files require sidecar files to save metadata edits, DNG files can store metadata directly in the file. I always capture in raw, then convert the raw files to DNG as one of the first steps in my workflow. I don't keep the original raw files from the camera. I'll talk about DNG in various places throughout the book.

Use DNG as your raw format and TIF as your layered work format
From these two master file formats you can produce derivatives of any kind, for any purpose.

Don't shoot in JPG
I believe the only situations that might benefit from capturing JPG instead of raw are those where you will not do any processing on the computer. Assuming that from this point on you'll be using Lightroom to work up your files, I strongly recommend that you always capture raw (and there's usually no need for RAW+JPG anymore.)

There's more about file formats in Chapters 2, 3, 4 and 5.

SAVING YOUR WORK

As you work on your photos, Lightroom automatically saves your adjustments in the catalog and continually generates screen previews based on the adjustments that have been applied. Your original file (regardless of its format) remains unaltered, giving you unlimited flexibility for changing your mind later.

However, storing all your editing instructions *only* in the Lightroom catalog carries some risk. For example, if you do all your processing in Lightroom and the catalog becomes corrupt (and you haven't made backups) you could lose that editing data, requiring the work to be redone.

This is why you must get in the habit of saving your work frequently when working in Lightroom, just like working with any other software. When you save metadata to files, in addition to being stored in the Lightroom catalog, the metadata processing instructions for the adjustments you make should also be saved to files *outside* the database. This can be done using sidecar files (for camera raw formats) or by saving metadata in the actual files themselves (for all other formats). Saving out the metadata helps ensure 1) your work won't be lost and 2) your edits travel with the original file wherever it goes.

Even when you save metadata adjustments into a file, the pixel data is not changed: the metadata is stored in a separate part of the file, and read back in when Lightroom (or other software) loads the image.

Back up often!
Backing up your Lightroom catalogs and image files is an essential part of the workflow. All hard drives will eventually fail; the effect of this occurrence can either be insignificant or a complete catastrophe, depending on your work habits. Chapter 2 contains a thorough discussion of backup strategies.

1

LIGHTROOM PREFERENCES

In most scenarios the default Preference settings in place when Lightroom is installed are ideal. However, when you've worked with Lightroom for some time, there may be settings you want to change to suit your computer configuration or work habits. Spend some time getting to know the options available in the Preferences dialog boxes; they are fairly straightforward, and with an understanding of Lightroom's interface and functionality the settings you want to change will become more evident.

On a Mac, Lightroom's Preferences are accessed under the Lightroom menu. On Windows, they're under the Edit menu.

In the chapters that follow, key preferences are explained in context of a particular aspect of the workflow.

PRESETS AND TEMPLATES

Throughout the program, Lightroom provides presets and templates to store settings and layouts. The default installation comes with some built-in presets and templates. As you work with Lightroom, you should save your own. This will dramatically speed up your workflow. You can also get presets and templates from other people; Google this.

The Lightroom presets folder is an important folder on your hard drive that you may access frequently the more you use Lightroom. To get there, open the Preferences, and on the Presets tab, click the button for Show Lightroom Presets Folder.

I'll discuss using presets and templates throughout the rest of the book.

CHAPTER 2

IMPORT

2

Importing photos into Lightroom

To work with images and video files in Lightroom you must first *import* them. This creates *records* within a Lightroom catalog. During an import, Lightroom reads the image files and makes records for each of them in the currently open Lightroom catalog file. File names, folder locations and metadata are all stored in the catalog.

It's important to understand that in all cases **the files themselves are not actually contained inside the catalog.** When you do an import, Lightroom just reads the files, makes data entries in the catalog for each file and links the Lightroom data to the file on disk.

Later, when you're working on photos, Lightroom *references* the original files on disk and keeps track of your edits within the catalog. Lightroom also generates numerous *previews* of the photos, which are constantly updated as you work.

Lightroom 3 provides a redesigned Import process that is faster and easier than previous versions. The new Import screen helps you see how Lightroom will handle the files being imported, quickly navigate through hard drives and folders to see their contents before importing, and speeds the import process with the use of presets.

In this chapter, I'll cover the three most common methods you'll use for getting files into your Lightroom catalog: importing from a hard drive, importing from a camera's memory card, and shooting with your camera connected directly to the computer ("tethered").

When you're done importing some photos, you can move on to Chapter 3, where you'll begin working with your photos in Lightroom's Library module.

Supported image file formats

Unlike Photoshop, which can open and save a dizzying array of image, graphic and video file formats, Lightroom is designed to work only with the most common formats generated by digital cameras and scanners. Lightroom can import, process and export the following types of files:

- Native camera raw files (from nearly all modern digital cameras)

- DNG (Adobe Digital Negative: open-format raw files)

- JPG

- TIF (TIFF)

2

- PSD (but only those with "Maximize Compatibility" enabled when saving from Photoshop)

- Digital movie files from current camera models, though all you get are basic previews and metadata features. It's not possible to play or edit video in Lightroom.

Lightroom cannot import files saved in any other format.

Note: Lightroom 3 *can* import files in the above image formats that use CMYK color mode, though any Develop adjustments you might apply to them would still be done in RGB.

65,000 pixel limit
Lightroom can import image files up to 65,000 pixels on the longest side.

Camera raw file support
Native camera raw files come directly from your camera with formats specified by the camera manufacturer and are encoded in a way that they cannot be directly modified. Common examples are Canon's .CR2 and Nikon's .NEF formats. Note that two raw files with the same file extension but from different cameras are likely to be programmatically different; your camera model's native format must be supported by Adobe for you to work with those files in Lightroom. Adobe imaging software supports nearly all digital cameras available on the market and support for new models is continually updated. However, when a new camera is released there may be a period of lag time during which your files cannot be read by Lightroom or Adobe Camera Raw.

What to do before importing
Prior to importing photos into Lightroom, you should establish a system for organizing and naming your files. Setting up a well-organized digital storage system for your images will make your work easier and provide peace of mind. With a solid information architecture in place, you can dramatically accelerate your workflow.

If necessary, you can skip ahead to review the recommendations given at the end of this Chapter regarding file naming and organization. At the very least, before you import photos, think about where the image files are, where you want them to be, and what kinds of additional processing you might want to do during the import.

(There's also a new option in Catalog Settings→File Handling (Mac Lightroom menu; Windows Edit menu) where you can set the format for Import Sequence Numbers.)

2

BASIC IMPORT WORKFLOW

Importing is one of the most important parts of the workflow and requires your complete attention. The steps you take in completing an import can largely determine the ease or difficulty of the rest of the workflow. Plan and execute your imports carefully and you will benefit from one of Lightroom's key strengths: *batch processing.*

Following is a simple rundown of the major steps you'll consistently use to import photos into Lightroom:

1. Choose the photos to import

2. Choose where the image files should be copied or moved (or left where they are)

3. Set the size of the previews to be generated during import

4. Rename the files, if they're being copied (optional)

5. Make backups of the files (optional)

6. Apply metadata, such as contact information, keywords and Develop adjustments (optional)

At home versus on the road

Your import process will likely be different when you're traveling—working from a laptop computer—than when you're at your main desktop workstation. Of course, if you use only one computer all the time, you may only need one import workflow. But if you use multiple computers in different situations, expect that your imports will vary from one computer to another depending on the files being imported and the location of your main image catalog. Chapter 9 has more information about working with multiple catalogs.

About batch processing

Usually you'll import multiple image files all at once (though you can import just a single photo). As such, this is the first instance of batch processing in our workflow. A batch is simply a group of multiple files that are all being processed the same way.

During an import, all the selected files we be processed using the same criteria. However, Lightroom gives you lots of ways to apply file-specific, variable data to your photos, such as a unique file name for each one. This is done using *templates;* we'll discuss these later in this chapter.

2

When processing many images at one time, the choices you make become increasingly important. Effective batch processing requires planning ahead, thinking carefully about the software settings, and considering the effects of your choices before going forward.

After you've run through the import process a few times, you'll easily remember the key settings to check before starting each Import. And new in Lightroom 3, you can save *presets* of your commonly used import settings.

⌘+Shift+I or
Ctrl+Shift+I
Open the Import screen from anywhere in Lightroom

THE NEW IMPORT WINDOW

When you click the Import button (see Figure 2–1) or use the File→Import Photos… menu command or shortcut, Lightroom opens a window where you configure all the settings for the current import (see Figure 2–2).

Figure 2-1

I'll discuss the specific settings for different types of imports later in this chapter. For now, let's just have a look around the new and improved Lightroom 3 Import screen.

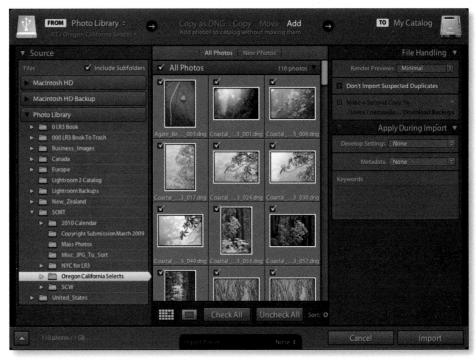

Figure 2-2

Keep in mind that at any time you can cancel and close the Import screen without actually performing an import. To do this, click the Cancel button near the bottom right, or press the Esc key.

2

The top panel of the Import screen contains the following info displays and controls:

- **From:** the *Source* from which the files are being imported

- **File Handling:** how they will be processed and added to the catalog, and

- **To:** the *Destination* for files that are being copied or moved.

The arrows indicate the import workflow, from left to right. See Figure 2–3.

Figure 2-3

From and To

Lightroom 3's Import window keeps track of the most recent folder used, and shows the space available on source and destination drives. Clicking the From menu (see Figure 2–4) provides access to recently used paths. Depending on the File Handling option selected, clicking the To field will provide controls for setting the final destination of the files (see Figure 2–5) or will simply say My Catalog. The contents of these two menus will constantly change as you work with Lightroom.

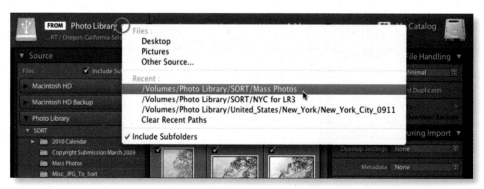

Figure 2-4

Figure 2-5

File Handling

In the center of the top panel, click the text button to set the way Lightroom handles the files: Copy as DNG, Copy, Move or Add (see Figure 2–6). Clicking these buttons will display a short description of what that option does. We'll go over all these in more detail momentarily.

Figure 2-6

Below the top panel, the left panel set is where you choose the Source of the import by clicking on folders or disk volumes (refer back to Figure 2–2). When you select a Source, you'll see the photos it contains in the center preview area.

On the right panel set, you can optionally specify additional processing for the photos being imported (also Figure 2–2). If files are being copied or moved, the contents of these panels changes to provide more options for Destination and File Renaming (see Figure 2–7).

For each import you do, you'll adjust the settings using the panels, menus and text-entry boxes on the Import screen. **Carefully confirm your import settings every time.** Go through the controls in the import screen methodically—from top to bottom,

Figure 2-7

left to right, and back again—to apply the settings appropriate to the photos that will be affected by the current import. Be sure you've correctly configured all the options in the import screen before executing the import.

When you're ready, click the Import button again (this time from the bottom right of the main Import screen) and the import will begin.

Really think about what you're doing

If importing is done incorrectly it can lead to disastrous results: lots of wasted time and potential loss of files. Think it through!

Import screen retains settings from previous import

The settings used for the previous import will remain in the Import screen until you change them. Also, be aware that depending on whether you're importing photos from a memory card, a folder on the hard disk, from another catalog (Chapter 9) or when you're *synchronizing* a folder (Chapter 3), **the options shown**

2

on the import screen will change. This is common throughout Lightroom: if an option is not available using the current settings, it is most often hidden from view.

WHAT HAPPENS DURING THE IMPORT

Depending on the type of import you're doing and the options you've selected, Lightroom will read each of the files in the selected folder(s), copy the files if directed to do so, create records in the catalog and builds previews for all the photos in the import.

As soon as you begin the import, the Import screen closes and the Library module loads with the Current Import image source selected. Photo thumbnails begin appearing in Grid view immediately as each file is imported.

When the top panel is visible, the progress indicator at left displays the approximate amount of processing remaining in each stage of the import, along with messages describing the current operation in progress; see Figure 2–8.

Figure 2-8

Folders get added too

When you import a batch of photos, the folder that contains them is also entered into the catalog and is listed in the Folders panel in Library (see Chapter 3).

Stopping an import in progress

If you start an import and realize you made a mistake or change your mind about something, it's often best to let the import finish and clean up after-the-fact. Stopping an import in progress increases the likelihood of bad data in the Lightroom catalog (especially if Lightroom crashes while trying to stop the import) and brings into question the accuracy and completeness of the files in subsequent imports.

For these reasons I believe you should be conservative with the number of files you attempt to import in one batch, especially when you're just starting out with Lightroom.

If you *do* decide to stop an import in progress, click the X next to the progress indicator in the Library module. **After clicking once, wait for Lightroom to finish what it's doing,** then remove the incorrectly imported files from the catalog and optionally delete any unwanted files from disk. (See Chapter 3 for information about removing/deleting files.)

Most importantly, if you're doing an import and the Lightroom application seems to freeze, or "hang", be patient. Don't force-quit Lightroom, or click anywhere on the screen during this time. Most often, Lightroom can recover from temporary memory issues. **If you ever force-quit Lightroom, for any reason, you increase the possibility of corrupting your catalog.**

You can start working right away

You can begin working on photos as soon as they appear in the Library Grid view. You don't have to wait for the entire import to complete in order to start editing and/or processing any photos that are already in the catalog. You can also switch from the Current Import source to another image source, or to any other module, while an import is in progress.

Completion sounds

In Lightroom's Preferences, under the Lightroom menu on Mac and the Edit menu on Windows, look on the General tab. About halfway down the middle of the dialog box (see Figure 2–x) are options to set a Completion Sound to play when Lightroom is done importing (or exporting) files. I find this to be a useful feature.

LIGHTROOM PREVIEWS CREATED DURING IMPORT

As Lightroom reads the pixel data from image files, previews are created, which are then also referenced by the catalog. In the Import screen you can specify the previews generated during import at the following sizes and quality levels (see Figure 2–9):

Figure 2-9

a. **Minimal**: Select this option to have your import complete in the fastest time possible. Only small thumbnails will be generated during the import. When you begin working with your images later, Lightroom will generate larger previews as necessary on-the-fly, which may cause slight delays in the response of the program as previews are built.

b. **Embedded and Sidecar**: Select this option to have Lightroom read any existing previews contained in the original files and use the current previews if they are up-to-date, or generate new ones if not. This is particularly intended for raw and DNG files. (I never use this option, because I only want to see Lightroom's most current previews.)

c. **Standard**: Select this option to have Lightroom generate thumbnails and standard-sized previews during Import. Standard previews are used to show photos full-screen. You can set the size and quality used for standard previews in Catalog Settings➔File Handling.

2

    d.   **1:1:** Select this option to have Lightroom render 1:1 previews (the largest size) during import, in addition to thumbnails and standard previews. This can significantly extend the time required to complete the import, however, working with the photos in Lightroom later will be noticeably faster.

Import photos from your hard disk

It's likely you've had many photos on your hard drive(s) prior to using Lightroom. The first major step to building your Lightroom catalog is to get your existing image files into the catalog.

During these imports, you can decide whether or not to make any changes to the files in order to conform to your current organization and naming conventions. When importing images from your hard drive, you have two basic choices:

- Just import the files, not modifying them in any way; or

- Process the files somehow during the import. This could include renaming, changing formats, applying metadata, etc.

The most basic kind of import is to just add the files into the catalog, nothing more. **In the example that follows, we'll be simply Adding photos on a hard drive into the current Lightroom catalog.**

Since we're not using Lightroom to move or copy the files, it's a good idea to take a few moments to confirm the file/folder structures you're working with and do any necessary clean up of your files before you import them.

Do some housekeeping first

Although you can (and sometimes should) move and/or rename files from within the catalog after they've been imported, doing some housekeeping in the Mac Finder or Windows Explorer ahead of time will make your imports easier.

At the very least, you will need to know the physical location on disk of the files you're going to import.

Following are the Import steps (in addition to the figures, below you can refer back to Figure 2–2 if you need to):

1.   Launch Lightroom and **make sure the correct catalog is loaded** (see Chapter 1).

2. In the Library module, click the **Import** button in the left panel, or use the menu command or shortcut to open the Import screen.

3. On the **Source** panel at the left of the screen, click to select the folder containing the photos to be imported. This list is a direct representation of your folder structure on the hard disk. You will probably need to dig through nested subfolders to find the correct folder. Note that Importing from an upper-level folder can also include all the photos in any subfolders underneath, and you can change this setting; see below.

By default, only "local" disks connected directly to your computer will be shown in the Source panel. To add a volume from your network, first be sure you're connected to the network drive with the necessary permissions. Then, click the From button, choose Other Source (see Figure 2–10), and navigate to select

Figure 2-10

the volume or subfolder. It will then be shown in the Source panel. Navigate to find your desired folder just as with local disks.

To select multiple folders in the list, hold the Ctrl and/or Shift key and click.

Docking folders

To make folder lists more manageable, Lightroom 3's Import screen includes a "Dock Folder" option. This hides the subfolders above the chosen folder, making it easier to navigate within the panel. Double-click a folder to dock and undock it, or right-click or Ctrl+click on a folder name, and from the popup menu, check or uncheck Dock Folder.

4. When you're choosing the folder containing photos to import, if you have multiple subfolders below an upper-level folder you selected, by default, the contents of the subfolders won't be shown. To change this, click the **"Include Subfolders"** checkbox in the Source Files list, or the button in the main preview area, to show all the files contained in the subfolders in the preview area.

To change this later, you can right-click or Ctrl+click on individual folders, and from the popup menu, uncheck Include Subfolders, or click the checkbox to enable/disable Include Subfolders globally.

2

5. When you've
selected a Source,
the From area
updates to show

the file path (as shown in Figure 2–11, above), and any image or video
files contained in the volumes/folder(s) will be displayed as thumbnail
previews in the center of the window (refer back to Figure 2–2).

Within the selected folders, Lightroom will only show thumbnails
for files whose formats it can import. If none are found in the chosen
source(s), the message No Photos Found shows in the preview area.

If a file has already been imported to the currently open catalog, or it's
unreadable for some reason, its thumbnail will be grayed out (see Figure
2–12).

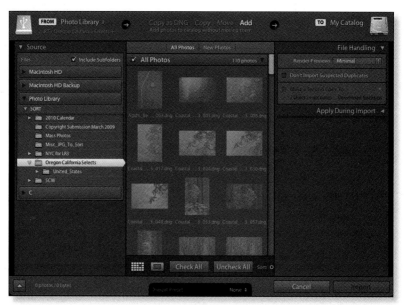

Figure 2-12

**A Lightroom catalog can only contain one instance of each photo; if
the photo is already listed in the catalog, you can't import it again.**

6. Use the scroll bar at the right side of the preview area to view all the
thumbnails (see Figure 2–12). It's a good idea to at least take a quick look
at the previews to confirm what photos will be imported.

2

7.   You can change the Sort Order and Thumbnail Size with the controls at the right of the Toolbar (see Figure 2–13).

Figure 2-13

8.   To see a larger preview of a single photo, double-click the thumbnail, or press the E key, or click the Loupe view button on the toolbar. You can zoom in closer on a preview by clicking with the magnifier tool (see Figure 2–14).

To switch back to the thumbnail Grid, double-click the large preview, or press G, or click the Grid view button on the toolbar.

Note: These Grid and Loupe views, and the zoom functions, are the same as those in the Library module

Figure 2-14

and are covered thoroughly in Chapter 3.

9.   **To include or exclude photos from this import,** you can click to activate or deactivate their checkboxes (shown on Figure 2–13). *Selected* thumbnails

2

Option+Click or Alt+Click thumbnails
Select and check/uncheck simultaneously

are indicated with a lighter cell color around the thumbnail preview. **Simply selecting or deselecting thumbnails by clicking on the cells does not change their checked status.**

To check or uncheck multiple photos at once, first use the shift or Ctrl key to select their thumbnails. Then, clicking a single checkbox will include or exclude all of the selected photos. The Check All and Uncheck All buttons make this easier (see Figure 2–15).

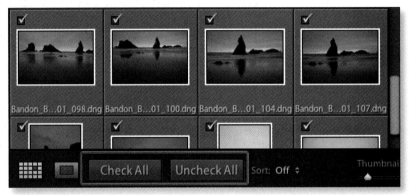

Figure 2-15

Or, with a large Loupe preview showing for a single image, click the checkbox in the Toolbar to include or exclude the file from the import (see Figure 2–14 on previous page).

You can also sort the previews by their Checked State.

10. With photos checked, a display at the bottom left corner of the Import screen indicates how many photos are

Figure 2-16

marked for import and the total aggregate file size of the batch (see Figure 2–16).

11. After you've made sure the proper photos are selected, make sure the **Add** button is highlighted in the middle of the top panel (go back to review Figure 2–6 if necessary). This tells Lightroom that we're only adding existing files to the catalog, and not copying, moving or renaming them in the process. To confirm this, the destination listed in the To section at the top right shows "My Catalog". (If you have a copy or move handling method selected, this will show the destination file path on a hard drive.)

12. Next, on the **File Handling** panel at the right side of the screen, from the **Render Previews** popup menu, choose the level of previews to create during the import.

I almost always use Minimal for Initial Previews. This allows the import to complete as quickly as possible, and later, Lightroom will render larger previews as needed.

Figure 2-17

1. Also on the **File Handling** panel, make sure Don't Import Suspected Duplicates is unchecked (see Figure 2–17). At this point, we don't want Lightroom deciding for us what's a duplicate and what's not. There may be the odd scenario where this option could come in handy; but I haven't found it yet. And if during the import Lightroom determines there *are* duplicate files, based entirely on an exact filename match, those photos won't be imported anyway, regardless of whether or not this is enabled.

2. On the **Apply During Import** panel, use these settings for this import; see Figure 2–18:

   a. **Develop Settings:** None*

   b. **Metadata:** None*

   c. **Keywords:** Leave blank*

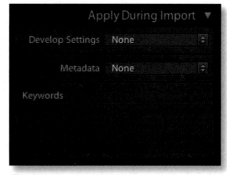

Figure 2-18

(*We'll talk more about these settings in a bit.)

3. Take one last look around the Import screen to be sure everything's correct, then click the **Import** button, or press Return or Enter, to start the import.

2

4. The Import screen closes and returns you to the Library Grid view with the Catalog panel showing the *Current Import* source (see Figure 2–19). When the import is completed,

Figure 2-19

this changes to say "Previous Import". Before editing photos, switch to a folder source (see Chapter 3).

If Lightroom fails to import any files, a dialog box appears at the end of the import that states which files failed, and why, and provides buttons to show the failed files in Finder or Explorer.

When importing existing files from disk, be careful applying metadata

Most times, you shouldn't apply metadata presets to existing files on your hard drive during import because **the files might already contain custom metadata.** The import screen doesn't indicate whether or not any metadata has already been applied to the files being imported, and if the files *do* have custom metadata applied, it isn't shown. You'll only know what metadata the files previously contained after they get into the catalog.

For images already on your hard drive, it's usually safer to apply any metadata and presets *after* the import, so you can review the files in Library and add your metadata as appropriate (see Chapter 3 for more on this).

However, if you are *certain* that no custom metadata has been applied to the files, *or you're okay with overwriting/modifying it,* you can apply your metadata template, add keywords and Develop presets during the import. Just be careful with this.

Lightroom respects xmp during import

If you're importing raw files and they have .xmp sidecar files, Lightroom will read the metadata settings from them, and the images will come into Lightroom with those settings applied. Same with DNG; any custom XMP settings found in a DNG when it's being imported will be used as the starting point for processing the file in Lightroom.

In the case of camera raw files that have been previously worked on, but *do not* have sidecar files, those previous edits *will not* come into Lightroom. Make sure any time you're working on raw files in other software that you save out the metadata to sidecar files. This is discussed further in Chapter 9.

2

Drag and drop folders onto Lightroom

With Lightroom running in standard window mode, reduce the size of the main Lightroom window so you can see your desktop. You can then drag and drop files and/or folders either onto the Lightroom window (or the Lightroom program icon). The import dialog box will open with the images selected, ready to complete the steps described above.

Import photos from your camera

After you've completed a shoot or filled up a memory card, you should get the files copied to your computer and backed up as soon as possible. Lightroom facilitates this and much more: you can use Lightroom to handle the transfer of files from your camera to your hard disk and automatically import them into the Lightroom catalog.

The one required step in this workflow is for Lightroom to physically copy the files from the memory card to the hard disk. You can also optionally have Lightroom:

1. Rename the files;

2. Convert native camera raw files to DNG (covered in the next section);

3. Apply a Develop preset; and

4. Add metadata such as copyright, contact info, keywords, etc.

If you do all the above steps, your photos can come straight into the Lightroom catalog loaded with metadata and looking good. This will allow you to move more quickly through editing the shoot (see Chapter 3) and get files into Develop for final processing (Chapter 4) with minimal effort.

Treat JPG as separate files

If you capture raw+JPG, and want to import both files for each capture, you need to enable this option in Lightroom Preferences→Import (see Figure 2–20).

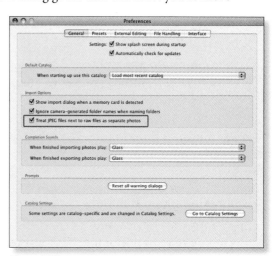

Figure 2-20

2

Following are the steps to copy files from your camera's memory card to your computer and subsequently import them into the Lightroom catalog:

1.   Launch Lightroom and **make sure the correct catalog is loaded.**

2.   Insert the memory card into a card reader (this is faster and safer than transferring from your camera itself). Lightroom may detect the card or camera directly attached and will open the Import dialog box. If not, click the Import button (or use the shortcut, etc.) to open the Import screen.

Show import dialog when a memory card is detected

This setting, in Lightroom Preferences→General (moved to the General tab in v3; see Figure 2–20 on previous page), is intended to automatically open Lightroom's import screen when you insert a memory card or connect a camera directly to your computer. However, this can be overridden by your operating system and other programs may also get in the way. If you want to use this feature you might need to change your system settings. On OS X, use the Image Capture application preferences and specify Lightroom as the application to launch when a memory card is loaded. On Windows, in the Autoplay control panel, choose Import using Lightroom and check the box for Do This Every Time.

3.   With the card mounted and Lightroom Import screen showing, in the top panel and Sources, you'll see the memory card listed (see Figure 2–21). Lightroom is usually very good at finding the subdirectory containing the photos. If not, navigate to the folder containing the image files on the card.

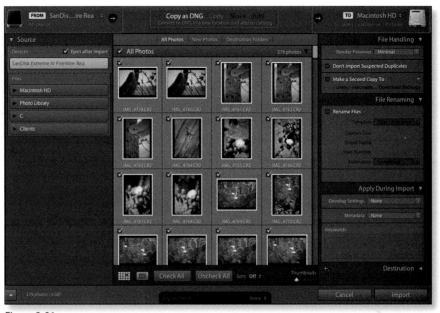

Figure 2-21

4. **Eject after import:** checking this box (see Figure 2–21) will do a safe removal of the media when the import has completed, so you can pull the card out of the reader immediately. Entirely optional.

5. Also optionally, make selections from the thumbnails. Thumbnails with the checkbox ticked will be imported; those unchecked will not. This is detailed in the previous section about importing from a hard drive.

    To import everything from the card, leave all the thumbnails checked. (I usually import all the images from a shoot because I want to avoid making editing decisions during import. The exceptions are obviously bad captures—blurry shots of my foot, for example—whose thumbnails I would uncheck.

    Scroll through the thumbnails to be sure of what you're importing.

6. By default, the file handling in the top panel will be set to **Copy** (see Figure 2–21). You can change it to Copy as DNG, which is what I prefer and is explained in the next section.

7. On the right side of the Import screen, notice the additional panels now showing under To, and that your default hard disk is shown as the destination (see Figure 2–21). To choose a different hard drive (or folder), click the To button and either choose the other drive if it's listed in the popup menu, or choose Other Destination… to navigate and select another drive.

Figure 2-22

8. In the **Destination panel** at the bottom of the right panel group, specify the directory where the files will be copied. You can do this in several ways. You can choose an existing folder, or you can create new folders by clicking the + button on the Destination panel header; see Figure 2–22.

2

Or, to create a subfolder under a specific folder in the list, right-click or Control+click on it, and from the popup menu, choose New Folder and use the system dialog boxes to make the folder. Be sure to give it an appropriate name.

Alternatively, with an upper-level parent folder selected in the folder list, check the box for **Into Subfolder** (see Figure 2–22). This provides several additional options for Lightroom's naming of folders as they are created. If you want to create a subfolder and give it your own name (as in the first method above), choose **Into one folder** from the Organize popup menu (see Figure 2–22). You can then type in the name for the folder in the provided text field. **This is almost always my preferred method.**

You could instead choose to have Lightroom automatically place the copied photos into folders named with a date format. From the Organize menu

Figure 2-23

choose By Date; this then allows you to choose from a set of predefined Date Formats in the menu below (see Figure 2–23).

Collapsing panels and Solo Mode

The import screen is one area in Lightroom where the panel tracks can get very long. As you're going through the steps to set up your import, you can close panels you're not using to make items easier to find.

Also, if you right-click or Control+click on a panel header you'll see a popup menu for hiding and showing panels. With **Solo Mode** enabled, as you open one panel, all the others will close. This option is specific to each left and right panel track and is my preferred mode. Solo Mode is available on panels throughout Lightroom and is mentioned in other places where it's particularly useful.

9. On the **File Handling panel** at the top right: use the **Render Previews** menu to set the size and quality level of previews generated for files in this import. The preview types are listed in order of size and quality.

10. Uncheck **Don't Import Suspected Duplicates.** At this point, we don't want Lightroom deciding for us what's a duplicate and what's not.

11. **Make a second copy to**: if you want to make an additional backup during the copy, check this box. I usually leave it unchecked, though, because I use Copy as DNG and it's the original raw files that get backed up, not the final DNGS. I'll explain this in more detail further in this chapter. If you want to back up your original capture files at this stage, use the popup menu and navigate to choose the backup location. Be sure that any backups you make are going onto a separate hard disk other than where the master copies are being saved.

12. **On the File Renaming panel**, tick the checkbox if you want to rename the files as they are being copied; see Figure 2–24. (See the Asset Management section later in this chapter for more about file naming strategies.) This enables the additional options below:

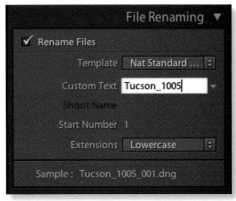

Figure 2-24

a. Template: this menu lets you choose the file naming template to be applied. Lightroom comes with built-in templates, and you can create your own. Choose a template from the list to load its options below.

b. For each variable contained in the template, enter your chosen values. For example, in the Custom Text field you can type in a text string that will become part of the file name. If you're using sequence numbers, you can choose the starting number for this batch.

c. You can choose whether to use lowercase or uppercase for your file type extensions.

d. At the bottom of the panel is an informational display that shows an example of how the current naming options will combine to form the final file names.

   Working in the Filenaming Template Editor is discussed in detail in Chapter 3.

2

13. On the **Apply During Import panel** you can specify additional metadata to be applied to the files as they are imported; see Figure 2–25.

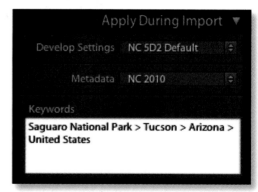

Figure 2-25

a. **Develop Settings:** optionally, choose a preset to apply to the files during import. Any Develop Settings you apply during import will become the starting point for processing those photos, and this step will be listed in the History panel as the initial Import state. See Chapter 4 for more information about Develop Presets.

b. **Metadata:** select a preset or make a new one if necessary. Metadata presets are thoroughly explained in Chapter 3.

c. **Keywords:** type to enter words and phrases descriptive of this group of images. Keywording strategies are covered in Chapter 3.

14. Click the Import Button or press **Return/Enter** to begin the import. The Import screen closes and returns to the Library module, within the Catalog panel and the Current Import source. When the import is completed, Lightroom will display all the imported images in Library Grid using the Previous Import image source (see Chapter 3).

Have Lightroom do as much as possible during an import

Lightroom is a powerful, batch-processing application with many options designed to save you time. The more functions you have Lightroom perform during Import, the less work you'll have to do later.

After Import, save metadata to files

If you've applied any metadata during import, save it out to the files immediately after the import is done. I usually use Select All, then Save Metadata to Files, using the keyboard shortcuts. See Chapters 3 and 4 for more information about Saving Metadata to Files.

Backup right away

Sync your backups immediately after an import completes. After your copy/ import procedures have completed, confirm the integrity of the files (usually, just quickly scrolling through them is sufficient) and make a backup. Make sure to back up to another media source, such as copying to a hard drive or burning a CD/DVD. **Copies made on the same hard drive are not really backups.**

Reformat the card in the camera
After transferring your files from the card to a hard drive and confirming backups, reformat your memory card *in the camera* before each new shooting session.

Never modify or delete the files on the card using your computer
Your computer file system and the file system on the memory card do not necessarily get along. **Never manipulate the files on your memory card in any way, including deleting, moving, renaming or modifying folders as this significantly increases the risk of data corruption.** Most importantly, never format the card using your computer. This can render the card unreadable by the camera.

Presets and templates used during import
Generally speaking, *presets* store settings; *templates* store formatted layouts. This distinction is not critical; throughout Lightroom you'll see frequent references to presets and templates and the use of one term versus the other is somewhat inconsistent. What's important is to recognize that presets and templates can save you lots of time by applying previously saved settings to your photos.

Finding your presets in the computer's file system
Preferences➔Presets tab➔Show Lightroom Presets Folder.

FILE NAMING TEMPLATES
Using file naming templates you can easily rename files as they are being imported. You can set up your own templates in either the Import screen or in the Library module, which is covered in detail in Chapter 3. To apply a file naming template during import, select it from the popup menu (shown previously in Figure 2–24), and as necessary, enter any custom text that will become part of the new names.

Custom Text
The Custom Text token allows you to manually enter text for part of your base file name during each import.

METADATA PRESETS
You can optionally select a metadata preset to be applied to the files being imported. With a metadata template you can embed your copyright notice, contact information and other optional information. This saves a lot of time by eliminating the need to manually apply metadata later.

2

Select a preset from the popup menu in the Import screen, or create and modify presets using the Edit Metadata Presets window, accessed from the import screen. You can also apply and edit metadata presets on the Metadata panel in Library where they are explained in depth; see Chapter 3.

Always include a copyright notice

At minimum, be sure a copyright notice containing your name and the year the photo was made is embedded in all your photos. Doing this during import ensures all your photos will contain your copyright notice from the outset of the workflow.

DEVELOP PRESETS

Develop presets allow you to automatically apply Develop module settings to photos as they are imported. This provides more control over your baseline image settings at the outset of the editing workflow and saves time in processing.

You can't configure Develop presets from the import screen; you must do this in the Develop module prior to starting an import (see Chapter 4).

Before you start saving Develop presets, you will likely need to manually process a few photos and take note of the common settings you frequently apply to help determine the adjustments to include in your presets.

One preset is not always enough

A Develop preset applied on import need not be the final stage of applying presets to an image. After it's been imported, in the Develop module you can apply additional, multiple presets. Note that if two consecutive presets both contain a setting for the same adjustment, the latter will override the former. For more information about Develop presets, see Chapter 4.

Import presets

Lightroom 3's new Import system now also provides the capability to save Import Presets. If you have common import settings

Figure 2-26

you frequently use, you can store them for quick retrieval later. (Import Presets can also store your selections for the other types of presets.)

Start with all the current settings that you want to save in your preset; you won't be able to change the settings stored in an Import preset. Then, at the bottom of the Import screen, click to open the popup menu and select Save Current Settings as New Preset; see Figure 2–26. Using the same menu, you can load saved presets and delete or rename presets later.

The Compact Import window

At the bottom left of the Import screen is a large triangle button that toggles between Show More Options and Show Fewer Options; see Figure 2–27. Sometimes you don't need to see all the thumbnail previews or options in the expanded Import screen. Showing fewer options compacts the Import screen to just show the essential elements; see Figure 2–28.

Figure 2-27

Figure 2-28

More import workflows

The two scenarios outlined previously, Import from Hard Disk and Import from Camera, represent the vast majority of situations you'll run into when importing photos into Lightroom. In some cases, slight modifications to those two basic workflows can help perform specific tasks. Here are some of the other scenarios to consider:

Copy photos as Digital Negative (DNG) and add to catalog

You can do this even for camera raw files already on the hard drive. This allows you to convert your camera raw files to Adobe's DNG format and subsequently import the resulting DNG files. If the raw files have sidecars, those edits will be integrated into the new DNG. You can then decide whether or not to keep your original camera raw files. (I don't.) DNG is discussed further in Chapters 1, 3, 4 and 5.

Move photos and import

This is similar to copy and import: Lightroom copies the selected files to a new location and imports the copies. But Lightroom then **deletes the old files at the original location.** Use this with care.

Manual copy now, Lightroom import later

There will likely be situations in which manually copying your files from the memory card to your hard drive is more desirable than using a Lightroom Import to perform the download.

2

For example, if you're pressed for time, a manual download using Finder or Explorer is the fastest way to simply copy the files from the card to the hard drive; you can deal with the Lightroom import later.

Also, a manual copy can provide quick indication of any problems with the files on the card.

When you've manually copied files this way, during the eventual Lightroom import you would use the same steps outlined in Import from Camera, but instead of choosing the card as the source, you'd choose the folder on your hard disk containing the previously copied files.

This optional workflow has many other potential applications. For example, using Lightroom's import functions, you could perform the same basic steps to:

- Convert your raw image library to DNG while importing to Lightroom;

- Copy files from one place to another while adding keywords and other metadata; or

- Move and rename a batch of files and import them into the catalog.

Tethered Capture

Tethered capture provides automated transfer of image files directly from your camera to your computer, and into the Lightroom catalog, as they are captured. Shooting tethered requires a live connection between your camera and computer, so it's most commonly used in studio environments.

Typically, photographers connect their camera to the computer using a USB cable. Many new camera systems also allow wireless transfer, eliminating the need to connect with a cord.

Lightroom 3 includes new methods for supporting tethered capture; previous versions required the use of the camera maker's utility software to facilitate the transfer. For users of Canon and Nikon digital SLRs, this is no longer the case— you can do it all with Lightroom. (If your camera make or model is not currently supported by Lightroom 3's tethered capture, you can likely still use the older methods as described in my previous book and numerous Web sites.)

The main benefit of shooting tethered is you can review your photos on a display that's larger and more accurate than the camera's LCD monitor. A secondary benefit is that in addition to residing on the camera's memory card, the photos are also immediately copied to your hard drive as they are captured.

2

Tethered capture also bypasses the main Import screen, handling the file transfers, processing and importing in the background as you continue shooting. Just press the shutter button, and in a few seconds, the capture shows in the Lightroom catalog with all the settings you've applied in the setup.

Below is an explanation of the steps to set up tethered capture in Lightroom:

1. Connect your camera to your computer using the provided cables or a wireless system. The first time you do this, your computer might need to install a device driver, and/or open the Auto Play window to ask you what you want to do with the camera. If so, you can just close these windows; there's nothing you need to set here.

2. In Lightroom, select File→Tethered Capture→Start Tethered Capture (see Figure 2–29).

Figure 2-29

3. In the Tethered Capture Settings window (see Figure 2–30, next page), configure the batch settings for this capture session. In the top part of the window, give this session a name, which is used to create a subfolder on your hard disk where these captures will be copied.

    Optionally, check the box for Segment Photos by Shots. When this is checked, Lightroom will place the photos from a "shot" into its own subfolder, located underneath the main folder set in the Destination (lower in the screen).

    For example, if you're shooting a session with three different models, each model could have their own "shots" named for the model, and the resulting photos will be grouped together in separate folders. Or, if you're doing product photography, each product could have its own shot. Of course, what comprises a shot grouping is entirely up to you.

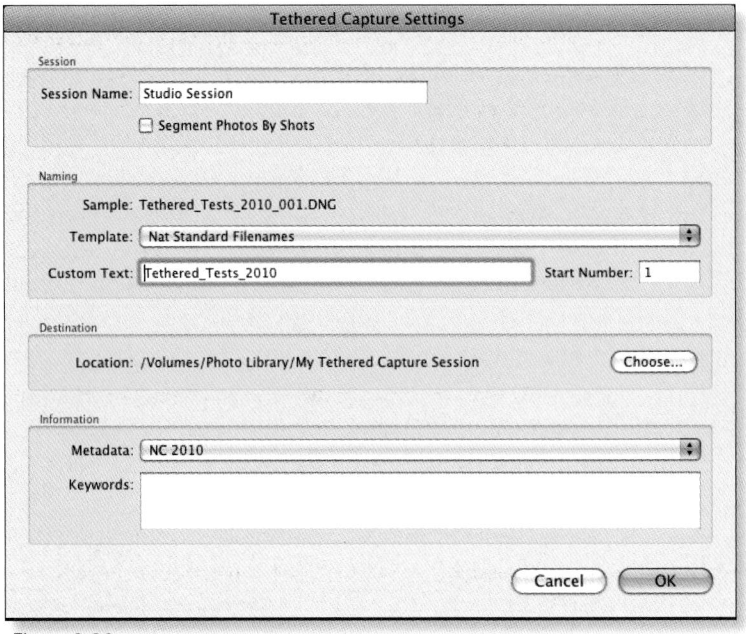

2

Tethered Capture Settings

Session

Session Name: Studio Session

☐ Segment Photos By Shots

Naming

Sample: Tethered_Tests_2010_001.DNG

Template: Nat Standard Filenames

Custom Text: Tethered_Tests_2010   Start Number: 1

Destination

Location: /Volumes/Photo Library/My Tethered Capture Session   Choose...

Information

Metadata: NC 2010

Keywords:

Cancel   OK

Figure 2-30

4. In the Naming section below, specify a **File Naming Template,** or create a new template by clicking the Edit command at the bottom of the menu. File naming templates are discussed in Chapter 3. (The file naming template editor now also includes a Shoot token that will use the Session Name when shooting tethered.)

5. Next, in the **Destination** section, specify the hard disk and folder where vthe files for this session will be copied to as they are transferred from the camera. (You can create a new folder at this time, but remember that the Session Name will generate a new folder, too.)

6. In the last section, apply your metadata template and optional keywords, as appropriate for the session.

7. When you're finished configuring tethered capture settings, click OK.

8. Lightroom then displays the Tethered Capture controls (see Figure 2–31). You can move the controls to a different place on your screen if you wish: move your cursor over the control bar and when it changes to a hand, click and drag.

Canon EOS 5D Mark II ⇕
Studio Session   125   2.8   100   Flash   NC 5D2 Default ⇕

Figure 2-31

9. If you need to change the settings for this session, click the gear icon at the right end of the capture control strip (circled above) to re-open the Tethered Capture Settings window. Or, to cancel the session, press the small X above the gear.

10. The large round button is a shutter control. You can click it to fire the shutter from your computer, or work as you normally would from behind the camera.

   Notes: at the time of my testing, Lightroom's shutter button did not replicate the full functionality of the camera's shutter button held down to capture in burst mode. Even holding down Lightroom's shutter button for several seconds still just produces a single shot.

   Also, the Lightroom shutter button will not trigger if your camera's mirror lockup is enabled (at least this is the case with my Canon 5D Mark II).

   The capture window also shows basic EXIF settings for each single shot, including as shutter speed, aperture, ISO and white balance, but you can't change any camera settings here.

11. You can apply Develop presets to the captures as they come into the catalog; click the Develop Settings popup menu to the left of the shutter button to select a previously saved preset. (Creating and saving Develop presets is covered at length in Chapter 4.)

⌘+T or Ctrl+T
Show and hide the tethered capture window

⌘+Shift+T or Ctrl+Shift+T
New Shot

12. As you capture images with your camera, they are automatically transferred to your specified folder and are processed and imported according to your Session settings. With the Auto Advance Selection menu option enabled, each new photo will be shown in Library as it is imported. You can hide the panels, and switch to Loupe for full screen previews, or Grid view for thumbnails in real time; see Chapter 3.

   During the time the photo(s) are being downloaded and processed, the main progress indicator shows in the Identity Plate in the left of the top panel. Another small, circular progress indicator appears next to the shutter release to show a file is being transferred and processed.

13. To have Lightroom automatically make each new image the selected photo when it comes into the catalog, make sure the option for Auto Advance Selection is enabled (under the Tethered Capture menu). This

2

is especially important if you're showing large Loupe previews.

14. To hide the tethered capture window while you're shooting, use the command under File→Tethered Capture→Hide Tethered Capture Window or the keyboard shortcut.

15. When you're done with the tethered capture session, click the small X at the right to close the controls and finish the session, or use the Stop Tethered Shooting menu command (see Figure 2–32).

Figure 2-32

16. When you come back later for another session, you'll find that Lightroom keeps track of cameras you've done tethered capture with, and you can select a different camera from the control strip. The Develop preset menu remembers the most recent settings, too.

Asset management for digital photographers

Asset management is a term used to describe the systems you use to store, organize, retrieve and back up your image files (or any other digital files, for that matter.) The systems you use for your photo library should be thoughtfully planned, implemented and maintainted. Independent from any software you may choose to process your photos, your image files must remain intact, accessible and secure now and in the future. You and your heirs must be able to manage your digital photographs quickly and easily for decades to come, underscoring the need for reliable systems for storing your photo files. It's essential that you plan out your storage system carefully, accounting for your current needs and budget along with a plan for growth.

Single-user environment

If you're the only one working with your image files your storage system can be very simple with few components. You can use internal or external hard disks or network storage. With the rate of advancements in disk drive systems and the corresponding increase in image file sizes it's important to create a cohesive plan for your image library.

Plan to upgrade your storage system every 16-18 months or sooner as you collect more images and as file sizes increase.

Use dedicated disk drives for your image library

It's better to *not* store your image files on your system disk. I recommend you store your photos (and usually, your Lightroom catalogs) on disk drives used only for that purpose. If you currently are storing your photos on a single internal disk, I recommend you set up new drives to use only for your imaging work.

Whenever possible it's easiest to use just one large disk for your entire image library. Fewer, larger disks are easier to manage than many small ones. A single disk also provides for easier backups. As your library grows and your disks fill to capacity, I highly recommend transferring everything to larger drives.

External USB 2.0 or FireWire (IEEE 1394) drives provide fast read/write times and can be easily moved to another computer as needed.

Workgroup environment

There are situations that benefit from, or require, the use of image files distributed over multiple drives and network servers. Lightroom handles this with ease, but with conditions. In a single Lightroom catalog, you can access image files stored on multiple disks and from network drives (though catalogs themselves must be on local drives). This is briefly discussed in Chapter 9; you can also search online for more about sharing Lightroom catalogs in network environments.

NAMING YOUR IMAGE FILES AND ARRANGING THEM IN FOLDERS

Your image files will be contained in folders, of whose structure you need to be acutely aware. Before importing photos into Lightroom it's best to establish a system for organizing your folders and files on the hard drive. Otherwise, you're likely to waste a lot of time looking for images, moving files around, and wondering which file is what.

How we arrange and name our files is one of the more subjective aspects of the digital photography workflow. While it stands to reason that you should use a system that fits your personal preferences and style of working, with all the variables involved, following a few standard guidelines will make your system easier to manage.

2

Folder structures

Deciding how to organize the folders in your image library can be the most daunting aspect of designing a *digital asset management* (DAM) system, but with careful consideration, you can implement a system that will serve you well for years. Here are a few things to keep in mind:

1. The number of folders in your image library will increase dramatically over time. **The system must scale** effectively with this growth.

2. Working with Lightroom, it's often advantageous to have all your photos organized in subfolders underneath one main, top-level folder (mine is called simply "Photo Library"). This makes it easier to keep your catalog links intact, even when moving your image library to other drives.

3. **Use as few folder levels as are necessary to support your organizational structure.** The number of nested folders (folders within other folders) can easily get out of hand; you don't want to have to "drill down" through many levels of folders to get to an individual file.

   Plan your photo folder architecture carefully. Consider what should be at the top level, what's beneath that, and so on. For example:

   2007
       091507_Grand_Tetons
       052107_Elizabeth_New_House
       100807_Maine

   or

   United_States
       Colorado
           Maggie_Homecoming_2008
           San_Juans_Summer_2008
             Silverton_080705
             Silverton_080706

   All the files from a single shoot should be contained in one folder. Files from longer shooting sessions, such as multiple-day trips, can be separated by folders named for days and/or locations.

4. **Keep original and derivative files in the same folder.** In general, it's best to not use separate folders just for different image file types, such as one folder for DNG, another for TIF, a third for JPG, etc. It's much easier to have all your files from a single shoot in one folder. The exception to this would be cases where you're exporting files for a particular purpose, such as sending to a client, etc. This is covered in Chapter 5.

Reworking your existing folders

The most important aspect of organizing your image library is to get everything into one place. If you have disorganized files and folders in different locations, start by putting them all into one top-level folder. Call it "Photo Library" or "My Photos"; whatever you like. You can use your User\Pictures folder temporarily for this, but eventually, **I strongly recommend moving your master photo library off your system disk.** Keeping your image library on a separate disk from your system makes managing and backing up your photo library easier, and also allows you to make updates to your operating system and applications without affecting your images.

Once everything is in one main folder rearrange/rename the subfolders to fit your new system. Do as much organizing of your files as you can before importing them into Lightroom.

Guidelines for folder and file naming

Even in this age of metadata, where software can perform all kinds of functions using information embedded inside image files, the names you give your files and folders is still very important.

The main reason careful naming matters is the frequent need to find, open and save files using your computer's file system. Navigating through dialog boxes, copying files between media and sending images as email attachments are commonplace activities. Using well-conceived names will make these tasks much easier. Name your folders and files using the following guidelines.

1. **Use as few characters as necessary** to provide all the pertinent information about the contents of the file or folder. Ideally, try to keep your base file name short characters, because as you create master and derivative files their names will become longer with codes or special designations. Keep it simple.

2

2. **Use Internet-friendly file and folder names.** When it's time to share files, having used Internet-friendly names from the start is a big time saver. Most importantly, *don't use spaces in names;* use dashes or underscores to separate words instead. *Don't use special characters* like "/", "$", "@", "%" and *no punctuation.* Parentheses () and apostrophes ' should be avoided.

   Wrong: Sam's Birthday 04/18/08
   Right: 041808_Sam_Birthday

3. **Use the same base file name for all the images from a single shoot.** Differentiate them with a serial number at the end of each file name.

4. **The names of your folders should be consistent with the names of the files they contain.**

The automatic file names the camera assigns to files are not useful in our workflow. Therefore, one of the key steps in the import process is to rename the files to something more meaningful. Your base file name should contain:

1. The date the photo was taken;

2. The subject or location of the photograph or an identifier such as client name, etc.; and

3. Serial (sequence) number.

Example folder and file names

yyyymmdd_location_sequence
20081025_bryce_canyon
    20081025_bryce_canyon_001.tif
    20081025_bryce_canyon_002.tif
    20081025_bryce_canyon_003.tif
…

SUBJECT-SUBJECT-MMDDYY-SEQUENCE
CLIENT-SHOOT-052603
    CLIENT-SHOOT-052603-01.jpg
    CLIENT-SHOOT-052603-02.jpg
    CLIENT-SHOOT-052603-03.jpg
…

Location_yymmdd_sequence_code
Vernazza_080224
> Vernazza _080224_0001.dng
> Vernazza _080224_0002.dng
> Vernazza _080224_0002_M.tif
> Vernazza _080224_0002_700px.jpg
> Vernazza _080224_0003.dng

…

The third set of previous examples is the convention I use. I start my names with the subject or location, because it's more important to me than when the photograph was made. When I'm looking for something, I like to have my folders organized alphabetically by subject. For example, if I'm looking for a photo I made in Colorado, it's easy to remember the location as the Great Sand Dunes National Park, but I wouldn't necessarily remember the dates I was there.

I also append a code to the end of the names of derivative files, such as "M" for Master (for layered composites), pixel dimension of the longest side (usually for Web JPG files), or text indicating the purpose of the file. This illustrates the importance of keeping your base file names short.

Do what makes sense to you

Many photographers like to organize their folders by date first, beginning with top-level folders for each year. It really doesn't matter, as long as your system is consistent. If you have large numbers of files in your historical archives that you don't feel deserve your taking the time to change their names, don't worry too much about it now. The important thing is to nail down a system and use it going forward. After you've lived with it for a while, you can decide if anything needs reworking and if older files should be renamed to fit the new conventions.

Backups

Every computer user knows that backing up your files is critical. Still, I'd be negligent if I didn't remind you *to actually do it*. Religiously. In the digital photography workflow there's absolutely no excuse to risk losing all your work. **Update your backups after every work session!**

People accidentally lose important computer data every minute of every day. Usually it's because of user error (deleting something unintentionally) but equipment failure is also common.

2

I can't over-emphasize the need for creating a practical system for backing up your work and updating your backups *very* frequently. When a hard drive fails mechanically or its data become corrupted, if you're prepared, you will be back on track quickly. Otherwise, be prepared to say goodbye to your photos.

In any photo storage setup, each primary disk should have, at minimum, one exact replica that is continually updated.

BACKING UP LIGHTROOM CATALOGS

Lightroom offers the ability to test the integrity of the database and make a backup of a catalog file. You should frequently allow these backups to be performed. New in Lightroom 3, backups are done when Lightroom quits.

During a backup process, only the current Lightroom catalog is backed up— the image files and preview packages are not.

Lightroom backup settings are found in the Catalog Settings dialog box, introduced in Chapter 1. On the General tab, set the backup frequency to **Every Time Lightroom Exits.** You can always skip backups if you choose. But at least this way, Lightroom reminds you!

When Lightroom asks if you want to do a backup, you can specify the location for the backup file. The backups are automatically placed in subfolders named with the date and time; see Figure 2–33.

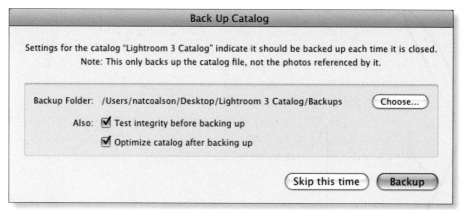

Figure 2-33

Only keep the most recent one or two catalog backups
Go to your backups folder to periodically delete old ones.

2

Drag-and-drop backup

You can also back up your Lightroom catalog and previews by dragging and dropping the main catalog folder onto another hard disk; this is a fine way to do it. However, keep in mind this skips the data testing stage that Lightroom performs when it performs a backup.

BACKING UP IMAGE FILES

Always maintain at least two copies of your image files on separate hard disks. Set up two hard drives, one as the master working library and the other as its mirror image. If possible, store a third backup at an alternate location. Update these backups frequently.

Backup after import

During any import in which files are being copied, Lightroom offers the ability to make backups of the files being imported. However, it is the *original* files that get backed up, not the new copies. For this reason I recommend you manually do a file backup immediately *after* imports are completed.

Syncing drives

Use backup software that can *synchronize* data between hard drives. **Sync your master and backup drives after every major work session.** You can also set up the software to automatically sync at specific times. For Mac, I recommend Carbon Copy Cloner and ChronoSync; on Windows I use Microsoft Robocopy and SyncToy.

Carbon Copy Cloner for Mac http://www.bombich.com/
Chronosync for Mac http://www.econtechnologies.com/
Microsoft SyncToy http://www.microsoft.com/prophoto/downloads/

Solid state media for backups

With the recent growth in capacity, solid state (flash) drives, such as removable USB "thumb drives", "jump drives", etc. provide a good option for both temporary backups and permanent archival. With no moving parts or magnetic data, they may survive longer than magnetic hard drives.

CHAPTER 3
LIBRARY

3

Organizing your photos in Library

After importing photos into the catalog it's time to edit the shoot. The goal is to go from the many images captured during a session to only the few, best photographs—those chosen to continue through the processing pipeline. The photo editing process is *iterative:* we review photos in multiple *passes* of editing until they are distilled down to the final *selects*.

SIMPLE EDITING WORKFLOW

During each round of editing, decide whether each image stays or goes. "Maybes" stay, at least for the current round. Try to look at the photographs as if someone else made them. Be your own toughest critic—you have too many good shots to waste time on bad ones! Move through your editing quickly, without over-analyzing. But also learn from your failures by going back to study them later. Is the shot successful or not? Does it have less-than-obvious potential that can be brought out in processing? Clearly define your reasons for giving each photo a thumbs-up or thumbs-down. Use the fundamentals of photography to make your choices: interesting subject or theme, strong composition, good exposure, etc.

Evaluate similar photographs *heuristically* (ranked in ascending order) to determine the best—and ignore the rest. Don't fret over your decisions. You can always come back later to confirm your initial choices—and you always have the prerogative to change your mind. For each pass, the editing steps are:

1. **Review:** evaluate the photographs on their strengths and potential. Concentrate on simply deciding if each photograph works or it doesn't.

2. **Rate:** apply Lightroom *attributes* (stars, labels and/or flags) to differentiate selects from rejects.

3. **Save:** save Lightroom attributes and metadata to the image files on disk.

4. **Filter:** show only those selects that have survived the current round.

5. **Repeat:** continue editing until only your best work remains.

These steps are first explained in basic terms. Then the remainder of this chapter explains each task in detail.

Don't use the Previous Import source for editing

Following an import, switch to the Folder source to edit the photos. The Previous Import source doesn't provide the full set of options that a folder does. (Both are discussed later in this chapter.)

3

⌘+Shift+F or
Ctrl+Shift+F
Enter full screen
mode and hide
all the panels

First pass

With all photos from the import showing in the Library Grid (see Figure 3–1), hide the panels and go through the shoot quickly. Apply one star to the best of this round. Optionally, mark with a reject flag any photos you want to delete. Whatever labeling system you prefer, do your best to use a consistent system of rating your photos. For example, all images with one star ideally should have the same significance in your catalog, such as indicating a first round select.

Figure 3-1

Use the arrow keys to move between images

In the Library Grid you can move left, right, up and down to select images with your arrow keys. At all other times (and in other modules) use just the left and right arrows to select the next/previous images shown in the Filmstrip.

As you go through your edit, you can switch to Loupe, Compare or Survey views as needed to evaluate larger previews or compare multiple images. We'll look at those in a bit. Also, sometimes you'll want to do some processing to make a decision about how to rate an image. With Lightroom you can make quick adjustments to photos as you edit the shoot. You can use the controls on Library's Quick Develop panel to quickly process multiple photos during editing. If needed, apply Quick Develop adjustments to help you make editing decisions… but don't get too mired in processing at this point. We're just picking our favorite shots.

3

When you're done with the first pass, Save Metadata to File, then apply a filter to show photos with one star only; see Figure 3–2. You can also Delete Rejects at this point, which is explained later in this chapter. If you edit your work tightly, this may be as far as you need to go in the editing process, and you can begin processing your selects in the Develop module.

⌘+Z or Ctrl+Z
Undo the last step. Repeat the keystroke to go as far back as necessary.

⌘+Shift+Z or Crtl+Shift+Z
Redo steps

⌘+A or Ctrl+A then ⌘+S or Ctrl+S
Selects all the images visible in the current source, then saves all Lightroom metadata to the files on disk

And during all editing, remember that you can always undo and redo steps!

Figure 3-2

Save your work frequently

After each round of editing, but before filtering, select all your images and Save Metadata to File. This ensures that ratings and any Quick Develop adjustments are saved on disk as well as in the Lightroom catalog.

A quick note about camera raw files and XMP sidecars

Because a raw file straight from the camera typically cannot be modified using software, any metadata applied to the file that you want to save on disk must be stored elsewhere. The most common method is the use of *sidecar* files in .XMP (Extensible Metadata Platform) format. A sidecar file is associated with a specific, individual image file and contains metadata changes made to the raw file in software such as Lightroom and Adobe Camera Raw. The sidecar must always accompany the original file in order for the metadata changes to be saved or read by the software. This is one reason I recommend using DNG for your raw originals instead of native camera raw files, because you can save XMP metadata directly into DNG files. More about DNGs later.

Second pass

If necessary, repeat the review and rating process to further refine your choices. Selects that make it through the second pass get two stars. When you're done, filter for two stars.

During editing, start applying more keywords to photos that make it through the current round. At the end, your final selects should contain a complete, unique set of keywords for each individual photo.

Additional passes

Continue to review and rate, applying three, four, up to five stars to the selects for each round. Repeat the process only as many times as necessary to get to your final selects. Sometimes one or two passes are all that are needed. Other times you might need to go through the shoot numerous times, filtering down your Grid view each time. Whatever the case, be sure that when you're done editing only your best work remains visible in the Grid.

Refrain from immediately deleting photos during editing

It slows the workflow, plus you might make a mistake. If you want to delete images, consider coming back later to do so. Better decisions might be made with some time gone by. Plus, in Lightroom it's easy enough to simply hide the photos you don't want to see, discussed later in this chapter.

After the final pass, add selects to a collection

When you get to the point where you have a strong representation of final selects, put them all into either an existing collection or a make new one. This can be done by manually making a collection and adding photos to it, or by using smart collections. Both are covered later in this chapter. **Typically, all further work on the selects should be done from collections.** Often, photos placed in the final collection(s) are the only images from the shoot that will continue into Develop. You can always return to the folder if necessary to have another look at the photos that were hidden during editing. In this chapter I'll explain why I think collections are so great.

Repeat

You can use the above basic steps for every edit. Lightroom is flexible; the order in which you perform specific editing tasks is not as important as using a consistent system.

The rest of this chapter explains Library's features and functions in detail.

3

Lightroom image sources

All the organizing and editing in Library is done using *image sources*. Sources determine which photos are shown in the *Grid, Loupe* and *Filmstrip* views. Lightroom's image sources and locations are:

- **Catalog Panel:** built-in sources with predetermined criteria.

- **Folder Panel:** representations of the actual folders on your hard disk.

- **Collections Panel:** virtual groups of photos within the Lightroom catalog.

- **Keywords Panel:** if a photo has keywords applied, they can be used to define or refine other sources.

- **Filter Bar:** filters are most effectively used to refine the other image sources.

⌘+Click or Ctrl+Click on multiple sources

You can combine multiple sources, from multiple panels, to create the exact selection of photographs you want to work on.

The Recent Sources menu

The *Source Indicator* is shown in text along the top of the Filmstrip. Clicking on this opens the Recent Sources menu. Use it to jump to any of the twelve most recently used sources plus the built-in Catalog sources and Favorite Sources. You can also clear the Recent Sources list. See Figure 3–3.

Figure 3-3

Favorite Sources: new in Lightroom 3, you can also save and retrieve Favorite Sources using this menu. (Favorite Sources remain even if you clear the Recent Sources.)

⌘+Control+1
or Ctrl+Shift+1
Open/close the
Catalog panel

CATALOG PANEL

The Catalog panel at the top left of the Library module lists several built-in image sources (see Figure 3–4).

Figure 3-4

The core criteria used for Catalog sources can't be changed, but filters can be applied to refine them, discussed later in this chapter.

All Photographs: shows all the photos in the catalog.

Quick Collection: shows all the photos in the Quick Collection.

Previous Import: shows all the photos added to the catalog during the most recent Import or Sync.

Additional Sources Sometimes on the Catalog Panel
Depending on the condition of your catalog and the work you've done, sometimes Lightroom will show additional sources on the Catalog panel, including:

- Missing Photographs, or Photos Missing from [folder name]

- Error Photos

- Added by Previous Export

- Previous Export as Catalog

Keep an eye on what's listed in the Catalog panel
Other temporary sources may also appear in this list from time to time. The Catalog panel can alert you to potential problems in addition to providing quick ways to retrieve photos you've recently worked with.

To remove one of these temporary sources from the Catalog panel, right click its name, and from the popup menu, choose Remove this temporary collection.

⌘+Control+2
or Ctrl+Shift+2
Open/close the
Folders panel

FOLDERS PANEL SOURCES

The Folders panel (see Figure 3–5) shows the hard disk and directory structures for all the photos that have been imported into Lightroom. The Folders panel does *not* show image files; as you select folders by clicking on them, their contents are shown in the *Grid, Loupe* and *Filmstrip*, which are discussed further in this chapter.

**Resize panel groups
by dragging their edges**
Wider panels can show longer folder names.

Figure 3-5

3

Hard Disk Drives and Volumes

At the top level of the folder/file hierarchy is the *volume*. A volume is usually an individual hard disk drive, but could also be a partition on a single disk or a multiple-disk array.

Volumes (and folders) shown in Lightroom correspond directly to the drive volumes on your computer's file system (Mac os x Finder or Windows Explorer). Volumes are listed in the Folders panel with their folders underneath; see Figure 3–6.

Figure 3-6

A single Lightroom catalog can contain images from any number of volumes. As you import images from folders on different drives, each volume also automatically gets added to the list in the Folders panel. Each volume has its own Volume Browser listing, which shows the status of the volume and optional statistics. Click the volume name to hide and show its folder contents.

By default, the Volume Browser also shows the available free space and the volume size. This can be changed. Normally there's a green "light" at the left of the Volume Browser indicating the volume is online with available free space. If the light is yellow or red, free space on the volume is low. If a volume is dimmed (gray), that volume is offline.

Figure 3-7

Control+Click or right-click on the Volume Browser header

To change the Volume Browser display options, or to show the volume in the Finder or Explorer; see Figure 3–7.

Offline/online

A disk volume that is connected and available to the computer is *online*. A volume that is not available to the computer is *offline*.

In Lightroom you can work with photos from offline volumes in Library, Slideshow, Print and Web, where Lightroom will use rendered previews if they are available.

You can't work on images from offline volumes in Develop and a few other controls are unavailable. This is because when processing an image, Lightroom renders new previews after each change is made, which requires re-reading the data from the actual image.

Volumes not listed in the Folder panel
Lightroom will not show or provide access to volumes until you import photos from that drive. If a volume is not listed in the Folders panel, it's because no photos from it have been imported into the current catalog.

FOLDERS AND SUBFOLDERS

Folders are the basic method for organizing your photos on the hard disk. Immediately after Import you'll begin editing your images within their folders (see Figure 3–8). When you import a photo into Lightroom, the folder containing that photo on disk will also be added to the Folders list.

You can directly manipulate the Folder hierarchy on disk from within Lightroom; if you move or rename folders listed in Lightroom's Folders panel, those changes **will also be made to the folders on disk.** Lightroom will give you an alert to confirm when doing this.

Figure 3-8

To add the parent folder of the selected folder to the Folders panel, **Control+Click or right-click the folder name, then choose Add Parent.**

Don't stay in folders too long
In Lightroom you can do a lot of work from within a folder source. But various stages of the editing workflow and some tasks will require more refined selections and the creation of derivative files for specific purposes. For efficiency, these situations benefit from the creation of other "virtual" organizational structures within the Lightroom catalog. As you move through your workflow on a group of photos, use the other sources instead of folders, especially collections and smart filters.

3

Show Photos in Subfolders

When the *Show Photos in Subfolders* menu option is active (see Figure 3–9), selecting a folder in the Folders panel will show its contents and **also the contents of any subfolders it contains.** You can also enable or disable this option from the menu that appears when you click the + button on the panel header.

Figure 3-9

Though this is the default condition, depending on your folder structure, this may be neither necessary nor desirable. For one thing, showing all the contents of subfolders can slow Lightroom's performance as it reads and makes previews for the many files in the subfolders.

With the Show Photos in Subfolders option turned off, selecting a folder will only show the contents of that folder and

Figure 3-10

not of the subfolders. This can dramatically improve performance and give you a more accurate read on the contents of individual folders. But a potential drawback to doing this is that the file counts of parent folders are also affected (see Figure 3–10). For this reason, I normally work with Show Photos in Subfolders on, and turn it off temporarily when appropriate.

MANAGING FOLDERS

Before importing photos into Lightroom, it's a good idea to first organize them as much as possible on the hard disk. **But once photos are in the catalog, it's usually best to manage them entirely from within Lightroom.** This ensures that Lightroom can keep track of all the files in its database. For example, you can drag and drop photos between folders in Lightroom and this will also move them on disk.

⌘+Shift+N or Ctrl+Shift+N
Make a new folder

Adding folders

When you add new folders in Lightroom they are also created on your hard disk.

Click + on the Folders panel header then choose Add Folder or Add Subfolder
Type the folder name and press Return or Enter.

Changes to folders in Lightroom also are changed on the hard drive

In almost all cases, making changes to the folders showing in Lightroom's Folders panel will also affect the actual folders on your hard drive.

Renaming folders

Renaming a folder in Lightroom renames it on disk. Right-click or Ctrl+click or on the folder name, **then** choose Rename from the contextual menu. Type the new name and press Return or Enter.

Removing folders

When removing a folder from Lightroom 3, you now have the choice of whether or not to also delete it from the hard disk. Control+Click or right-click on the folder name, then choose Remove Folder from the contextual menu. Press Return or Enter to finish.

Finding a folder on your hard drive

You can easily locate a folder anywhere on your hard disk. Control+Click or right-click on the folder name. From the contextual menu choose Show in Finder or Show in Explorer. This will locate the folder and select it on your file system.

Import into This Folder

Lightroom now provides a quick way to add photos into a specific folder. Right-click or Ctrl+click on a folder and select the command from the menu. The Import window opens with the chosen folder as the destination.

MANAGING PHOTOS

After photos have been imported into a Lightroom catalog, those image files need to remain accessible to Lightroom for you to do most of the work with them. For example, you can't do any Develop edits without having the actual files accessible by Lightroom. You *can* do metadata edits like keywording, rating etc. but if you want to actually process the files you need the original image files available on disk.

(If you have a fast enough internet connection, you can put image files on a network server; Lightroom can work with any image files you can gain access to, even over a network.)

When you have access to the actual files, renaming or moving photos in Lightroom also makes those changes on disk.

3

Renaming Photos

Renaming photos in Lightroom also always renames the image files on disk (see Figure 3–11). Renaming files is something you should consider carefully. If a batch of images is improperly named, you should rename the files correctly as early as possible in the workflow. Use the menu command or shortcut to open the Rename Files dialog box. Select Custom Name from the File Naming drop-down menu and enter the name in the Custom Text field or use one of the other file naming presets.

F2
Open the Rename File dialog box

Rename 1 Photo
File Naming: Nat Standard Filenames
Custom Text: Boston_104026   **Start Number:** 1
Example: Boston_104026_001.dng   Cancel   OK

Figure 3-11

Rename a Batch of Images During Editing

If you do your file naming *after* the Import, rename the photos after you remove any rejects. Along with other potential workflow advantages, this helps keep your numbering sequence unbroken.

File naming templates

One of Lightroom's most useful batch processing capabilities is renaming files. With file naming templates you can set up a standardized base file name using whatever conventions you prefer. The templates are then used to rename files during import, or later in the Library module.

The filename template editor window (see Figure 3–12) is accessed from the File Renaming: panel on the import screen (see Chapter 2), the Library→Rename Photos menu in Library or the Metadata panel in Library.

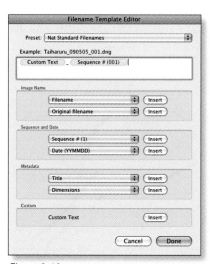

Figure 3-12

The filename template editor provides a wide range of controls to set up your template. Enter type directly in the text box and/or click the Insert buttons to put tokens in the name. A token is a preformatted type of information, such as date, sequence number, etc. Carefully construct your base file name template in the text box. When it's the way you want it, save it from the Preset menu at the top.

Finding a photo on your hard drive

⌘+R or Ctrl+R
Go to a selected file in Finder or Explorer

From within the Lightroom catalog, you can easily locate an image file anywhere on your hard disk. Control+Click or right-click on the photo. From the contextual menu choose Show in Finder or Show in Explorer; this will locate the image within your hard drive's file system.

Finding a photo in the Lightroom Folders list

Occasionally, when working in a source other than a folder, you may need to find the folder, within Lightroom, that contains the image. Control+Click or right-click the image. From the contextual menu choose Go to Folder in Library.

Note that if you're already working in any Folders image source, this menu command is not available.

Removing photos

You can remove images from Lightroom without affecting them on the hard disk, or you can use Lightroom to actually delete files from the disk (see Figure 3–13).

Figure 3-13

Select the affected image(s) and press Delete. A dialog box appears giving you three options:

- **Delete from Disk:** Remove the photo(s) from the Lightroom catalog and move the image file to the system trash.

- **Remove:** Remove the photo(s) from the Lightroom catalog but leave the image on the disk. You won't be able to work on the photo in Lightroom any more unless it's re-imported or synchronized.

- **Cancel** and do nothing.

3

Be very careful when deleting folders or photos

When you remove folders or delete photos from Lightroom, any edits or adjustments you made to those photos in Lightroom will also be removed. If you haven't saved out the metadata, that work will be lost. (You could re-import the files, but your Lightroom changes will not be restored.) If you make a mistake when removing photos or folders, you can immediately Undo the deletion(s).

Some thoughts about deleting photos from the master catalog

Many photographers permanently delete rejected images to conserve disk space and maybe also to conserve a little ego (none of us wants to look at our worst images). If you choose to do this, I recommend giving it some time before you do.

During editing it is faster, cheaper, easier and safer to simply hide unwanted photos from view rather than actually delete them. Deleting images in the heat of the moment introduces the risk of accidentally trashing something important. If you wait to do it at a later date you're less likely to make a mistake.

Plus, we can often learn more from our failures than from our successes. Trashing your worst shots right away can cramp your creative development and impede the learning process. Keep the bad photos for a while and take the time later to really understand what worked and what didn't. Think about how you would do it differently next time.

In my twenty-plus years of professional imaging work, managing huge volumes of digital files, there have only been a handful of times when I accidentally deleted something that I shouldn't have… and for which there was no backup. It always happened in the midst of the production workflow, when I was doing several things at once and not paying enough attention to what I was doing. So for now, I keep everything but the most obvious wasted pixels and I go back later to permanently delete photos that really deserve it.

As your image library grows to tens or hundreds of thousands of images, it may become necessary to delete unwanted images in order to save potentially significant amounts of disk space. Plan to come back to your library periodically in the future to re-confirm your editing decisions and delete unwanted files for good. You'll have better perspective with the benefit of hindsight. For now, just use the Lightroom image sources, filters etc. to conceal the images you don't want to work on.

HANDLING MISSING PHOTOS AND FOLDERS

Remember that the names and locations of your image files and folders are recorded in the database at the time of import. This means if you move anything in your file system outside Lightroom, especially when Lightroom is not running, the database will not automatically update and you will need to manually relink the files in the catalog.

Also, in some situations, it's possible that the files *haven't* been moved, but Lightroom has somehow lost track of them. An example of this is when using an external drive on Windows, where the drive is assigned a default letter each time it's turned on. It's possible that the same drive will be assigned a different drive letter the next time it's connected. Lightroom won't be able to find the files because the drive letter is part of the file path stored in the catalog.

Whatever the reason, if Lightroom can't locate a file or folder, you'll receive notification. Usual causes and remedies for broken links:

- **The file or folder was moved or renamed outside Lightroom:** relink the files from within Lightroom.

- **The volume is offline:** connect the hard drive(s) to the computer.

- **Something is wrong with the database:** verify, repair and/or update it.

Don't leave broken links hanging around

If you have missing folders or photos showing in your catalog, you should either relink them or remove them as soon as possible. Database housekeeping is essential: when using any database-enabled program (like Lightroom) it's important to keep the database as clean as possible, with no extraneous data or records known to be bad. This will make things easier to find, improve performance, speed backups and generally make the program more pleasant to use.

Finding missing folders

If a folder name contains a question mark (see Figure 3–14) it means the folder and its contents cannot be located by Lightroom. To process these photos, you will first need to relink the folder.

Figure 3-14

Control+Click or right-click on the folder name

Choose Find Missing Folder from the contextual menu. Navigate through the dialog boxes to find the missing folder and click Return or Enter to finish. Lightroom will update the links in its database.

3

Update Folder Location: this command allows you to point Lightroom to a different source folder on a hard disk, whether or not Lightroom thinks a folder is "missing". This is useful if you've copied or moved files and need Lightroom to use the new location, even though the existing catalog links are not broken.

Finding missing photos
If a thumbnail shows a question mark (see Figure 3–15), Lightroom can't find the image file on disk and you cannot process it in Develop.

Click the question mark on a thumbnail
Navigate through the file dialog boxes to find the image file on disk. Press Return or Enter to relink the photo.

Finding one missing file will also find others
In the dialog box, click the checkbox to Find Nearby Photos. Once you've successfully relinked a missing folder or file to the correct location on your hard disk, Lightroom will find and relink all the others, if possible.

Figure 3-15

Find missing photos
This command, under the Library menu, identifies any missing photos in your catalog and filters the Library view to show them. You can then determine whether to relink or delete them.

SYNCHRONIZING FOLDERS

If you've made changes to the contents of a folder outside Lightroom, such as adding or removing images, renaming files, etc., you can *synchronize* the folder in Lightroom. Synchronize Folder compares what's in the catalog with the contents of the folder on disk and allows you to update the catalog accordingly. For example, if you use Adobe Bridge, Adobe Camera Raw,

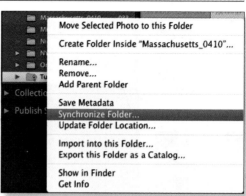

Figure 3-16

Photoshop or Elements to edit photos outside the Lightroom catalog, you'll need to synchronize them in Lightroom when you're done.

Control+Click or right-click on the folder name
Choose "Synchronize Folder..." from the contextual menu (see Figure 3–16) to open the Import window where you can see previews of the changed to be made during the sync. Also, and maybe more importantly, metadata entries remaining from your Previous Import, such as keywords and copyright notice, can be inadvertently applied to photos added to the catalog during the sync process. Check those fields before executing the sync. Press Return or Enter to sync the Folder.

COLLECTIONS AND FILTERED SOURCES

In addition to the ability to manipulate actual files and folders on disk from within Lightroom, there are even more powerful options for finding, organizing and sorting your photographs using *virtual* sources created in the database.

Collections are like "virtual folders"; they exist only in the Lightroom database. A single photograph can be a member of any number of Collections without requiring additional copies of the file on disk. Collections are an example of Lightroom's ability to reference a single image in multiple ways from within the database. *Filters* define image sources using criteria you specify and are used to refine other, higher-level sources. Collections and Filters are discussed in detail later in this chapter.

KEYWORDS AS SOURCES

You can create image sources using the Keyword List panel; see Figure 3–17. When you place your cursor over a keyword an arrow appears to the right. Click the arrow to view images containing that keyword. Note that this will only find photos with that keyword *in the current source.* In other words, if you want to search for photos with a specific keyword within a folder, make sure that folder is selected first before clicking the keyword arrow.

Figure 3-17

For searches on multiple keywords, use the text filter
To set up image sources using multiple keywords, use the Filter Bar controls instead of the Keyword List (discussed later in this chapter).

3

G
Go to Library
Grid from
anywhere in
Lightroom

Working in Grid view

Much of your work in Library will be done using *thumbnails* of your photos. In Library, the Grid view (see Figure 3–18) shows thumbnails inside *cells* arranged in rows and columns. There are two parts of the thumbnail; the image preview itself and the cell (the gray area surrounding a thumbnail). They behave differently and provide different options. Thumbnails are useful for seeing groups of photos together and contemplating their relationships to one another and when applying settings to multiple photos.

Figure 3-18

Your initial rounds of editing can primarily be done using thumbnails; they are good indicators of strong composition, as you're not distracted by minute detail as with larger previews. Lightroom provides lots of control over the presentation and functionality of thumbnails.

Panning in the Grid

Position your mouse on the border between thumbnails—the cursor turns into a hand and you can scroll the Grid up and down.

Page Up and Page Down in Grid
To jump between full-screen sets of thumbnails use the Page Up and Page Down keys.

- (dash)
Make
thumbnails
smaller

= (+)
Make
thumbnails
larger

Changing Thumbnail Size
You can change the thumbnail size by dragging the slider on the Toolbar.
See Figure 3–19.

Figure 3-19

Smaller Thumbnails in Filmstrip
Like the other panels, you can resize the Filmstrip by dragging its (top) edge. This
changes the size of thumbnails in the Filmstrip.

SORT ORDER
Working in most image sources you can change the *sort order* in which the
thumbnails are shown. The Library Grid toolbar contains a menu for selecting the
sort order; see Figure 3–20. The button to the left (labeled az or za) reverses sort
direction. In Lightroom 3 you can now sort by aspect ratio.

Figure 3-20

User Order
This is a special sort order where you can rearrange the thumbnails however you
want by dragging them around. **User sort order is only available in Folders and
Collections (not Smart Collections) sources.**

Click and drag thumbnails to arrange them
Click and drag with your mouse to rearrange the thumbnails in the Grid. This will
automatically set the Sort Order menu to User Order. (You can't do this within the
Catalog sources.)

Drag using the center of the thumbnail image
When selecting or dragging photos, always click on and drag from the image part of
the thumbnail.

Other Sort Orders
Image files that get added to the catalog during editing or synchronizing (often
with varying file types) may appear in the Grid in an order that can be confusing. If
you look for a photo thumbnail in a certain place in the order and it's not there, try

3

looking at the last images in the source. Newly added photos often end up there. Once you find the new photos at the end, you can modify the sort order or tag them differently to change where they appear in the sort order.

⌘+Option+Shift+H or Ctrl+Alt+Shift+H
Hide/show badges in the Grid

Click a Badge
Edit the image using that tool

THUMBNAIL BADGES

In Library Grid, the thumbnails by default will show one or more small *badges* when any metadata (keywords, cropping, adjustments, etc.) has been applied to that image, or if the photo is in a collection. See Figure 3–21.

Badges in the Filmstrip

The icons in the Filmstrip can show badges, too; configure this in Preferences➔Interface. (Note that some Filmstrip badges won't show if the thumbnails are very small.)

Figure 3-21

In Lightroom 3, there are new options for showing badges in the Filmstrip; go to Preferences➔Interface.

J
Cycle through the Grid view styles

⌘+ Shift+H or Ctrl+ Shift+H
Switch between compact and expanded Grid thumbnails

⌘+J or Ctrl+J
Open the View Options window

GRID VIEW STYLE

There are two styles of Grid thumbnails: *Compact* and *Expanded*. Both can be customized using View Options (see Figure 3–22).

VIEW OPTIONS

This window configures the display of the thumbnails in Grid view and the Info Overlays in Loupe view. Click the tabs at the top to switch between Grid and Loupe views. When you're done changing the settings, close the window. The information you choose to show depends a lot on personal preferences and circumstances.

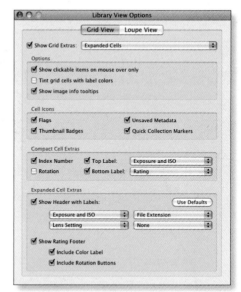

Figure 3-22

Selecting and deselecting images

Most operations in Lightroom require one or more images to be *selected*. The most obvious way to select images is to click them, but there are some faster, easier selection methods available.

It's important to understand that usually there is at least one image selected, if only by default, unless you take action to deselect them.

You can select a single image, multiple images or all images in the current source. The order in which multiple photos are selected is important. You can also select None (no images selected).

The Grid and Filmstrip show the same selections; see Figure 3–23. Selected photos are highlighted in light gray to stand out against the other unselected photos. This means that you can select images in the Grid, and then see and work with those selections using the Filmstrip in other modules.

Figure 3-23

Select images using arrow keys
In the Library Grid you can quickly select images using the arrow keys on your keyboard—left, right, up, down. Or, in all the modules, use just the left and right arrow keys to move through images horizontally in the Filmstrip.

Hold Shift while pressing the arrow keys to select multiple contiguous images (those next to each other in the sort order).

3

THE ACTIVE PHOTO

Figure 3-24

When multiple photos are selected, the first one you selected is the "most selected" and referred to as the *active* photo. The active photo is highlighted brighter than the others (see Figure 3–24) and has unique properties within the selection. Most importantly, the active photo behaves **as if no other images were selected.**

⌘+Left/
Right Arrow
or Ctrl+Left/
Right Arrow
Change the active photo with multiple photos selected

The active photo also:

/
Deselect the active photo

- Is used for the histogram;

- Is Processed in Develop; and

- Has settings that can be synced (or copied and pasted) to other images.

By default, when you switch between image sources, the first image in the source becomes active.

With multiple images selected, click a thumbnail preview to make that photo the active one, or use the shortcuts.

⌘+A or
Ctrl+A
Select all

SELECT ALL

There are many situations where you will want to select all the images in the current source, such as when adding to a collection, modifying keywords and Saving Metadata to File.

Use the Select All command under the Edit menu, or use the shortcut. All images in the current source become selected (see Figure 3–25).

If you had an image selected before running the Select All command, it becomes the active photo. If no image was previously selected, the first image in the source order becomes the active photo.

Figure 3-25

⌘+D or
Ctrl+D
Select None -
"deselects" all
photos

SELECT NONE

This is one of the most important commands used throughout the editing workflow. It's a very good habit to deselect any previously selected images before moving on to work on others. Otherwise, you might accidentally apply adjustments or other changes to a photo without intending to!

If your thumbnail Grid shows some empty space with no thumbnails at the end, you can click there to Select None; see Figure 3–26. Otherwise, use the shortcut.

Figure 3-26

ADD, SUBTRACT, INTERSECT

These specialized selection commands allow you to make complex photo selections quickly based on several criteria. These selections commands are *Boolean*; think of them in terms of yes/no, on/off or active/inactive. You can start with one selection and then modify it to include only the images you want.

Many selection commands will invert the selection status of the any photos already selected: selected images become deselected; deselected images become selected.

Under the Edit menu there are a bunch of selection commands:

- Select Only Active Photo

- Deselect Active Photo

- Select by Flag

- Select by Rating

- Select by Color Label

Always know what's selected
Keep track of your selections at all times. When scrolling in the Grid or Filmstrip it's possible to have images selected but not visible on the screen.

3

This can cause trouble: you could easily apply changes to photos that you didn't mean to. Pay careful attention to which images are selected at all times, and be deliberate in making your selections.

⌘+Click or Ctrl+Click

To add to or subtract from a selection hold the ⌘ or Ctrl key and click additional thumbnails in either the Grid or Filmstrip.

Shift

To add a contiguous range of photos to a selection. With one image selected, hold the Shift key on your keyboard and click another thumbnail. All the images between the two will become selected.

With multiple photos selected, click a photo's cell (not the thumbnail preview) to deselect all the others.

⌘+G or
Ctrl+G
Stack
selected
photos

Grouping thumbnails into stacks

Think of stacks like good, old-fashioned slides. Stacks save space in the Grid and are also useful when you've shot a sequence of similar images and want to group them together. Stacking images can save time during editing.

⌘+Shift+G
or
Ctrl+Shift+G
Unstack
selected
photos

Examples: many landscape photographers often capture a sequence of photos, all with the same composition, with only the light in the scene changing over time. Portrait photographers might have a series of shots that all have very minor differences in the pose of the subject.

By stacking these kinds of shots together you can clean up the thumbnail Grid view, significantly reducing distraction during editing. Later, when you're ready to choose the *champion* shot (the winner between several competing shots) expand the stack to finish editing those photos. Then, when you're done choosing the final selects, you can unstack the photos, or move the champion to the top of the stack and collapse it again.

Stacks can only be applied in Folder image sources.

A stack can be *collapsed*, which will then only show the thumbnail for the top photo, or *expanded* to show all the photos in the stack; see Figures 3–27 and 3–28.

A couple of limitations: stacks are not available in collections, and a single photo can only be a member of one stack. If you try to make a stack and it doesn't work, it's likely because the current source doesn't allow stacking or that one or more of the images already belongs to another stack.

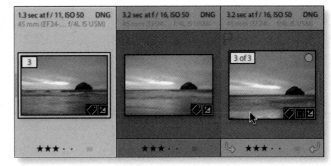

Figure 3-27   Figure 3-28

Choose Library➔Photo menu➔Stacking➔Group into Stack
… or use the shortcut. The active photo will go at the top of the stack by default, but you can change the stacking order at any time afterward.

The top image in a stack shows the photo count for the stack in the upper left corner of the thumbnail. Click this to expand and collapse the stack.

Right-click or Ctrl+click on the stack photo count badge to open the stack contextual menu.

Filters and stacks
When filters are applied (see later in this chapter), unflagged and unrated images within a stack won't show, which can really cause confusion. To avoid this, make sure all the photos in a stack are marked with the same attributes (discussed later in this chapter).

Shift+S
Move to top of stack

Shift+[
Move up in stack

Shift+]
Move down in stack

Changing the order of images within the stack
To change the order of images within the stack you must first expand it. Click the photo count badge or the two thin lines at the right edge of the top image in the stack. Use the arrow keys to select the image you want to reposition and use the stack contextual menu commands or the shortcuts to move the image within the stack.

Auto stack by capture time
First, choose a folder, then control+Click or right-click on one of the thumbnails. From the contextual menu, choose Stacking➔Auto Stack by Capture Time. Set your desired time interval by adjusting the slider; the number of stacks that will be created will show

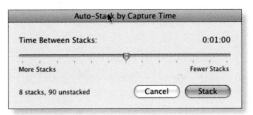

Figure 3-29

underneath. Press Return or Enter. Lightroom will create stacks in the current source for all photos matching the given criteria. See Figure 3–29.

3

Working in Loupe view

Loupe view displays a single, large photo (see Figure 3–30). You can zoom in and out of the Loupe preview using preset *zoom levels* based on ratios of image pixels to screen pixels. When the image is magnified you can *pan* the image to examine different parts of it more closely.

E or Return/ Enter
Go to Loupe view

Shift+E
Loupe view in the second window

Figure 3-30

The full screen image shown in Loupe view uses the Standard preview size. If you zoom in to 1:1 or greater, Lightroom will load the 1:1 preview. When you first enter Loupe view or zoom in close to a photo, Lightroom may need to build the preview. If this is the case, you'll see a message at the bottom of the image that says Loading…. This will take varying amounts of time depending on the size of the preview being built.

ZOOMING IN AND OUT OF IMAGES IN LOUPE VIEW

Lightroom gives you several ways to zoom in and out of images. Each method has its own usefulness; in some situations, one way is easier or faster than the others, so it's worthwhile to learn all the methods for zooming.

To show an image full size in Loupe view, double click it, or press E or Return/ Enter. To go back to Grid, double click again, or press G. Pressing Return/Enter cycles through Fit/Fill, most recent zoom and Grid.

3

⌘+= or Ctrl+=
Zoom in

⌘+- or Ctrl+-
Zoom out

Spacebar
Toggles
between Fit
or Fill and the
most recently
used zoom
level

Return or
Enter
Cycle between
Grid, Loupe
and the last
used zoom
ratio

Z
Zoom to last
used zoom
level and
position

To zoom in further, use the Navigator panel zoom selectors or the keyboard shortcuts. Using the shortcut zooms in and out based on the four zoom levels shown on the Navigator, discussed in Chapter 1.

Click-release versus click-hold

You've probably already figured out that you can click the Loupe preview to zoom in and out with each click. Try this, too: click *and hold* the mouse button to zoom in, and *without letting go,* drag the hand tool to move around the preview. Then release the mouse button to zoom back out to the previous view.

Panning the image in Loupe View

When you're in any zoom ratio except Fit, you can pan around the image by clicking and dragging with the hand cursor. See Figure 3–31.

Zoom clicked point to center

There is a preference setting that re-centers zoomed images around the clicked zoom point. I find this useful most of the time. Go to Preferences→Interface→Tweaks.

Figure 3-31

Page Up, Page Down in Loupe

Using these keys allows you to "scroll" over a Loupe preview in equal "columns" whose widths are determined by the zoom ratio and the width of the Loupe preview. Start at the top left of the image, and press Page Down repeatedly. When you've reached the bottom of the photo and you press Page Down again, Lightroom will jump the preview to the top of the next column to the right. This is very useful when checking photos for artifacts and doing retouching such as removing dust spots, as it ensures you can see every part of the photo, which can be uncertain using only manual panning.

I
Cycles
through the
two available
info overlays,
and no
overlay

SHOWING PHOTO INFO IN LOUPE

Lightroom provides optional text overlays that show statistics about the image file, capture settings and other useful information; see Figure 3–32. Using View Options you can configure the elements making up the info overlays.

1/4 sec at f / 11, ISO 400, 132 mm
(EF28-135mm f/3.5-5.6 IS USM)
0 EV

Figure 3-32

3

Comparing two images

Compare view lets you evaluate two images side by side (see Figure 3–33). Select two photos and click the Compare button on the toolbar, or press C. The active photo becomes the *select* and the second image becomes the *candidate*.

C
Compare view

Tab or Shift+Tab
Hide the side panels or all panels

L
Cycles through the three Lights Out modes

Figure 3-33

When you enter Compare view, first take a look at the Toolbar; you'll notice some controls for working in Compare.

In Compare (and Survey) view it's helpful to hide the panels to allow maximum room for the images. Also, use Lights Out to dim or black out the entire screen except for the images.

Link Focus

With Link Focus, you can zoom into the exact same place on both images to check for critical focus, examine small details, etc. Make sure the Toolbar is visible, and click the lock icon to enable Link Focus (see Figure 3–33). You can then zoom in and out and pan both images at the same time.

Changing photos in the Select and Candidate positions

The toolbar in Loupe Compare contains buttons for switching or swapping photos in both select and candidate positions (see Figure 3–33). Hover over each button to see its tool tip.

Left and Right Arrow Keys

With two images loaded in Compare view, use the left and right arrow keys to load the next photo in the current source or selection into the Candidate position.

The up arrow will promote a candidate photo to the Select, simultaneously making it the active photo.

Comparing multiple images

Survey view is for comparing more than two images. All the selected images are scaled automatically to fit into the Survey window (see Figure 3–34). Survey is most useful for a maximum of 8-10 images; for more than that you're usually better off using the Grid.

N
Survey view

Figure 3-34

To enter Survey view, select multiple images from the Grid or Filmstrip and click the Survey button on the Toolbar, or press N. Note that the photos you see in Survey are all selected, so as when working with any group of multiple photo

3

selections, it's important to keep track of the active photo. In Survey, the active ("most selected") photo is indicated by a white outline. Clicking a photo makes it the active photo.

Once in Survey view, you can add, remove or rearrange the previews. Drag a preview to put it in a different position. Remove a photo from Survey by clicking the X in the bottom right corner of the photo (you must put your cursor over the images to see the controls). Add photos to the view by selecting them from the Filmstrip while holding the ⌘ or control key. Press / (forward slash) to remove a photo from the Survey selection.

T
Hide/show toolbar

Toolbar or Not Toolbar?

I usually hide the toolbar in Survey view, but there are times when the toolbar is helpful or required to carry out certain tasks. **In all modules, at all times, don't forget to hide and show the toolbar:** you can either make more room for photos by hiding it, or show it to provide access to more controls—some that are not found anywhere else in Lightroom. Press T to hide or show the toolbar.

Rotating and flipping photos

You can rotate and flip images when viewing either Grid thumbnails or Loupe previews. Remember that this only affects the previews in Lightroom; the original file on disk is not altered.

⌘+] or Ctrl+]
Rotate clockwise in 90-degree increments

ROTATING PHOTOS

In Grid, the thumbnails show arrows for rotation. View Options lets you configure this to show the rotation arrows all the time, or just when hovering your cursor over a thumbnail. If you have multiple photos selected, you can rotate them all at once. Click on the arrows to rotate the photo(s) by 90-degree increments. (To rotate an image by an amount other than 90 degrees, use the Crop/Straighten Tool in Develop; see Chapter 4.)

⌘+[or Ctrl+[
Rotate counter-clockwise in 90-degree increments

Select all photos of a specific orientation

You can use filters, discussed later in this chapter, to select all the photos of either a Landscape or Portrait orientation. (In the filter, though, it's referred to as "aspect ratio"; this is a bit misleading.) You can then rotate all the selected photos at once.

FLIPPING PHOTOS

Photos can be mirrored around their horizontal and vertical axes.

To flip images in Library, select the photos to be flipped, and choose the menu command **Photo→Flip Horizontal or Photo→Flip Vertical.**

Flipping photos is different than View→Mirror Image Mode, which affects *all* the images in the current catalog. This can be useful for showing people portraits of themselves, since we're used to seeing ourselves in a mirror.

The Secondary Display window

Lightroom offers support for a secondary display that can be configured separately from the main window. The second window can be used to show full-screen Loupe images while you choose from thumbnails in your main window, or vice versa. You can also use the second window for Compare and Survey views, while keeping your main window in another view.

Shift+E
Loupe view on Second Window

To open the second window, click the secondary display button on the top left of the Filmstrip. See Figure 3–35.

At the top left of the second window are the same view modes as the main window: Grid, Loupe, Compare and Survey; see Figure 3–36.

Figure 3-35

Live Loupe

At the top left of the second window, choose Loupe. At the top right, choose Live. Move your cursor over the thumbnails in the main window and the second window will instantly show each photo under the cursor.

Figure 3-36

Locked

At the top left of the second window, choose Loupe. At the top right, choose Locked. Locked mode retains the same image until you explicitly choose to update it. This can be helpful in client reviews, as you can push images to the second display only when you intend to. Control+Click or right-click on a thumbnail for the contextual menu and choose Lock to Second Window.

The Second Window is also discussed in Chapter 1.

3

Metadata

Metadata is one of the most useful, important properties of any digital image. Literally, it means "data about data". Metadata is plain text information embedded in a special section of the image file's program code. Metadata can describe all kinds of things about an image file and is used in a variety of ways by a computer system processing that file.

Because metadata is stored in a different part of the file than the pixel data it can be created and manipulated independently from the pixel data. Image capture devices, such as digital cameras, write metadata into image files as they are created (EXIF metadata). Imaging software, such as Lightroom and Photoshop, can also write metadata into files and modify that metadata later.

Probably the most well-known types of metadata are keywords, titles and captions, and star ratings. Search engines look for keywords and display results containing them; photo sharing Web sites can display embedded captions and titles for images; even your computer operating system will recognize and display star ratings for photos that have them applied.

Lightroom also uses metadata to make image adjustments. For example, when you change the exposure, sharpening or white balance settings, those adjustments are stored as metadata in the catalog, and can also be saved onto your hard disk as XMP data, but the pixel data in the file on disk is never altered. More on this in Chapter 4.

When you're working with your photos, don't skimp on metadata. Start applying metadata to your photos during Import and continually add and refine metadata throughout editing and processing—especially keywords on your final selects.

Keep in mind that much of the work you do with metadata today will save significant time and effort later, and will make it much easier for you (and other people) to find your photos far into the future. Make it a habit to constantly enhance the quality and quantity of metadata in your photos.

Metadata for video files

Lightroom 3 is the first version of the program to offer support for working with video clips. You can see thumbnail and loupe previews in Library, along with text indicating the duration of the clip. Although you can't play or edit video directly within Lightroom 3, you can use all the metadata features, including keywording, collections and filtering for video files. Video is also a file type criteria for smart collections (discussed below). However, note that (depending on the video file format) not all Lightroom metadata would be included on an export of those video files.

⌘+4 or Ctrl+4
Open/close the
Metadata panel

THE METADATA PANEL

Lightroom's Metadata panel, on the right panel group in the Library module, contains information about the digital image file such as name, location on disk, capture settings, etc. as well as any custom metadata you add to the photo.

You can change the metadata shown on the panel by choosing from the popup menu in the panel header (see Figure 3–37), which has been updated in Lightroom 3; choose one of the options to show different groupings of metadata.

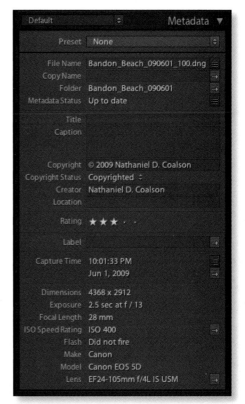

Figure 3-37

Metadata panel actions

The buttons to the right of many of the items in the Metadata panel provide shortcuts to a range of editing and updating features. To see the function of a button, place your cursor over it without clicking and wait a few seconds for a tool tip to appear (see Figure 3–38). Pay special attention to right-facing arrows: these provide time saving shortcuts to useful functions.

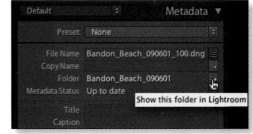

Figure 3-38

Title and Caption

Metadata titles and captions are useful in many ways. Most of all, they help other people find your photos and learn more about them. An image title should usually be a name or short phrase. Captions are often several sentences, describing the who, what, where, when, why about the photo. Depending on the subject of the photo, the caption is usually journalistic, describing a person, place, or event.

Titles and captions are very helpful in presenting your work using the Slideshow, Print and Web modules, as they can be configured to display along with the

3

photos. In Web galleries, title and caption contribute significantly to search engine indexing and phrase-based relevancy of images on the Web. In addition to keywords, search engines will often read the contents of the Title and Caption fields and use those fields in their ranking algorithms.

EXIF

The camera writes EXIF metadata into the image file when you take the picture. EXIF includes all the camera settings at the time of capture. Most EXIF metadata cannot be edited in Lightroom but it can be useful when making processing decisions. Examples of some EXIF metadata (see Figure 3–39) shown in the Metadata panel are:

- Dimensions - resolution in pixels

- Exposure

- Exposure Bias

- Flash

- Exposure Program

- Metering Mode

- ISO Speed Rating

- Focal Length

- Lens

- Subject Distance

- Capture date/time (Date Time Original, Date Time Digitized and Date Time)

Figure 3-39

- Camera make, model and serial number

- Artist

- And possibly others, depending on your camera model

Click the arrow button next to the Date to show photos taken on that date.

Editing a photo's capture time

If the clock on your camera was incorrect at the time of capture or your image file does not have a date embedded, you can change the image capture time in Lightroom. Choose the menu command Metadata→Edit Capture Time (see Figure 3–40). You can adjust by specified date and time, shift by set number of hours (time zone adjust) or change to file's creation date, if different than the other dates. The dialog box states that the operation cannot be undone, but you could always change the time again to correct any errors.

Figure 3-40

Assigning your name to the Artist field

Use the utility software that came with your camera to connect your computer to your camera. You can then enter your name using the software, which will then be stored within the camera. All the photos digitized with the camera will then have your name embedded in them. Note that if you buy a used camera or sell your camera to someone else this should be updated immediately.

Apply and jump to next photo

When you need to apply one type of metadata to different photos using different values, try this: instead of pressing enter after typing in your metadata, press ⌘+right arrow, or Ctrl+right arrow. This applies the typed text to the current image and jumps to the next image with the same metadata field highlighted.

GPS and Altitude

If there is GPS and/or altitude metadata embedded in the file, Lightroom will display it. If no GPS and/or altitude metadata is found, the fields do not show in the panel.

3

Jump to Google Maps

If GPS data is shown, click the button next to the coordinates. This opens your default Web browser and loads that location on the Google Maps Web site. To go to Yahoo! maps instead of Google, hold the Option or Alt key while clicking.

Audio Files

If you recorded voice notes with your image files, Lightroom will show and allow you to play them on the Metadata panel. A few cameras support audio recordings; otherwise, you can pair a separately recorded audio file. The base filename of the audio clip must exactly match that of the image file for Lightroom to find it. Click the button next to the audio clip filename to play the file.

Just as with GPS data, If no audio sidecar file exists for a photo, the field doesn't show in the Metadata panel.

IPTC

IPTC metadata is comprised of a wide range of standardized categories for information about an image. The most important fields—author, creator, copyright notice, contact information and keywords—are but a few of the many types of IPTC metadata available. Lightroom shows IPTC metadata at the bottom of the Metadata panel (see Figure 3–41) and provides controls to edit these general IPTC metadata categories:

- Contact

- IPTC Core and Extension

- Image

- Workflow

- Status

- Copyright

To add, change or remove metadata from any of these fields, click to activate the field, then type or delete the text. You can apply the same metadata to many photos selected

Figure 3-41

at once, but if you find that you are entering the same metadata over and over, you should set up a metadata preset, which is discussed in the next section.

IPTC **Extension**
Lightroom 3 includes an expanded set of IPTC metadata called IPTC Extension. This new schema provides additional types of information that can be embedded in image files, and together with IPTC Core is referred to as the IPTC Photo Metadata standard. For more details visit http://www.iptc.org/.

Add copyright metadata to every image
Even if you apply no other custom metadata this is the one section you really must complete to assert your rights as a photographer:

Copyright Status: for setting the copyright status of your own work, in nearly all cases you'd choose "Copyrighted"; "Public Domain" and "Unknown" are provided also.

Copyright: type your copyright text here, i.e. © 2010 Nathaniel D. Coalson. On Mac, press Option+G for the copyright symbol. On Windows, type Alt+0169 on the numeric keypad, or on the regular numbers with Num Lock activated.

Rights Usage Terms: enter "All Rights Reserved" or "no use without written permission", etc.

METADATA PRESETS

As with all presets in Lightroom, metadata presets can save you huge amounts of time. In addition to working with metadata presets in the Import screen, you can create and modify them using the menu on the Metadata panel (see Figure 3–42).

Figure 3-42

Setting up standardized metadata presets
Like the other parts of the workflow, you should establish and use a consistent system for your metadata presets. Use the same diligence in maintaining your presets and templates as you do with your file and folder systems.

Give your presets clear, consistent names. I use my initials at the beginning of all my custom presets and templates so they are grouped together in alphabetical lists and I can find them easily.

The contents of a preset should be only those items that can be reasonably applied to many images simultaneously. Contact information, copyright notice, etc. make good candidates for presets. Conversely, keywords do not, since they are very image-specific.

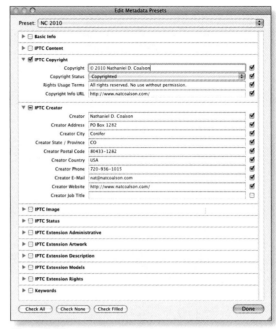

Figure 3-43

Typically, my presets vary only in the year of copyright. All the other information, such as my address, phone number, and Web site remain consistent. This means that when entering a new year, all I need to do is make a new preset with a copyright change for that year.

See Figure 3–43 for an example of the Metadata Preset Editor.

Blank fields in a metadata template

If you make a metadata preset that includes blank fields and apply that preset to photos that had data in those fields, the blank fields will overwrite the existing metadata. For this reason, choose carefully the fields you include in a preset, and it's usually a good idea to uncheck any blank fields to prevent them from being included in the preset.

To see all the Lightroom presets saved on your computer, choose Preferences→Presets

…then click the button "Show Lightroom Presets Folder". This opens the presets folder in Finder or Explorer. To remove presets from Lightroom, you can delete them from their folders. Do this with Lightroom closed; the changes will be visible when you restart the program.

SYNC METADATA

With multiple photos selected, this button on the right panel set (see Figure 3–44) and its corresponding menu command synchronizes file metadata (but not Develop settings) between multiple photos. The settings from

Figure 3-44

the active photo will be applied to the rest of the selected photos. In the Synchronize Metadata window (very similar to the Metadata template editor), tick the boxes for the metadata to be synced. Anything that remains unchecked will not be modified in the target photos.

(The Sync Settings button synchronizes Develop settings; see Chapter 4.)

METADATA STATUS

Metadata status compares the metadata for a file in Lightroom and the actual file on disk and will indicate the state of the photo's metadata as compared to Lightroom's stored version of it. If there is a conflict, Lightroom displays a status indicator in the Metadata panel, and optionally on the thumbnail also (see Figure 3–45). If there is no conflict, the icon does not appear.

Up to Date: as far as Lightroom knows, all is in sync: what's in the file on disk matches the Lightroom metadata.

Figure 3-45

Has Been Changed: metadata in Lightroom is out-of-sync with the metadata contained in the file. This can mean either that Lightroom data is newer or the file's is newer; take the time to investigate before changing anything. Reading Metadata from File or Saving the Metadata to File changes this indicator to Up to Date.

It's possible that changes have been made outside Lightroom that the application is not yet aware of; sometimes Lightroom doesn't know the current status of the file's metadata and you won't see an indicator.

Show unsaved metadata

Press ⌘+J or Ctrl+J to show View Options (see Figure 3–46) and click the checkbox to enable the badge that shows unsaved metadata. This will display a special icon on the thumbnail when the file metadata is different than the metadata in Lightroom. Clicking the icon gives you the option to save metadata out to the file.

Figure 3-46

3

What's the correct version?

Whenever you're changing file metadata it's important to understand exactly what version is correct before proceeding. Other software can change your image file metadata even if you don't actually open the file using that software. Bridge is one such application; building previews for image files in Bridge often will alter file metadata, resulting in a conflict with Lightroom. If you know the metadata in Lightroom is the most current, save it out to the file. Otherwise, check the files in question to figure out when and how the metadata was changed before reading metadata into Lightroom. Of course, if you only use Lightroom for processing your photos, you won't need to worry about this.

⌘+S or Ctrl+S
Save metadata
to file

Saving Metadata to Files

To save all the current Lightroom metadata out to the image files on disk, use the Save Metadata to File command. This writes all the Lightroom metadata, including Develop settings and keywords, to the files. If your files are DNG, TIF, PSD or JPG, the metadata is written directly into the image files. Native camera raw images use XMP sidecar files to store the metadata.

Saving your work is as important in Lightroom as in other software applications, but it's all too easy to work on and on without Lightroom prompting you to save. Though all your changes are automatically saved into the database, they are *only* in the database until you save the changes out to the files and/or export new files. So save often!

Don't use Automatic Save

Catalog Settings provides an option to automatically save your metadata to the files as you work. I generally don't recommend this, for several reasons. First, many computers will experience a decrease in performance with this option enabled. Second, even on a fast machine, I don't want Lightroom accessing my files that frequently. Lightroom will save out the metadata after *every* change made to *any* setting. That much file access increases the possibility of file corruption. Third, and maybe more importantly, if Lightroom is always saving out metadata as you work, you won't be able to use the Read Metadata from File command to go back to a previous version.

Usually it's best to just regularly save out the metadata yourself (though one exception might be when managing photos in workgroup environments.) To see whether Lightroom is automatically saving metadata, check the option in the Catalog Settings→Metadata tab.

XMP sidecars are now listed on Metadata panel

In conjunction with the conflict status icon, Lightroom 3 will now show you when a raw file has a sidecar saved next to it on disk. Look on the Metadata panel, below the File Name field.

Reading Metadata from Files

If you've edited your file outside Lightroom (such as in Bridge, Adobe Camera Raw, Photoshop etc.) and want to update Lightroom to show the latest changes, you can read in the metadata from the file using the command on the Metadata menu. This will overwrite the photo's metadata in the Lightroom catalog.

Confirm your decision

Be careful using the Read Metadata from Files command; it will potentially overwrite all your current Lightroom metadata for selected images. Be sure it's what you really want to do before going ahead.

Keywords

Keywords (also often called "tags") are words and short phrases used to describe the content, theme and subject of a photo. Keywords can also be used to address metaphors, abstract concepts and graphical elements of the composition.

In most cases, keywords are essential metadata that should be applied to every photo, especially those that will be posted online: search engines commonly read keywords embedded in image files, and display search results based on the contents of this metadata.

Keywords also have lots of potential for use within your local Lightroom catalogs. You can use keywords to find and organize photos in your archives, even if those keywords are never shown to the public.

You can apply keywords during Import, and then enhance them in Library, where you work with the Keywording and Keyword List panels.

KEYWORDING STRATEGIES

For most photographers, every image in your catalog should have at least a few keywords assigned to it, and usually, more is better. Obviously, there's no point wasting time applying keywords to photos you will never use, but as has been discussed previously, this can be difficult to determine today.

Most importantly, your final selects should have many keywords applied when you're done processing them. Years from now, locating specific images will depend on the richness of the metadata you've applied, especially keywords.

3

And though an image can have many keywords, it's good practice to be careful with the words you use. Think about keywords in terms that a viewer unfamiliar with the photograph might use to describe it, and use keywords both general and specific.

As important as the choice of words is, it can be tricky. For example, if you make a photograph of a crowded city street, would it make sense to add a keyword for every single item shown in the picture (e.g. Manhole, Lamp Post, Car, Pavement, etc.)? Does this add real value, or are more generalized descriptions right for this photo? It's up to you to decide.

A photo of an eagle in flight could use keywords like Animal, Bird, Raptor, Predator and, of course, Eagle. But what about Freedom, Feathered, Talons, Airborne? Effective keywording is a creative exercise in language.

And with regard to language, if you're an English speaker, there's no reason you must limit your keywords to English alone. I frequently use phrases—especially names—from the local dialect. For example, my Italy collections also contain the keyword "Italia"; Tuscany is also "Toscana", etc. (This is most effective using *synonyms*, discussed in just a bit…)

Within a photo's metadata, keywords are separated by commas, and optionally, spaces (which I prefer). You can use single or multiple words. I recommend using specific, distinct phrases as keywords. For example, if I shoot in Rocky Mountain National Park, I will use the phrase "Rocky Mountain National Park" as a keyword, because it's a name, and not "Rocky, Mountain, National, Park". However, depending on the photo, I might also include the word "Mountains" as a separate keyword.

As you apply keywords to photos, they become stored in the current catalog. You can manage your keyword lists independently from your other photo editing work. You can also import and export keyword lists, which is discussed further in this chapter.

It's up to you to decide how far to go with your keywords; the point is, use them. Start adding keywords at the very beginning of the workflow, and continue adding and refining your keywords for selects as you move them through the pipeline.

If you feel that keywording is taking too much time, keep in mind that this work will pay off later, and stick with it. If you use Lightroom's shortcuts and batch processing features, your keywording will be much easier. Take control of your keywording, and I guarantee that managing your catalog will become much easier for you, and the photos you want people to find on the Web will become much more visible online.

Apply keywords to as many photos as possible at one time

As you go through your editing workflow, apply keywords in progressively finer detail. Start with the most generic terms that apply to the most photos, and gradually add more specific keywords to smaller groups and individual photos.

⌘+2 or Ctrl+2
Open/close the Keywording panel

KEYWORDING PANEL

The Keywording panel shows the keywords applied to the selected photo(s). It also contains text entry fields for you to add, remove and modify keywords. If a photo has keywords applied, the thumbnail will show the keyword badge. Clicking the badge opens the Keywording panel.

Click the small black triangles to see all the options in the Keywording panel (see Figure 3–47).

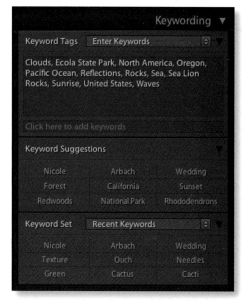

Here, you can type in Keyword Tags, or click to apply keywords

Figure 3-47

from the Keyword Suggestions and Keyword Sets. Lightroom's Auto Complete feature helps finish words for you as you type; this behavior is controlled by the option in Catalog Settings→Metadata.

The popup menu at the top of the panel allows you to choose how keywords are shown in the panel:

Enter Keywords: in this mode, all the keywords applied to a photo are shown in the large text box in the top portion of the Keywording panel. **This is the only mode that allows you to edit keywords in this panel.** Click in the text box to add, change or delete keywords from the selected photo(s). Press Return or Enter when you're done.

When multiple photos are selected, keywords showing an asterisk (*) are only applied to *some* of the selected images. In other words, if a keyword does not have an asterisk, it is applied to *all* the selected photos. To quickly apply a keyword to all the selected photos, simply delete the asterisk. (However, adding an asterisk is not practical; to remove keywords from some photos use the other methods described below.)

3

Keywords and Containing Keywords: this mode displays the keywords applied to the selected photo(s) along with their hierarchies, which is discussed below.

Will Export: this mode displays the keywords that will be applied to the photos when you export them using any method, including Slideshow, Print and Web. Depending on how you've set up your keyword list, some keywords may not export. This is covered in the next section.

⌘+K or
Ctrl+K
Puts the
cursor in
the Add
Keywords
text field

Add Keywords

In the Keywording panel, where it says "Click Here to Add Keywords" (see Figure 3–47 on previous page), if you only want to *add* keywords to selected photos—not change or remove them—use the Add Keywords field. When you're done typing, press Return or Enter to apply the keywords to the selected photos.

Return/Enter or Esc

Always press Return or Enter when you're done typing text into any field in Lightroom. Or, press Esc to leave that text entry field without committing the changes.

Keyword Suggestions

As you keyword photos, Lightroom keeps track of other images to which you've applied similar keywords and, based on capture times, provides suggestions. There are up to nine keyword suggestions available at any given time; all of the suggested keywords must already exist in the current catalog. The suggestions are constantly updated so, usually, when you apply a new keyword, the suggestions may change. Click a suggested keyword to apply it to the selected photo(s).

Option+0
or Alt+0
Load
the next
keyword set
in the list

Keyword Sets

Keyword Sets are designed to speed up your work when adding keywords to photos with similar subjects or themes. You can make Keyword Sets using any criteria you like. Each Keyword Set contains up to nine words.

Lightroom comes with several built-in keyword sets: Outdoor Photography, Portrait Photography, Wedding Photography. There is also a selection for Recent Keywords.

Select a set from the popup menu to load that set of keywords. The keywords contained in that set are then shown in the panel. Click the keywords to add them to selected photo(s) or use the keyboard shortcuts for *Set Keyword* (see below).

You can modify these sets and create your own sets. To edit a keyword set, open the popup menu and select Edit Set… The resulting dialog box (see Figure 3–48) lets you add, change or remove keywords from that set. You can enter any keywords you like in this box; if they don't already exist in the catalog, they will be added the next time they are used. If you make changes to a keyword set, click the Change button to apply the changes.

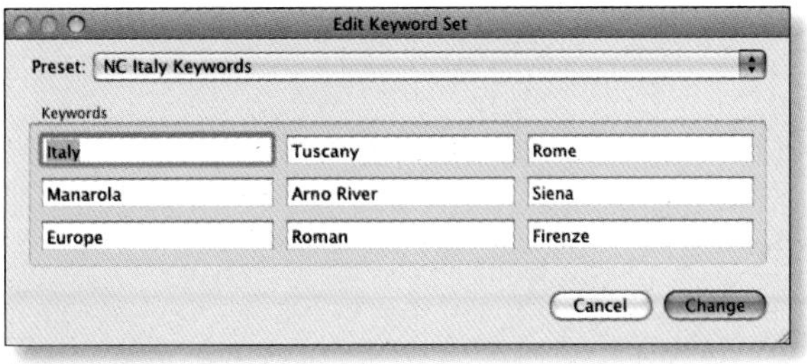

Figure 3-48

Option+1–9
or Alt+1–9
Applies the
corresponding
keyword to
the selected
photo(s)

Set Keyword

The nine most Recent Keywords or those from another Keyword Set can be applied to selected photos using a keyboard shortcut, the Painter (covered later in this chapter), or the Photo→Set Keyword menu command.

Press Option or Alt

To show the numeric keyboard shortcuts in the Keyword Set section of the panel.

⌘+3 or Ctrl+3
Open/close the
Keyword List
panel

KEYWORD LIST PANEL

Keywords are stored within each catalog. The Keyword List panel (see Figure 3–49) shows an alphabetical list of all the keywords in the currently open catalog. Since it's sorted alphabetically, you can't change the order of keywords in the list, but you can group keywords together in hierarchies or add numbers or special characters to keywords to control where they show in the list.

As you add keywords to photos using the various methods described here, they are automatically added to the Keyword List. You can use the Keyword List to add and remove keywords to/from photos and to modify the keywords themselves.

When images are selected, the Keyword List panel shows which keywords are applied to the selected photo(s). A checkbox to the left of each keyword indicates whether or not it's applied to

Figure 3-49

3

the photo. A check mark indicates all selected photos contain that keyword(s); a dash indicates the keyword is only applied to some of the selected photos (like the asterisk in the Keyword Tags field), or that a single selected photo only contains some of the keywords within a hierarchy.

With one or more photos selected, you can add or remove keywords to or from a photo by clicking the check box to the left of the keyword. You can also add keywords by dragging and dropping them from the list onto the photo, or vice versa.

To remove a keyword from a photo, you can uncheck it from the list or use the controls in the Keywording panel.

You can also add and remove keywords by right-clicking or control+clicking on the keyword, and then selecting the appropriate command from the popup contextual menu (see Figure 3–50).

Figure 3-50

Shift+K
Applies the target keyword to the selected photo(s)

Finally, you can select the popup menu option to "Use this as keyword shortcut" which allows you to apply that target keyword using the keyboard shortcut. When this option is enabled, a + symbol shows next to the target keyword in the list.

Creating and editing keywords

Create new keywords in the catalog by clicking the + button at the top of the Keyword List panel. This opens the Create Keyword dialog box (see Figure 3–51). In the Keyword Tag field, enter the name for the keyword. Explanations of the other options are below.

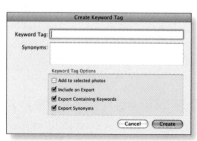

Figure 3-51

Edit a keyword by right-clicking or control+clicking it. From the popup contextual menu, choose Edit Keyword Tag… You'll get the Edit Keyword Tag dialog box, which functions identically to the Create Keyword box.

In both of the aforementioned dialog boxes you have several options for controlling the behavior of the keyword being edited.

Keyword Name: this is the keyword itself. If you've made a typo or spelling error, you can correct it here.

Synonyms: When you create a new keyword or edit an existing one, you have the option to include *synonyms* for the word. Synonyms are words that mean the same thing as the main keyword. On a case-by-case basis, you'll have to decide whether it's better to add a synonym or make a separate keyword. For example, the keyword "Autumn" could have the synonym "Fall". This is likely more efficient than setting up "Fall" as its own keyword. "Vacation" could have the synonym "Holiday", and so on. Of course, you could also have a second entry for Holiday in a different, more generic context. Lightroom uses synonyms when generating suggestion lists.

Include on Export: keywords that have this box checked will become embedded in all photos it's applied to when those photos are exported. This includes Web galleries and files made with the Print to JPG command in the Print module.

If this box is not checked, the keyword will not be included when the photo is exported. This feature is very useful when you're using keyword hierarchies for internal organization but don't want certain keywords to be exported (see below). For example, I have a keyword called "Geographic Locations", under which are nested keywords for many specific regions and countries around the world. I want the specific place names to be included on export, but not the "Geographic Locations" tag.

Export containing keywords: if a keyword is nested in a hierarchy, this option determines whether or not the parent (upper-level) keywords will be included on export.

Export synonyms: determines whether or not a keyword's synonyms will be included on export.

Add to Selected Photos: does just that; if photos are selected, they will instantly have the keyword applied when it is created or edited.

Renaming keywords

To change a keyword, right-click or control+click on it, and from the popup menu choose Rename. This opens the Edit box with the name highlighted. Type in the new name for the keyword, and when you're done, press Return or Enter. All photos containing that keyword will be updated.

Deleting keywords

Deleting a keyword from the catalog will also remove it from any photos to which it was applied. Right-click or control+click on the keyword, and select Delete… from the popup menu. Lightroom will prompt you with a warning. Click Delete to accept.

3

Purging unused keywords

This command allows you to remove all the keywords from the catalog that are not applied to any photos. **Library module→Metadata menu→Purge unused keywords.**

Finding keywords in the list

At the top of the Keyword List panel is a text search box you can use for finding keywords within the list (see Figure 3–52). By default, the search box says "Filter Keywords". As you type in the field, the keyword list dynamically updates to show only those keywords containing that string of text. To remove the filter, click the X at the right side of the box.

Figure 3-52

Keyword hierarchies

In the Keyword List panel you can create keyword *hierarchies,* which are multi-level groupings constructed of *parent* and *child* keywords. Think of keyword hierarchies like folders and subfolders in a file system: you have one "top level" folder, with multiple "subfolders" underneath. Same with keywords in Lightroom (see Figure 3–52).

In the Keyword List, hierarchies are indicated by a triangle arrow at the left (see Figure 3–53). Click the arrow to expand or contract the hierarchy.

Figure 3-53

Keyword hierarchies provide several very significant benefits. For one, hierarchies allow you to keep your keyword list clean and orderly by grouping keywords into larger categories.

Using hierarchies also greatly speeds the application of groups of common keywords to photos, all at one time. When you drag-and-drop a lower-level child keyword onto a photo (or multiple photos), *all the keywords above it in the hierarchy will also be applied.*

You can also set the options differently for each keyword within a hierarchy. For example, within a single hierarchy, you could have some keywords that won't be included on export. This approach provides infinite possibilities for using keywords as organizational tools.

With hierarchies, you can also have multiple instances of a keyword, grouped depending on syntax. For example, the word "Blue" could be under "Colors" and also under "Feelings". As you're keywording photos, you'll find many words that have different meanings based on the context in which they are used; hierarchies accommodate this easily.

To make a hierarchy, click and drag a keyword to place it over the keyword that will become the parent. The parent becomes highlighted. Release your mouse button to drop the keyword onto the parent, and the child becomes nested underneath.

You can also make hierarchies using commands from the contextual popup menu. Create a child keyword underneath a parent by right-clicking or control+clicking the keyword, and from the popup menu, select "Create Keyword Tag Inside [XYZ]…". The new keyword will automatically be placed under the parent within the hierarchy.

Or, right-click or control+click on a keyword, and from the menu, choose "Put new keywords inside this keyword". Any new keywords you make using any method will be automatically added as children of this keyword until you disable the option.

Use drag-and-drop when you want to move a keyword out of a hierarchy. Simply click on the affected keyword, and drag it to a new position outside the parent. Lightroom displays a blue line to indicate the location where the keyword will be moved to (see Figure 3–54).

Figure 3-54

Entering hierarchies during Import

In text entry fields, such as the Import screen and the Keywording panel, you can manually type hierarchies. This is especially useful if you've already set up a hierarchy and want to apply it during import, where there is no access to the Keyword List panel. To add a hierarchy during import, start by typing the keyword at the bottom of the hierarchy, and use the "greater than" symbol instead of commas, and the Import window will auto-fill in the rest of the hierarchy.

Example: Denver > Colorado > United States > North America

Managing your Keyword List

The keywords stored in your Lightroom catalog have a unique, important place in the workflow and deserve regular attention all their own. It's a good idea to

3

do the bulk of your keywording work separately from other photo editing tasks. Periodically update your Keyword List: check for typos and spelling errors, create or fix parent/child hierarchies, update keyword sets and synonyms and purge unused keywords.

Remember that when you change any keyword in the list, Lightroom automatically updates all the photos containing that keyword.

Import/Export Keywords

You can import and export lists of keywords to and from Lightroom. These are simple text files with a .txt extension. Today, many photographers are sharing keyword lists with each other. Getting keyword lists from other photographers can assist you in deciding how you want to set up your own list. You can also use Import and Export keywords to keep Keyword Lists on multiple computers and catalogs in sync.

Metadata➜Import Keywords…
To import a keyword list into your catalog.

Metadata➜Export Keywords…
To export a keyword list file from your catalog.

Some of the places you can get keyword lists on the Web (Google these):

- Controlled Vocabulary

- Sean McCormick

- Nick Potter

- D-65

- Fleeting Glimpse

- Birdkeywords.com

When you get keyword lists from other people, you can open them in a text editor or spreadsheet to see their contents. You can modify your own or others' keyword lists using your text editor prior to importing it into Lightroom. In many cases this saves lots of time, because you can establish hierarchies using simple word processing: in a keyword text file, Lightroom hierarchies are determined by tab levels.

When you import keywords into your catalog, all your previously existing keywords remain intact. In the case of any conflicts, your original catalog keywords will take precedence. This means that if you've already got an extensive keyword list, any time you're importing more keywords, it's likely that some of those keywords and/or hierarchies in the list being imported won't come into the catalog.

Matching items will be ignored if they are in the same hierarchy order. It's a good idea to evaluate both your list and the list being imported to determine any conflicts so you can resolve them before or after the keyword import.

Using keywords to refine image sources

When you move your cursor over a keyword in the Keyword List panel, you can show all the photos in a chosen image source by clicking the arrow to the right of a keyword in the Keyword List. This applies a Library filter using that keyword as text search criteria. Hold ⌘ or Ctrl to select multiple keywords in the list.

The image source you're working in is a critical factor here. For example, if you want to see all the photos in your entire catalog that contain a given keyword, make sure you have the All Photographs catalog source chosen first. You can also use any of the other kinds of image sources for keyword filtering.

Don't use keywords as you would a collection

Finding photos by keywords is usually most effective as a method of refining another source. To gather sets of photos for longer term storage, it's better to use collections, particularly smart collections based on keywords.

Attributes

When you assign *attributes* to photos you can then quickly and easily sort them in many ways. Lightroom's attributes are:

- **Star ratings:** one to five stars, or no stars

- **Color labels:** named colors, any string of text, or no label

- **Flags:** pick flag, reject flag, no flag

With just these three sets of attributes you can differentiate between your photos in many ways.

3

There are several ways to apply or remove attributes on photos. Attribute controls are available on the Toolbar, but they are not all visible by default. Click the triangle button at the right side of the toolbar to enable or disable items in the Toolbar (see Figure 3–55).

Figure 3-55

RATINGS (STARS)

Numbers 1–5
Set the photo rating to that number of stars

]
Increase rating incrementally

]
Decrease rating incrementally

0 (zero)
Set the rating to no stars

Shift+0–5
Set rating and selects next photo

Star ratings (see Figure 3–56) are a very common method of ranking photos and other digital media. They are designed to be used as a *heuristic* ranking model, e.g. five stars is better than one. By default, photos come into the database with no stars, unless they had stars applied in another program.

Like many photographers, I begin rating with one star, going up to two, three, etc. to a maximum of 5. But some people start at 3 and go up or down from there. You can use whatever system you choose, but it's practical to use an ascending order of ratings. In any case, using a standard system can speed up your workflow and ease decision-making.

Figure 3-56

Take into consideration that when you're editing a batch of photos, let's say in a folder source, that the level of ratings necessary to complete that round of editing may differ. With some batches of photos, you might only need to use one or two stars to identify the keepers. Other times you may need to use more stars to further refine the selects from rejects. This is one potential drawback of using a heuristic model in different sources. But in most scenarios, those with the most stars are the best photos in that group.

Apply a star rating to one or more selected photos by clicking the stars in the Toolbar or the expanded thumbnails (see Figure 3–56), or by using the shortcuts.

Clicking on the current rating resets the photo to "unrated".

Star ratings are persistent throughout Lightroom; that is, if you apply stars in a folder source and then add those photos to a collection, the rating will be retained.

3

Numbers 6–9
Red is 6, yellow is 7, green is 8, blue is 9. Purple doesn't have a shortcut

Shift+6–9
Assign the color label and selects next photo

COLOR LABELS

You can apply a color label to a photo to indicate a specific meaning for the photo (see Figure 3–57). For example, a photographer might apply a green label to indicate portfolio images to be exported from a collection. Or you could mark a set of images blue to indicate they are to be stitched into a panorama. Or label photos purple to indicate they had been reviewed by a client.

In Lightroom, color labels correspond with accompanying text. The defaults are Red, Yellow, Green, Blue and Purple.

Figure 3-57

I don't often use color labels. If I need to differentiate between photos with the same rating, I usually use keywords or titles and captions. However, I've known many photographers for whom using color labels is an essential part of their sophisticated workflow. This is one example of how workflows can be personalized based on your own preferences.

The key to using labels effectively is using them consistently in the same way. Otherwise, confusion results. If you use a color in one folder of photos to mean a certain thing, and then use a different meaning in another folder, it becomes difficult to keep track of what's what.

You can apply standard color labels by clicking the color label swatch on the Toolbar or expanded thumbnails, by typing text into the Metadata panel, or with the shortcuts.

Color labels are also persistent throughout Lightroom; if you apply a label to a photo, it will be retained on all instances of that photo within the catalog.

Color label sets

You can make multiple Color Label Sets that have different definitions for the colors. Choose Metadata➔Color Label Set to edit the current set or make new ones (see Figure 3–58).

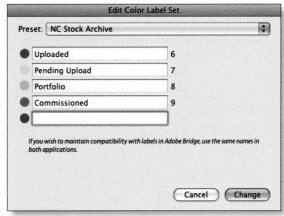

Figure 3-58

127

3

If you have used Bridge to apply color labels, be aware that the names of the default color labels differ in Lightroom and Bridge. Lightroom offers a built-in color label set that matches that of Bridge but it's not the default.

Custom label names

On the Metadata panel, you can type *any* text into the Label field (see Figure 3–59), but the five standard colors listed above are the only ones that will actually show a color on the thumbnail.

Figure 3-59

The important thing to understand is that the Label field itself is simply editable text (whereas flags and stars are invariable) so you can enter anything you want for the label definition. But if you want the thumbnail to show a color you must use the standard color names.

Photo→Auto Advance

With Auto Advance enabled, as you apply any attributes to images in Library (flags, stars, etc.) Lightroom automatically selects the next image in the current source.

Disappearing thumbnails

During an edit, if you change any of the attributes of a photo and it disappears from view, it's because filters are enabled. Change or disable the filter set (discussed in the next section).

P

Marks photo(s) with a pick flag

Shift+P

Marks a photo with a pick flag and advances to the next photo

FLAGS

Pick flags and their opposites, reject flags, may be the simplest form of editing decision—yes or no. You can apply a pick flag by clicking the flag icon in the top left of the photo's thumbnail (see Figure 3–60) or you can use the keyboard shortcuts.

Unlike ratings and labels, flags are specific to the source in which they are applied. For example, if you apply a pick flag to a photo in a folder, and then put that photo in a collection, the photo will be unflagged in the collection. (You could reapply the flag in the collection.) This is intended behavior; flags are meant to be used mainly in source-specific editing.

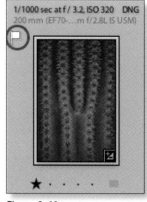

Figure 3-60

Pick flag status is not written to xmp metadata

I prefer to use stars for most of my editing because the star ratings can be saved out to the files or read by other software. **Flags are only visible in Lightroom.**

X
Marks photo(s) as reject

⌘+Delete or Ctrl+Backspace
Delete Rejected Photos

U
Removes any flag from the photo (marks it as unflagged)

Marking Rejected Photos

Using the *reject flag* helps hide unwanted photos and speeds their removal from your catalog. When they're unselected, thumbnails for rejected photos are dimmed in the Grid View. See Figure 3–61.

⌘+Delete or Ctrl+Backspace

After marking photos as rejected, this filters selected photos as rejected so you can then remove from the catalog (or delete from disk). Use the shortcut or select the Photo→Delete Rejected Photos menu command.

Figure 3-61

Keeping only your picks with Refine Photos

If you use Reject Flags, Refine Photos helps facilitate automated mass-deletion of photos from your Library. When you run Refine Photos, images that had Pick Flags will be set to Unflagged, and previously Unflagged photos will get a Rejected flag. You can then use Photo→Delete Rejected Photos to quickly remove all the rejects from the current source. Use Library→Refine Photos to run the Refine Image command.

Library filters

This is one of the most powerful and important features for organizing and sorting your photos in Lightroom: applying *filters* determines which photos will be shown in the preview area and Filmstrip. Filters can also be used to search your catalog for specific images.

Filters are configured using the Filter Bar at the top of the main preview area (see Figure 3–62) and from the top, right section of the Filmstrip (see Figure 3–63).

If the Filter Bar is not showing, use the shortcut or the option under the View menu.

****
Hide and show the Filter bar

Library Filter : Text | Attribute | Metadata | **None** | Filters Off ⇕ 🔒

Figure 3-62

Figure 3-63

3

Typically, you will start with photos from an image source, such as a folder or collection, then apply filters to see only the photographs you want from within that source. Thus, filters are used to refine other sources. When you've created a filtered view, you can add those photos to a collection for easier access later.

⌘+F or Ctrl+F
Opens the Text filter bar and inserts the cursor in the text search field. Type a string of text to search for and press Return or Enter.

Lightroom comes with some built in filter sets, including Flagged, Rated, etc. Load these filters using the popup menu on either the Filter Bar or the Filmstrip (see Figure 3–64).

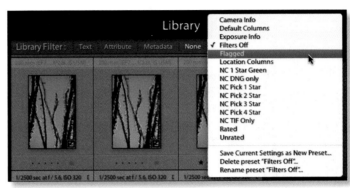

Figure 3-64

You can also set up your own filters based on a wide range of criteria, including image file properties and metadata such as keywords and attributes. Filters can be combined to create any kind of file grouping and can be saved as presets for later use.

By default, filters are specific to the folder or collection source to which they are applied, and are saved automatically, so different sources can have different filters enabled.

In Lightroom 3, the filter state is no longer tied just to the current source. Now, filter settings can be "locked" so the filter's criteria persist even when switching between sources. Click the lock icon on the Filter Bar to lock the filter in place (see Figure 3–65).

Figure 3-65

Showing the whole Filter Bar

If the Lightroom application window and main preview area are not wide enough, the right side of the Filter Bar will not be visible (see Figure 3–66).

Make the window larger and the panels narrower, or hide unused panels, to see the entire Filter Bar.

Figure 3-66

3

TEXT FILTER

The Text filter is essentially a search engine. It's most useful for searching for keywords, file names, and any other text that may be associated with image files or virtual copies. The text filter can find a string of text contained—or not contained—anywhere in the file data.

Step One. Start by selecting the main image source you'll be filtering (see Figure 3–67). If you want to filter the entire catalog, use the All Photographs catalog source, as I did here. Otherwise, choose a folder or collection to start with. (Collections are discussed in the next section of this chapter.)

Figure 3-67

Step Two. Then, with the Filter Bar visible, click on the Text filter (see Figure 3–68). The text filter options become visible below.

Figure 3-68

3

Step Three. Use the menus to set up your search criteria (see Figure 3–69). The first menu default is "Any searchable field", which will look for the text string anywhere in the files. To narrow the criteria, open the menu and choose from the other options, which include Filename, Title, Keywords, etc.

Figure 3-69

Step Four. Next, set how the filter will search using the text (see Figure 3–70). The options are Contains, Contains All, Contains Words, Doesn't Contain, Starts With, and Ends With.

Figure 3-70

Step Five. Finally, type in the text to search for (see Figure 3–71). As you type, Lightroom dynamically updates the filtered view to show only the files matching the criteria you've selected.

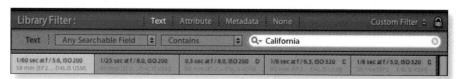

Figure 3-71

To start over and reset the text search to show all the unfiltered photos in the source, click the X at the right of the text search field (see Figure 3–72).

Figure 3-72

Special search characters
Add ! (exclamation mark) in front of a word to exclude it from the search
results. + before a word activates the "Starts With" criteria for that word. + at
the end of a word activates the "Ends With" criteria for that word.

ATTRIBUTE FILTER

This is the core set of filters used for the Lightroom editing sequence outlined
at the beginning of this chapter: star ratings, pick flags, and color labels.

Step One. As before, start by selecting the main image source you'll be
filtering: if you want to filter the entire catalog, use the All Photographs catalog
source. Otherwise, choose a folder or collection to start with.

Step Two. In the Filter Bar, click Attribute to enable the filter (see Figure
3–73).

Figure 3-73

Step Three. Click the buttons in the Filter Bar to set what attributes will be
used for the filter (see Figure 3–74). The main options are Flag, Rating, Color
and Kind.

Figure 3-74

>   **Flag:** filter based on flag status—unflagged, picks, or rejects. You can
>   click multiple flags to refine the criteria; click a flag again to remove it
>   from the filter criteria.

>   **Rating:** filter based on the number of stars applied. Between the word
>   Rating and the first star is a menu option to choose Rating is greater than
>   or equal to, Rating is less than or equal to, or Rating is equal to. Click a
>   star to set the desired rating level for the filter.

>   **Color:** filter based on a color label, unlabeled, or a custom label. Click
>   multiple colors to create an aggregate filter of labels. Click a label to
>   remove it from the filter.

3

Kind: filter based on original (an actual file on disk), virtual copies, or videos. Click to add multiple kinds to the filter if you like.

Tooltips

Remember that when you hover with your cursor over an item for a few seconds, a tooltip appears. This is a great way to learn and memorize what the buttons do.

METADATA FILTER

You can create image filters based on any file metadata, including EXIF information such as exposure setting, lens used, capture date, flash on or off, etc.

Step One. Start by selecting the main image source you're filtering.

Step Two. Click the Metadata button in the Filter Bar. The default Metadata filter loads, with four sets of criteria: Date, Camera, Lens and Label (see Figure 3–75). You can use these columns as your starting point and add, remove and change them however you like.

Library Filter:		Text	Attribute	**Metadata**	None		No Filter ÷ 🔒
Date		Camera		Lens		Label	
All (2 Dates)	370	All (1 Camera)	370	All (2 Lenses)	370	All (1 Label)	370
▶ 2010	370	Canon EOS 5D...	370	EF24-105mm f...	88	No Label	370
				EF70-200mm f...	282		

Figure 3-75

Step Three. Optional—To add or remove columns from the metadata filter, place your cursor over the column header and a small icon appears at the right (see Figure 3–76). Click here and use the menu to add or remove the column.

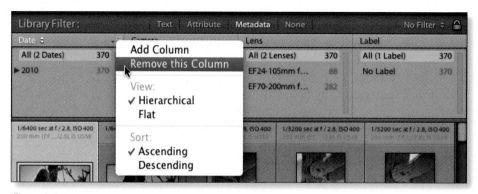

Figure 3-76

Step Four. To change the metadata being used in a filter column, click the column header to select a type from the popup menu (see Figure 3–77).

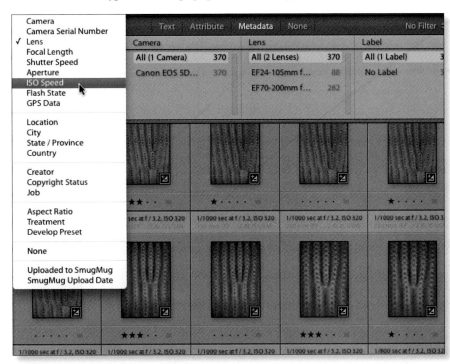

Figure 3-77

Step Five. From within each column, continue to select the metadata values to use for the filter.

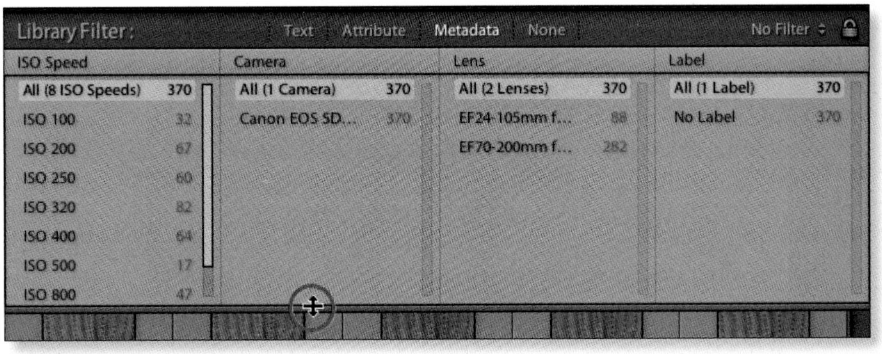

Figure 3-78

You can click and drag the bottom edge of the metadata filter to enlarge or reduce it (see Figure 3–78).

3

Selecting multiple values

You can select multiple criteria within the metadata columns. Hold Shift to select a contiguous range of options. Control or Ctrl selects individual, non-contiguous criteria (see Figure 3–79).

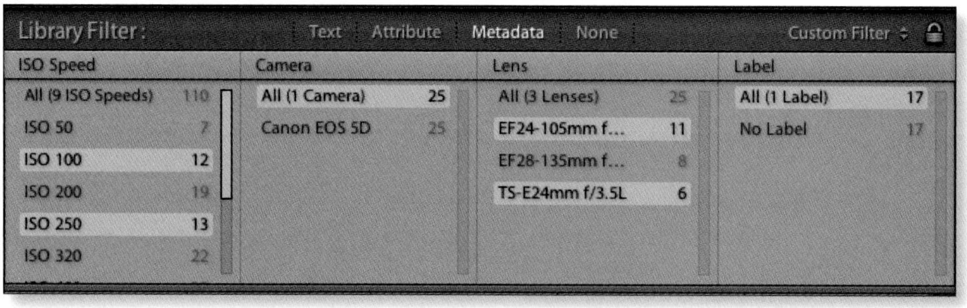

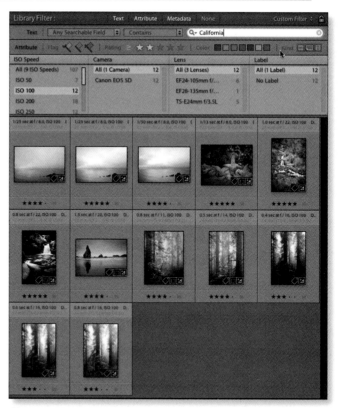

Figure 3-79

COMBINE MULTIPLE FILTER TYPES

Hold Shift or Ctrl when clicking the filter names to add controls for multiple filter types at the same time. For example, you could use a Text filter with Attributes added. Or Text with Metadata, etc. A highlighted label indicates that filter is active; see Figure 3–80. Click the name of the filter to enable or disable it in the current filter set.

If you spend time configuring a complex filter set, you might consider saving it for later; see next page.

Figure 3-80

3

NONE

Clicking None on the Filter Bar (see Figure 3–81) deactivates the current
filter set.

Figure 3-81

Filter controls on the Filmstrip

At the top right of the Filmstrip is a second set of filter controls (see Figure
3–82). These provide essentially the same on/off functionality as the filter bar
and you can select saved filter presets, but you can't configure complex metadata
filters here.

Figure 3-82

⌘+L or Ctrl+L
Turn filters
on/off

The filter switch

The filters section on the Filmstrip includes a switch that disables or enables the
current filter (see Figure 3–82). This may produce a result similar to clicking
None on the Filter Bar, but will only turn off the current single filter criteria
(not multiple criteria). To turn everything off, use None on the Filter Bar, or the
shortcut.

Don't modify filters just to disable them

If you want to temporarily show photos that don't match the current filter set,
you don't need to modify the filters, just turn them off. For example, if you have
a filter enabled to only show picks and need to see the unflagged photos also,
don't remove the pick flag from the filter; turn the filter off using None or the
Filmstrip switch. This allows you to keep
filter sets intact for later use.

SAVING FILTER PRESETS

To save a filter preset, get the filter set up
the way you want, then click the menu at
the right side of either the top Filter Bar
or the filters section on the Filmstrip (see
Figure 3–83). From the menu, select Save
Current Settings as New Preset. Give your
preset a meaningful name; it will then be
listed in the filters menu.

Figure 3-83

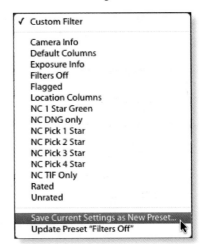

3

Lightroom Collections

Like filters, collections are one of Lightroom's great advantages over other imaging software.

Think of collections like "virtual folders": these groupings of images exist only within the Lightroom database.

You can make collections for any purpose, subject or topic and you can use as many collections as you want.

A single photo or virtual copy can belong to any number of collections. Adding or removing a photo from one collection doesn't necessarily affect it in others.

You can group your collections together in *collection sets*.

B
Add or remove
photos from
the Quick
Collection
or Target
Collection

QUICK COLLECTION

The Quick Collection is a built-in collection that is best used as a temporary holding place during editing or organizing. It's a useful tool for combining search results and filtered views. For example, during editing, you could add photos to the Quick Collection as an intermediate step to getting them all into one permanent collection later.

⌘+B or Ctrl+B
Go to Quick
Collection
or Target
Collection

There is only one Quick Collection available in each catalog. Access the Quick Collection in the Catalog panel; see Figure 3–84.

Figure 3-84

To add or remove photos from the Quick Collection press the B key, or hover your cursor over a thumbnail and click the gray circle in the top right corner.

Photos that are in the Quick Collection (or the Target Collection) show a gray dot on the top right of the thumbnail image; see Figure 3–85. To remove a photo from the Quick Collection, click the dot, or press B.

Figure 3-85

COLLECTIONS

Regular collections are those you create yourself, manually. Unlike smart collections (which are covered next), these "dumb" collections aren't based on any predefined criteria. You can create collections yourself for whatever purpose you choose, and add photos to them however you see fit.

I've set up numerous collections to hold client work, portfolios, exhibition entries and Web galleries. I have other collections containing work in progress, and collections for otherwise uncategorized images looking for a more permanent home in my catalog.

Using collections—instead of working in the original folders—reminds and assures me that my editing for those photo shoots was completed, and I'm now seeing only the final selects.

As you move through the workflow, I strongly recommend that you end up working more from collections than you do the actual folder sources. This is one primary benefit of using a database-driven system.

⌘+Control+3 or
Ctrl+Shift+3
Open/close the
Collections panel

⌘+N or Ctrl+N
Make a new
collection

Make a new collection and add photos to it
Click the + button on the Collections panel header and choose Create Collection (see Figure 3–86). Type a name for

Figure 3-86

the collection and configure the other options to your liking. For example, if you have images selected, you can automatically add them to the new collection. Press Return or Enter to create the collection.

To add photos to a collection later, drag their image thumbnails onto the collection name in the panel, or use the Target Collection option discussed below.

If you try to add a photo to a collection and you're not able to, it's because the photo is already in that collection. If it's not visible within the collection view, check the filter status.

Multiple instances of a single photo
By default, when you put a photo into a collection Lightroom creates a new *instance* of the photo in the database. In this case, the instance is linked to the original: changing one will change the other. For example, if you add a photo to a collection and then convert it to black and white, the original file in the folder source will also show those changes, and vice versa.

However, when adding photos to a collection it is also possible to create a new *virtual copy* of the file in that collection. A virtual copy is a special kind of instance of the original and exists only within the catalog. However, a virtual copy's link to

3

the settings applied to the original is effectively severed: changing a virtual copy doesn't affect the original, or vice versa. Virtual copies are discussed further in Chapter 4.

⌘+' or Ctrl+'
Make a virtual copy

Name the vc and find the original

In Library's Metadata panel is a special field, Copy Name (see Figure 3–87), where you can give a vc a unique name. Also, next to that is an action button which, when clicked, will locate and select the original from which the vc was made.

Figure 3-87

Removing photos from a collection

To take photos out of a collection, select the photo *from within the collection* and press Delete. This will immediately remove a file from a collection without presenting a confirmation dialog box. This is undo-able; just be sure to undo the removal before going on to other work. Deleting the photo from a collection doesn't affect instances of the photo in other collections or the original file on disk.

Moving and copying photos between collections

From anywhere in Lightroom—a folder, catalog source or another collection—you can drag and drop a photo onto a collection to add it to that collection. In this case the photo still remains in the previous collection; you can delete it from there if you like.

Control+Click or right-click on a collection

To access many useful commands on the collections contextual menu.

Control+Click or right-click on a thumbnail, choose Go to Collection

If the photo is in one or more collections (regular collections only; not smart collections), they will be listed here. Select one to go to that photo in the collection; see Figure 3–88.

Figure 3-88

Collections badge

Lightroom 3 also adds a new collections badge that will show on a thumbnail in Grid view; see Figure 3–89. Collections badges only show in folders and sources

Figure 3-89

other than the specific collection itself, though if the photo is a member of other collections, it will be displayed. Click the badge to go to the photo in that collection.

Set as Target Collection

You can specify any existing collection as the destination for photos when the B key is pressed. Control+Click or right-click the name of the collection and choose Set as Target Collection from the contextual menu (see Figure 3–90). A white plus symbol next to the collection indicates it is targeted. Pressing B will now assign photos to the target collection, and not the Quick Collection. To turn targeting

Figure 3-90

off, uncheck the option from the menu and the Quick Collection will again become the target collection.

SMART COLLECTIONS

Smart collections are configured with options similar to filters. You can set up smart collections to source images from anywhere in the catalog, using a wide variety of metadata criteria. As you work with photos and their settings are changed, Lightroom will dynamically add or remove them from the smart collections. You could make smart collections for photos made in the last 30 days, photos that need keywords, photos to prepare for a client, photos to be sent to a lab for printing, etc. All would be based on file metadata, and updated dynamically. Note that smart collections cannot have custom (user) sort orders.

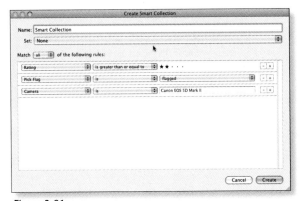

Figure 3-91

Make a new smart collection

On the Collections panel, click the + button and choose Create Smart Collection. Type a name for the collection and then configure its criteria.

3

By default, a new smart collection just contains one rule. Use the plus or minus buttons to add or remove criteria (see Figure 3–91 on the previous page). Press Return or Enter to create the smart collection. Use the dropdown menus and/or text fields to define the rule for this smart collection.

Option or Alt

To provide additional, "advanced" options when adding criteria to a smart collection.

Note: Since smart collections work automatically from photo metadata in the catalog, you can't directly add or remove images from smart collections by dragging and dropping them.

Import and Export Smart Collections

You can transfer your smart collections between computers. Right-click or Ctrl+click on the smart collection name, and choose Import or Export from the contextual menu.

COLLECTION SETS

Like folders can contain subfolders and keyword hierarchies have parent and child keywords, *collection sets* can contain both collections and smart collections. Figure 3–92 shows collection sets, each with several collections nested inside. Collection sets are a great way to keep your collections organized into larger categories. A collection set is designated in the Collections panel list by a special icon.

To make a new collection set, click the + button on the collections panel header and select Create Collection Set.

Figure 3-92

You can drag and drop collections within the panel to rearrange them or nest them under different collection sets.

To rename a collection set, right-click or control+click on its name and select the option from the popup menu; see Figure 3–93.

Figure 3-93

3

DELETING COLLECTIONS, SMART COLLECTIONS AND SETS

Figure 3-94

To delete a collection or set, select it in the list, then either click the minus button on the panel header (see Figure 3–94) or right-click/control+click the collection name and select Delete from the popup menu.

Deleting a collection will not affect any original photos in disk, or instances of photos that might also be in other collections.

Deleting a collection set will also delete all the collections within it.

Processing photos in Library

Sometimes when you're editing photos from a shoot you'll want to do some processing to help your decision-making process. Maybe you have a group of shots that are underexposed, or the white balance is off. In these cases, you can use tools and panels in Library to evaluate photos and apply simple adjustments to them.

⌘+0 or Ctrl+0
Open and close the Histogram panel

HISTOGRAM

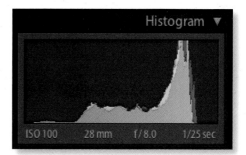

Figure 3-95

Processing decisions can be made easier by evaluating the *histogram*; see Figure 3–95. This oft-misunderstood tool is simply a bar graph. It shows the digital values contained in the photo, with blacks at the left and whites at the right. The height of the levels in-between indicates the relative number of pixels at that brightness value within the image. The histogram is explained in more detail in Chapter 4.

Using the Histogram panel in Quick Develop can give you a better understanding of the data in the photo. Knowing what you're starting with can help you decide where you want to go in processing your photos. But don't obsess over the histogram!

QUICK DEVELOP

The Quick Develop panel in the Library module (see Figure 3–96) contains a limited subset of the image adjustment controls available in the Develop module.

⌘+1 or Ctrl+1
Open/close the Quick Develop panel

Using the Quick Develop panel is very different from using the full Develop module. Though the names of the adjustments are the same, and those adjustments produce essentially the same visual changes in the individual photo(s), it's *how* the adjustments are applied that makes all the difference.

In Library's Quick Develop panel, all the adjustments are *relative:* the changes you make are applied **on top of any existing adjustments.** For example, if you start with a Saturation setting of +6 and click a single-arrow button to apply a +5 Saturation increase, the resulting value will be +11.

Figure 3-96

Conversely, when you set an adjustment in the Develop module, the slider value—or the number you type—is *absolute.* That means that the numeric value applies precisely that amount of adjustment. In the Develop module, if you apply multiple adjustments to a photo, the effects of two sequential adjustments are not cumulative. These adjustments are absolute and the numeric value is what it is: +.50 Exposure applies a half stop exposure adjustment to the photo; +35 Clarity applies exactly that amount of processing to the photo. If you start with Saturation set at +8 and change it to +12, the value becomes +12, not +20.

Also, in Library's Quick Develop, you can apply adjustments to multiple photos at once, and because of the relative nature of those adjustments, each photo will potentially be processed differently (whereas adjustments you make in Develop affect only the active image). To apply Quick Develop settings to multiple photos, select them in Grid view—if you're previewing a single photo in Loupe view, Quick Develop adjustments will only be applied to that image.

To apply Quick Develop adjustments in Library, whether to one or multiple selected photos, click the buttons in the Quick Develop panel to adjust those settings. The adjustments and their effect on photos are described in more detail in Chapter 4.

Right-facing arrows increase the value for each setting; left arrows decrease that value. Single arrows increase or decrease by small values, double arrows increase the adjustments in larger increments. (Hold your cursor over each setting to see tool tips.)

Small and large arrow buttons and their adjustment values:

- Exposure 1/3 stop, 1 stop

- Fill Light 5, 15

- Brightness and Contrast 5, 20

- Recovery 5, 20

- Blacks 1, 5

- Clarity 5, 20

- Vibrance 5, 20

You have two places you can directly apply adjustments to photos—Library and Develop—but in each module, keep in mind that the changes are applied differently. This aspect of parametric, metadata editing is crucial for understanding how Lightroom works with your photos.

The Preset menu on the Quick Develop Panel

You can apply saved Develop presets to photos using the Quick Develop Panel. Or, to remove all Develop settings from the selected photo(s), choose General – Zeroed from the menu. All other metadata remains intact.

Show all the Quick Develop settings

Click the black triangles to access all the settings on the Quick Develop panel (see Figure 3–96).

Press Option or Alt

This toggles Clarity/Sharpening and Vibrance/Saturation on the Quick Develop panel.

Crop presets in Quick Develop

Using Quick Develop, you can quickly and easily apply crop presets to multiple photos in Library. (To use custom crop presets you'd have to create them first; see Chapter 4 for more on this.)

3

Reset All

This button on the Quick Develop panel (see Figure 3–97) resets the settings for all the photos selected when in Grid view, or the single photo showing in Loupe view.

Figure 3-97

V
Convert selected photo(s) to black and white

Convert photos to black and white

Using the Quick Develop panel or the keyboard shortcut you can convert color photos to black and white from within the Library module. Black and white conversions are discussed further in Chapter 4.

⌘+Shift+S or Ctrl+Shift+S
Sync settings

⌘+Shift+R or Ctrl+Shift+R
Reset to Adobe Default settings (see Chapter 4)

SYNC SETTINGS

In Library, you can synchronize Develop settings between multiple photos. When you Sync Settings, the settings from the active photo will be applied to all the other selected photos.

First, select the photo from which you want to copy the settings, then select the other photos to have the new settings synced to. Click the Sync Settings button. A dialog box opens, allowing you to choose what settings will be synced. These are Develop adjustments only; not keywords or other metadata. To sync metadata, use the Sync Metadata button instead.

⌘+Shift+C or Ctrl+Shift+C
Copy settings

⌘+Shift+V or Ctrl+Shift+V
Paste settings

COPY/PASTE SETTINGS

You can copy Develop adjustments from one photo and paste them to other photos. Copy/Paste is similar to Sync Settings. However, there's one major difference: when you copy settings, they are stored in memory, and can be pasted to other photos later. Conversely, Sync Settings operates on just that single instance. Otherwise, the Copy Settings dialog box is identical to Sync Settings in appearance and function.

Select an image, then press the keys to open the Copy Settings dialog box. Choose what Develop settings to copy from the selected photo.

Select one or more images that will receive the pasted settings. Pressing the Paste shortcut applies the copied settings to all the selected photos. Only settings that are different will be pasted.

3

Option+⌘+K
or Alt+Ctrl+K
Activates the
Painter

MAKING FAST METADATA CHANGES WITH THE PAINTER

The Painter is a powerful way to modify photo settings and metadata. With it you can add, remove or change all kinds of metadata and Develop adjustments very quickly.

To use the Painter, first be sure the Toolbar is showing (T). Click the Painter icon to activate the tool. Then, from the Paint: popup menu choose what kind of settings you want to modify (see Figure 3–98); the Painter icon changes accordingly. Next, configure the options for the changes you'll be applying. Then simply click on thumbnails in the Grid or Filmstrip to apply the Painter setting(s). See Figure 3–99.

Figure 3-98

Figure 3-99

To use the Painter to remove some kinds of metadata, such as keywords, hold the Option or Alt key. The Painter icon changes to indicate you're in erase mode. Click on photos to remove the specified metadata or adjustments from them.

Paint Target Collection

Using the Painter you can add or remove photos in the Target Collection. This can be much faster and easier than dragging and dropping or using the contextual menus (though in most cases, I still prefer the B-key shortcut).

When you're done, click the button in the Toolbar or press Esc to turn off the Painter tool.

Converting raw files to DNG in Library

If you're capturing raw files with your camera (as you well should) then I believe converting to DNG in Lightroom is definitely the way to go.

DNG (Digital NeGative) is Adobe's non-proprietary, openly-documented raw format. DNG files can be made from any original, native camera raw file.

A raw file converted to DNG preserves all the original, linear data and offers additional benefits, most importantly the capacity to directly save XMP metadata into the DNG file, eliminating the need for sidecar files that would be required to save edits to raw files.

3

(If you don't care about all this technical mumbo-jumbo, the simple answer is "yes, use DNG".)

I convert my Canon CR2 files to DNG very early in the workflow (usually during import); though it can be done at any time. After converting to DNG and backing up, I don't keep my CR2 files.

You can convert camera raw files to DNG from within the Library module, without needing to do an export. You can convert to DNG at any point in your workflow.

Library menu➔Convert Photo(s) to DNG
In the dialog box (see Figure 3–100), apply the settings for the conversion. (I prefer and usually recommend using the default settings.)

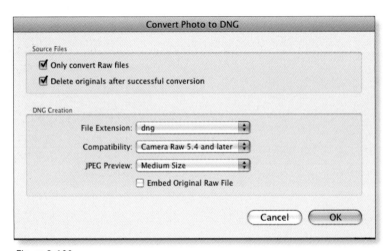

Figure 3-100

DNG is also discussed in Chapters 1, 2, 4 and 5.

Publish Services and Comments

New in Lightroom 3 is the ability to "publish" photos to hard drives and Web sites directly from Library; see Figure 3–101. This provides exciting new capabilities for integrating Lightroom with outside services. For example, on Web sites that support user comments,

Figure 3-101

Lightroom can automatically sync those comments into your catalog. (That's what the new Comments panel is for.) Publish services are discussed in detail in Chapter 9.

Backing up and optimizing your catalog

As described in Chapter 2, Lightroom 3 includes some important changes for how we back up our catalogs. Backups are now done on quitting Lightroom, instead of when launching. **The options for controlling how often Lightroom backs up a catalog are under Catalog Settings.** Keep in mind that only the catalog itself is backed up; not image files or previews. I back up my catalog after every work session where I've made any kind of significant changes within the catalog, so I keep this set to "Every time Lightroom exits"; I can just skip a backup if it's not necessary.

Also, the Optimize Catalog command has been moved to the Lightroom menu on Mac and the File menu on Windows. I recommend you optimize your main catalog every couple of weeks worth of work, at minimum. (The Optimize Catalog command runs the SQL Vacuum procedure, which cleans, compacts and repairs the catalog.)

I'm not going into a lot of detail about backup again here; we all know it's important. Take good care of your catalogs—it's quite possible that there will be problems with corrupted data at some point, and having a recent, optimized backup of your catalog will minimize the inconvenience.

CHAPTER 4

DEVELOP

4

Perfecting your photos in Develop

After you've edited the shoot, identified your selects and put them into collections using the Library module, it's time to make each photo look as good as it can.

Along with the organizational power in Library, the Develop module is one of Lightroom's core strengths. Master the Develop controls and you may find that you can complete all the processing you desire entirely within Lightroom. (In cases where you also want to work on your images more in Photoshop, Lightroom provides a streamlined workflow for sending photos to Photoshop, and then back to Lightroom when you're done; Chapter 9 includes instructions for Lightroom's "round-trip" procedure for editing photos in Photoshop.)

Obviously, processing individual photos involves a number of variables, and what works in one instance won't necessarily work in another. Some images will require very little adjustment, and others more. But even with the greatest care taken at the time of capture, *every* raw image stands a chance of being improved—often significantly—during processing.

DEVELOP MODULE PANELS

In the Develop module, the left panel set (see Figure 4–1, opposite page) contains the Navigator, Presets, Snapshots, History and Collections; we'll look at those later. I usually work with the left panels hidden to give the photo as much room as possible in the preview area; see Figure 4–2.

The right panel set provides all the adjustment controls and tools you'll use to Develop your photos. Lightroom 3 contains significant additions and improvements in the Develop module adjustments. Take a minute to look around; open and close each panel to get an idea of the adjustments available.

Make the panels as wide as you can to provide the greatest refinement for the sliders. Position your cursor over the edge of the panel, and you'll see the cursor turns into a double arrow (see Figure 4–3). Click and drag outward to expand the panels to the maximum width.

The Develop module is also one of the places within Lightroom where I almost always work with the panels in Solo Mode. This avoids the need

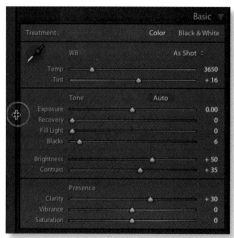

Figure 4-3

Figure 4-1

Figure 4-2

to scroll through the right panel track, which can get quite long. Right-click or Ctrl+click on any panel header to enable Solo Mode from the popup menu (see Figure 4–4).

If you keep the Filmstrip open (see Figure 4–5) you can easily switch between photos without needing to go back to the Library module.

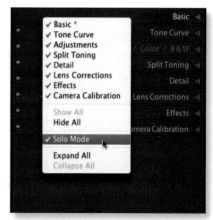

Figure 4-4

Figure 4-5

TYPICAL DEVELOP WORKFLOW

To get the best results with the least amount of effort, you should follow a standard set of steps for all your work in Develop. In this chapter we'll cover all the individual adjustments you can make, and you'll learn how to dramatically speed up your workflow using Develop presets. First, let's outline the order of the Develop workflow you'll use to process most of your photos:

1. Global rendering

    1.1 Default settings and Auto settings

    1.2 Camera Calibration: Process and Profile

2. Crop and straighten

3. White balance

4. Tone adjustments

    4.1 Exposure

    4.2 Blacks

    4.3 Brightness

You'll find that the majority of your photos will benefit from applying all or most of these standard adjustments, so we'll examine these in detail. Then, in the latter part of this chapter, we'll also take a look at some of the possibilities for special creative effects you can achieve within the Develop module.

Process as far as you can in Lightroom

Many photographers who have been using Photoshop, or other image processing software, for a long time have a natural inclination to do a minimal amount of work in Lightroom, wanting to switch to the other program as soon as possible to finish the photo. (If you're one of these folks, I believe you're cheating yourself!)

4

Practice processing the image as far as you possibly can, using Lightroom alone, before switching to another program…you won't regret it! When you've mastered the Develop controls in Lightroom you will not spend nearly as much time in other software.

About composite images

Any photo that is made of more than one original capture is called a *composite*. **Currently, Lightroom can't produce composites.** To combine multiple images you need to get them out of Lightroom and into other software, like Photoshop. Processing individual images that will become part of a composite requires special consideration. If, during processing, you start thinking of combining multiple exposures—in any fashion and for any reason—you'll need to start considering exports and external editors; covered in Chapter 5 and 9, respectively.

For now, as you're looking at processing individual images in Develop, learn to make the most of the tools available. You may find that in some cases—especially those that at first glance appear to require blending exposures—can be fully accomplished in Lightroom.

You will find images that in the past may have required compositing now can be successfully processed with just one capture in Lightroom.

MAKE A PLAN FOR PROCESSING

Before beginning your processing in Develop, take a few minutes to evaluate the photo and make a quick plan for the work you're going to do. (You could instead do this in Library, as the last step of editing.) It might help to jot down some notes to help visualize the sequence of steps you will take. This doesn't need to be elaborate; just take a moment to envision the final result you're looking for.

As every image is unique, each will benefit from different enhancements to make the photograph look its best. These decisions are highly subjective; the choices you make will reflect *your* creative vision of how the image should look. (Of course, if you're working for a client, their vision might guide the creative process, too.)

However, there are some common criteria you can use when determining the appropriate improvements to a photo. Some enhancements, like noise reduction and sharpening, are quite objective, as there are established standards of technical and aesthetic quality to consider. For example, in most cases, we would agree that digital noise is undesirable and should be minimized, or, many people would agree when a photo looks "crooked" or "blurry". Of course, there are exceptions to every rule.

Keep in mind that every step of the workflow affects and is affected by every other step. For example, sharpening the image may increase noise. Adjusting color may affect contrast, etc. So it might be necessary to go back and forth between steps to perfect the image.

Remember that repeatedly following the same general sequence of steps will help you work more efficiently, more effectively and with greater creative freedom.

Learn to differentiate between technical and aesthetic characteristics
Critiquing photography—whether your own or someone else's—requires analysis of the effectiveness of the photograph's creative impact as well as the technical execution. Though neither necessarily takes precedence, artistic and technical considerations should be evaluated separately. Technical characteristics include resolution, sharpness, and the appearance of artifacts, while compositional choices and the portrayal of subject matter are more aesthetic. Lighting could be considered from both technical and aesthetic perspectives. Practice seeing all the elements of a photograph independently.

Think about post-processing while you are shooting
Once you're comfortable quickly changing settings on your camera while shooting, start to consider how you will process the file later. Taking production issues into account while you're shooting will help you get better captures and make post-processing easier.

MAINTAINING MAXIMUM QUALITY

As has been discussed in previous chapters, one of the primary goals of digital image processing is to retain as much data as possible from the original capture throughout the imaging pipeline. Regardless of the types of adjustments you make or special effects you apply in Lightroom (or any other software) it's usually best to process your images as minimally as you can.

This requires you to plan several steps ahead as you adjust images and, in general, to perform your processing tasks in a consistent sequence. Go through your processing methodically, taking the time to finish each photo before moving onto the next. In some cases, batches of images can be Developed the same way; Lightroom accommodates this with ease.

The order of tasks
Lightroom's Develop controls can be adjusted in any sequence you like. You can go back and forth between panels and settings to progressively refine

4

your images and Lightroom will apply the adjustments to the final image in the ideal way to maintain the most possible data. However, the order in which you perform your image editing tasks is important for several reasons:

- **Different adjustment controls affect image data in similar ways.** For example, increasing the Brightness value and adjusting the midpoint of the Tone Curve produce similar changes in the appearance of the photo.

- **Some adjustments affect others.** Continuing the example above, *increasing* the Brightness value and *decreasing* the midtone areas of the Tone Curve would produce counteracting adjustments and decreased quality.

- **Tone and color should be evaluated and adjusted independently.** You'll often find that once you get the tones right, the colors will also fall into place. For this reason, it's best to do as much tone correction as possible before moving on to adjust color. (The exception is white balance.)

- **Work gets done faster if it's done the same way every time.** Though some images will require more work and additional processing steps than others, following a consistent sequence of steps allows you to be more efficient through repetition. This allows you to spend more time on the photographs that really benefit from additional attention.

If it doesn't improve the image, turn it off

When experimenting with adjustment controls or applying settings with the intention of achieving a specific effect, if you find that the adjustment is not an improvement, undo the adjustment or reset the slider to its default.

⌘+Z or Ctrl+Z
Undo the last operation. Continue pressing to go further back in History

Don't make an adjustment that counteracts another

This wastes time and data and diminishes quality. As you're processing a photo, take care that the adjustments you make don't actually put you further from your goals. Always use the best tool for the job and use as few adjustments as necessary to achieve the desired appearance.

⌘+Shift+Z or Ctrl+Shift+Z
Redo the last undone operation

Undo/Redo

Unlimited undo and redo removes the fear of experimentation. In Develop you can't irreparably harm an image—but you can surely make it look bad! Lightroom maintains an unlimited history of all the processing work you do on an image from the import forward. So feel free to play!

Don't use undo/redo like before/after

Lightroom offers controls for seeing the image with and without the current adjustments. Before/After is covered toward the end of this chapter.

Global rendering settings

Start your photo processing by doing the *global* adjustments—those that affect the entire image—and progressively work towards fine tuning the details (*local* adjustments). For example, do your retouching after adjusting tone and color.

Lightroom has a few settings that affect the baseline rendering of your photos. Let's look at those first.

ADOBE DEFAULT

When you import photos, Lightroom must *render* the image data to generate previews. This means that every capture coming into Lightroom could be affected by some kind of processing, even if you don't apply any adjustments yourself. In these cases, Lightroom will render the captures using the *Adobe Defaults*, which you can override.

In the case of raw or DNG files, sometimes the Lightroom defaults may render your photos with less than "optimal" quality. **This can skew your perception of what the capture actually contains, and what needs to be done during processing.**

By default, TIF, PSD and JPG files are *not* adjusted when they come into Lightroom. Their settings are *zeroed;* no processing is being done to the images. (However, this, too, can be changed.) In these cases, the Lightroom preview will show you how the photo looks with no adjustments.

If you apply your own Develop preset during import, you will see initial previews closer to what you expect. We'll look at Develop presets later in this chapter.

Make your own default

Work with your photos for a while to determine the Develop settings that provide the optimal rendering for the majority of your files. You can then override the default settings to create your own baseline for rendering newly imported images.

Hold down the Option or Alt key; this changes the Reset button on the bottom right panel to say "Set Default". Click the button and make a choice from the dialog box to set the default using all the current settings, or to restore the Adobe default.

Set Default...

4

PROCESS VERSION

Here's a fundamental new feature in Lightroom 3 that's really important to understand: *Process Version* denotes a change in the core processing routines that Lightroom uses to demosaic and render image files, generate previews for them and in some cases will also determine the available adjustment controls.

During the development of Lightroom 3, Adobe refined and improved the basic raw processing algorithms used in all their software. Put one way, this means that older process versions are "not as good" as newer ones. Looking more carefully, you might recognize that new process versions also enable more capabilities in working with the image data… but this doesn't necessarily mean your pictures processed using older versions aren't valid.

(If Lightroom 3 is the first version of Lightroom you're using, you don't need to be concerned with the rest of this particular section.)

If you've used earlier versions of Lightroom, or Photoshop with the Adobe Camera Raw plug-in, you should be aware of what's changed. Be aware that Process Version can affect all photos in the catalog, regardless of file type.

There are currently two process versions, 2003 and 2010, named for when they were created. When you import new photos into Lightroom 3, they will automatically be assigned the 2010 Process Version.

Photos in your catalog that were imported with previous versions of Lightroom will have the 2003 Process Version applied. In these cases, your photos will look exactly like they did before; Lightroom 3 is not going to change them automatically.

But for your prize selects, you might consider changing to the 2010 Process Version, because you might be able to make photos look even better than they did before. Also, some of the new tools in Lightroom 3, require using the 2010 Process Version.

Based on what kinds of adjustments were applied using the 2003 Process Versions, you may see more, or less, of a change when switching to the new process version.

Photos using the 2003 Process Version will display an icon containing an exclamation mark in the bottom right of the Develop Loupe view; see Figure 4–6.

4

Figure 4-6

⌘+8 or Ctrl+8
Open/close
the Camera
Calibration
panel

To change to the 2010 Process Version, click the notification icon, or choose from the Settings menu options. (If you use the icon, a dialog box opens, explaining what will happen if you proceed.)

You can also change process version on the Camera alibration panel; see Figure 4–7.

You can use Lightroom's Before/After feature to compare a photo with the different process versions; Before/After is discussed toward the end of this chapter.

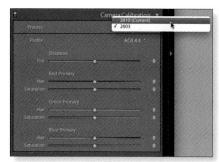

Figure 4-7

4

CAMERA PROFILES

In addition to Process Version, another important starting point for establishing the best possible default rendering for your photos is to apply a camera profile using the Camera Calibration panel (see Figure 4–8).

Note: camera profiles can only be applied to camera raw and DNG images. Other file types will show "Embedded", though you can still tweak slider adjustments here (but I don't' recommend it.)

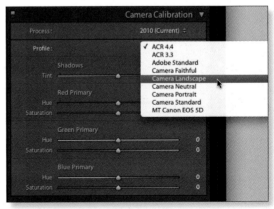

With the current camera profiles installed, Lightroom will show only the profiles applicable for the camera

Figure 4-8

used to make the capture. If your camera is not listed, you can use the default Adobe profiles or create your own.

In some cases, you may see several versions of Adobe Camera Raw (ACR) profiles. The numbers indicate during what version(s) of Adobe Camera Raw the original matrix-style profile was created for that camera model. If there is more than one listed, this indicates the profile for that camera was updated in the newer version of ACR.

The newer Adobe Standard profile replaces the older ACR profiles. (For camera models released after ACR 5.2, the profile menu will not list the ACR profiles.)

In addition to the Adobe profiles, depending on your camera make and model, you will also very likely see camera-specific profiles listed. These mimic the picture styles in the camera and the camera-maker's dedicated software.

Some images benefit from different profiles

Try each of the various profiles until you get the best results. Choosing a different profile can dramatically improve the baseline rendering of your captures!

Installing/uninstalling camera profiles

At the time of this writing, Adobe's camera profiles are automatically installed when you install Lightroom (version 2.2 and higher), DNG Converter (v5.2 and higher) or Adobe Camera Raw (v5.2 and higher). If you installed earlier

4

versions of these products, you might have the old, beta profiles still installed on your system. These can be removed by deleting them from the folder; however, be aware that any presets made using those beta profiles will no longer function correctly.

The default locations of the camera profiles are:

Mac os x: Macintosh HD/Library/Application Support/Adobe/CameraRaw/CameraProfiles

Windows Vista and 7: C:\ProgramData\Adobe\CameraRaw\CameraProfiles

Windows 2000/xp: C:\Documents and Settings\All Users\Application Data\Adobe\CameraRaw\CameraProfiles

Make your own camera profiles

Though the Adobe profiles can often get very close to the optimal rendering on many images, you will usually achieve the best results by profiling your own camera. More information and instructions for doing this are at Adobe's DNG profile editor Web site at http://labs.adobe.com/.

Camera calibration sliders

Prior to the introduction of camera profiles, the Camera Calibration slider adjustments were commonly used to apply baseline rendering values stored in Develop defaults. Camera profiles have made the Camera Calibration slider adjustments obsolete, and I generally recommend you don't make adjustments to these sliders or use them in presets. However, due to the fact that many Lightroom users have processed photos and created presets using these sliders in the past, it's likely that they will remain a part of Lightroom.

AUTO SETTINGS

You will find Auto adjustment buttons in several places throughout Lightroom's Develop panels (see Figure 4–9) and menus (and Library's Quick Develop).

Figure 4-9

4

Preferences→Presets→Apply Auto-Tone Adjustments

Lightroom has a preference setting to either automatically apply Auto-tone adjustments or not (see Figure 4–10). The default is off. For the most control over Developing your photos, check your preferences to verify this. Otherwise, Lightroom will auto-process your photos.

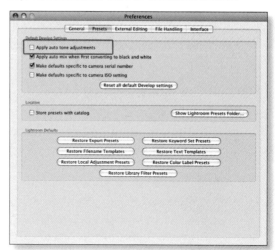

Figure 4-10

Crop and straighten

As the first step in evaluating each image, carefully consider whether it could be made stronger with different cropping (see Figure 4–11). Since cropping removes parts of the photo—and thus changes the composition—this can be the most significant modification you make to an image. Before you go much further into processing, take a few moments to crop and/or straighten the photo as necessary. (Note that because all digital images are rectangular, *straightening* a photo in Lightroom always involves cropping.)

Figure 4-11

Be willing to crop photos in Lightroom whenever it makes an improvement.

Are there distracting elements along the edges or in the corners? Are there areas of empty space that detract from the main subject? How is the overall balance of the composition? If the photo had been shot in landscape orientation (horizontal), would a portrait (vertical) crop make it better? How about a square crop?

Also decide if the image looks "straight"—especially if there is a prominent horizon line or a strong edge that should appear level to convey the right "feel" for the image. You may need to rotate the image slightly (which requires cropping in Lightroom). Alternatively, would the photograph be more interesting if it was rotated even further?

Lightroom always crops (and processes) images using the full resolution of the files. There are no resizing/resampling controls directly within Lightroom; to resize an image you must Export it, which is covered in Chapter 5. Don't be concerned with the size or resolution of the image when you're working in Develop; it is what it is.

Crop in-camera

It's always best if you don't have to crop or rotate in post-processing; in both cases, you'll lose resolution. While shooting, whenever possible, slow down and take your time to perfect your compositions.

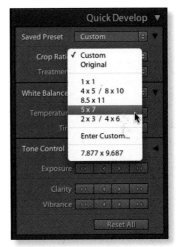

Figure 4-12

Apply Crop Presets in Library Quick Develop

To quickly Crop one or more photos, select them, and choose the desired preset, or custom option, from the Crop Ratio menu in the Quick Develop panel in Library; see Figure 4–12. Note that the applied crop will be centered on all the images; you can then go into Develop to adjust crops for individual photos as necessary.

CROP OVERLAY TOOL

Lightroom's crop and straighten tools are in the *tool strip* on Develop's right panel set, just below the Histogram (see Figure 4–13).

Figure 4-13

4

Activating the tools opens the *tool drawer* underneath the tool strip; see Figure 4–14. The tool drawer contains the controls for each tool. When the crop overlay is active, some crop settings are also found on the Toolbar.

Figure 4-14

R
Activate the crop overlay

Click the crop tool button in the tool strip (or use the shortcut) to enable the crop overlay, which is then displayed over the image.

Option or Alt
Crop from the center of the photo

Drag the corners or the sides of the overlay to adjust the crop; see Figure 4–15. The crop overlay always remains straight and centered in the image preview area; the photo moves underneath it. Drag the photo to reposition it within the crop overlay.

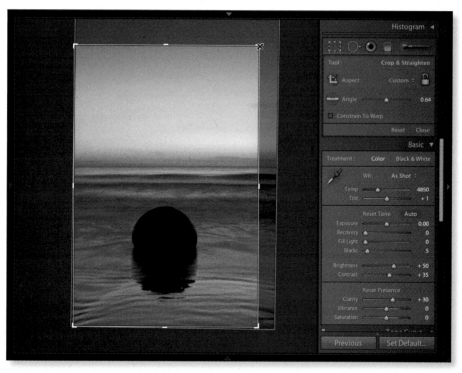

Figure 4-15

To apply the crop when you're done adjusting, press Enter or R, or the Done button in the Toolbar, or the Close button in the tray. Alternatively, to cancel cropping without applying the changes, press Esc.

4

Try Lights Out when cropping

Press L once or twice to darken or black out everything on your screen but the image—it's much easier to see how the cropped image will look; see Figure 4–16. (Lights Out is discussed in more detail in Chapter 1.)

Figure 4-16

ASPECT RATIOS

The *aspect ratio* of an image refers to its length and width, expressed as a ratio. For example, 2:3 means that the photo's short side is 2 units and the long side is 3 units. These units can later be translated into real world measurements, such as size in inches for printing.

When cropping in Lightroom, you can *constrain* the crop to a precise aspect ratio or apply a free-form crop that is not locked to any aspect ratio. The padlock button (see Figure 4–17) toggles

Figure 4-17

4

whether or not the aspect ratio is constrained. Next to it, a popup menu allows you to choose a ratio or to create your own.

Use standard aspect ratios when possible

In Lightroom you can crop a photo any way you like, without regard to specified aspect ratios. It's always best to let the composition of the image determine the optimal crop. However, your plans for printing and framing the photo may introduce other constraints. For example, using a 4:5 aspect ratio will allow an 8x10 print in a 16x20 frame. Envision how you will finish the photo, and when appropriate use a standard aspect ratio.

ROTATING AND STRAIGHTENING

You can rotate your photo to make it appear more level, or you can use rotation as a creative effect.

The easiest way to arbitrarily rotate the photo is to place your cursor outside the crop overlay; the cursor turns into a curved double-arrow. Click and drag to rotate the photo under the crop overlay; see Figure 4–18. You can also double-click on either the Angle label or its slider to reset it.

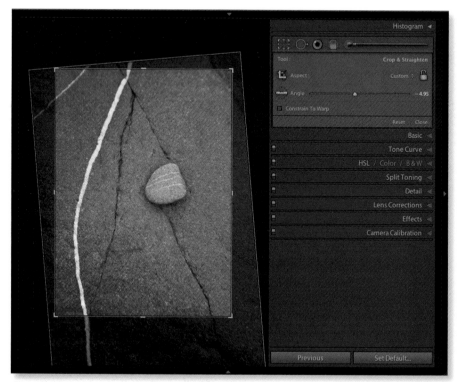

Figure 4-18

Alternatively, you can use the following methods for rotation:

- Click and drag with the Straighten tool;

- Drag the Angle slider; or

- Enter a numeric value in degrees (see Figure 4–19).

Figure 4-19

Use overlays to assist with rotation
If you want to straighten a horizon or other prominent line in the photo, use the grid overlays to help line things up; see below.

O
Cycle crop overlays

Shift+O
Change overlay orientation

GRID OVERLAYS

Lightroom's crop tool provides the following overlays (see Figure 4–20). These are based on long-held principles of design and are included to aid composition while cropping:

- Rule of Thirds

- Golden Ratio

- Diagonal Lines

- Triangles

- Golden Mean

- Grid

Figure 4-20

4

Changing orientation

You can use the crop tool to turn a landscape-oriented image to a portrait and vice versa; see Figure 4–21 and 4–22. Press the X key; it toggles the crop overlay between portrait and landscape orientation.

Figure 4-21   *Figure 4-22*

The crop frame tool

With the crop frame tool (see Figure 4–23), you can draw a freehand crop in either portrait or landscape orientation. When using the crop frame tool, the aspect ratio controls apply in the same way as when manipulating the crop overlay directly.

Figure 4-23

4

Constrain to warp

This checkbox works in conjunction with Lens Corrections, forcing the crop within the boundaries of the Transform controls. If no Transform adjustments are applied, this checkbox has no effect on the crop. Lens Corrections are discussed later in this chapter.

⌘+Option+R
or Ctrl+Alt+R
Reset crop

RESETTING THE CROP

To reset the crop overlay to its original settings, click the Reset button in the tool drawer or use the shortcut. (Note: both crop and rotation will be reset at once.)

White balance

With digital capture, you can control how the color of light in the scene affects the colors captured. *Color temperature* is measured in degrees Kelvin and refers to the measured color of light sources. For example:

- Bright sunlight at midday is approximately 5000k;

- Open shade is around 6500k; and

- Tungsten light bulbs are about 2800k.

Color temperature dramatically affects the overall colors in a digital photograph so understanding how the color temperature of light affects the digital capture is essential. *White balance* lets you manipulate the global rendition of colors in a photo, based on color temperature.

Does the image appear to have a *color cast,* or overall tint, that may be affecting color accuracy (see Figure 4–24)? You've certainly seen photos shot indoors, under tungsten light (standard bulbs), that appear very yellow. This is because the white balance used was intended for daylight,

Figure 4-24

which has a much cooler color. (Yellows and oranges are *warm* colors; blues and purples are *cool* colors.)

4

After cropping, adjust the white balance to remove any apparent color cast and fine-tune the rendering of color in the image. Of course, you can also use white balance to creatively warm or cool the image for effect.

After a process version and camera profile is selected, the white balance adjustment will have the largest effect on the overall rendering of the image. In Lightroom, even black and white images are affected by the white balance settings.

Bear in mind that, like all other adjustments, white balance is usually subjective and you shouldn't worry too much about whether the white balance is "correct". What matters most is that you like the way the picture looks.

However, in situations where you need to precisely reproduce color (such as product or fashion photography), a reference target must be included in the photo in order to correctly neutralize the white balance. Popular reference targets include the ColorChecker from X-Rite and WhiBal cards from RawWorkflow. com. Simply capture an image that includes the gray card, and use the eyedropper to set the white balance (see opposite page).

In Lightroom, white balance value can be assigned to a photo using the following methods:

- Temperature and Tint sliders, and corresponding numeric entry. I usually prefer to use the sliders to adjust white balance. (Note that the sliders show the color effect of moving them a certain direction; see Figure 4–25);

Figure 4-25

- Popup menu containing white balance preset values; and

- White balance eyedropper.

With any method, you can reset the white balance back to its original value by choosing As Shot from the popup menu or by double-clicking the WB: text in the panel.

4

WHITE BALANCE PRESETS

The fastest, easiest way to apply standard white balance values is to select from the preset values in the popup menu; see Figure 4–26. While doing so, pay attention to each preset's effect on the slider settings. This is a good way to learn the numeric values for specific lighting conditions. After choosing the preset closest to your desired look, you can fine-tune the white balance using the sliders and/ or numeric entry.

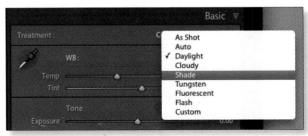

Figure 4-26

Lightroom vs. camera settings

In many cases, the numeric values for Lightroom's white balance settings uses will be different than those used in the camera. For example, the Daylight setting on my Canon 5D Mark II uses a temperature of +4850 and a tint of +1, whereas Daylight in Lightroom is +5500 and +10. Depending on the photo, this may not be an important distinction, and white balance on a raw capture is only a metadata value, so you can apply any numeric settings you want in Lightroom.

THE WHITE BALANCE EYEDROPPER

W
Activate the White Balance eyedropper

⌘+Shift+U or Ctrl+Shift+U
Apply auto white balance

To activate the white balance Eyedropper click the tool (see Figure 4–27) or use the shortcut (from anywhere in the Library or Develop modules). Move the cursor around the image; a small grid overlay appears, depicting enlarged pixels under the cursor (see Figure 4–28 next page). If the Navigator is visible, it will show a dynamic preview of the white balance that would result from clicking in a particular spot. Click on an area of the image that you believe should be neutral gray and the white balance will be adjusted to neutralize that area. Other colors in the image will be adjusted accordingly. Press W again or press Esc to deactivate the tool.

Figure 4-27

4

Figure 4-28

White balance options on the Toolbar

With the Toolbar visible and the white balance eyedropper active, you can change the options for the eyedropper; see Figure 4–29.

Figure 4-29

Auto Dismiss: when checked, this will deactivate the WB eyedropper as soon as you click a spot in the photo.

Show Loupe: this checkbox determines whether or not a grid preview is shown to help you pick a location in the photo to use for WB.

Scale: when the Loupe is enabled, you can change the scale of the WB Grid.

Sometimes tone should be adjusted before white balance

When possible, adjust the white balance first. However, in some cases, the exposure may be so far off it may be difficult or impossible to properly evaluate white balance. A strong color cast in an image can affect the perception of both tone and contrast.

Tone adjustments

After white balance, the next Develop tasks to perform are *tone* adjustments.

"Tone" refers to the range of dark to light values in the image, without regard to color. An image containing tones from very bright whites to very dark blacks has a wide tonal range. Most "properly exposed" photographs can be expected to show this, but of course, some images will naturally have a narrow tonal range. More than any other aspect, tone sets the *mood* of the photograph.

Every capture contains a finite amount of data, with dark and light and levels in between, and though some contain a wider range of tones than others, once you get the file into Lightroom the goal is to optimize the captured tones to meet your vision of what the final photograph should be. Whether the finished photo ultimately reveals a wide range of tones or a narrow one (see Figure 4–30), always try to make the most of the available data. In the examples below, the photo on the left contains a wide range of tones, while the photo on the right contains a narrow range of tones.

Figure 4-30

An image with an overall light, bright appearance is referred to as a *high key* image whereas one with mostly dark tones and deep shadows is *low key*.

The tonal data captured is dependent on the accuracy of the exposure. Is the photograph underexposed or overexposed? Is it too dark, or too light, overall? Carefully evaluate the exposure of the photograph and determine how it relates to the optimal tonal structure..

Contrast refers to the relationships of dark tones to light tones. Does the image "pop" with depth and dimension? Or does it appear flat and dull? A *high contrast* image contains a strong variation of light to dark tones, whereas a *low contrast* image has tones compressed to a narrow range (see Figure 4–31 next page).

4

Figure 4-31: High contrast, low contrast

Evaluate the tones of elements in the photo relative to one another. Using the elements in the scene, decide what should be brighter, what should be darker, and how all the tones should fall in between. In most cases, you should finish evaluating tone and contrast before moving on to color.

This requires first determining where the black and white points should fall and, based on that, how the rest of the tonal data should be distributed throughout the image. This takes practice; evaluating the image and knowing where to place the tones for best effect is not a simple or automatic process. Fortunately, there are some long-held standards you can use to guide your decision-making:

Shadow (black point): in the RGB color model, solid black has the same numeric value in all three channels. Some images can benefit from having some pixels set at solid black. In Lightroom's Basic panel, the Blacks slider adjusts the black point, transitioning up toward the midtones.

Highlight (white point): highlights are the brightest spots in the photo. In some cases, the brightest pixels might be pure white; again, equal in all color channels. However, to show detail in highlights, they need to contain some pixels with values at some levels less than pure white. Lightroom's Exposure slider adjusts the white point, transitioning down toward the midtones.

Midtones: this refers to tones in the middle of the scale—halfway between solid black and pure white. (This is not the same as *middle* gray or *neutral* gray.) The Brightness slider adjusts midtones in Lightroom, transitioning down toward the black point and up toward the white point.

The actual numeric values of the pixels in these zones will vary depending on the color model used. This is why the terms *shadows, highlights* and *midtones* are used to generally describe the same places on the tone scale, regardless of color model or numeric values.

Again, keep in mind that tone is separate from color. All you should care about at this stage is how light or dark a particular part of the photo should be. Use your intuition and trust your eyes. Take as much time as necessary to get the tones right and the remainder of processing becomes easier.

HISTOGRAM

⌘+O or Ctrl+O
Open and close the Histogram panel

The Histogram (see Figure 4–32) is a bar graph showing the distribution of tonal values in the image. The black point is at the left side of the horizontal axis; the white point is at the right. Midtones are at the middle of the horizontal scale. The values displayed on the vertical axis represent the relative number of pixels at each tonal level.

There is no such thing as a "correct" Histogram. As every image is different, every Histogram will be unique. However, the shape of the

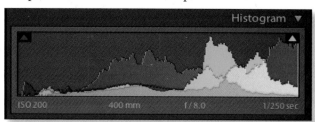

Figure 4-32

Histogram can help you make decisions about how to process the tones in an image. Usually, the width of the data shown in the Histogram is more important than the height; the Histogram for an image with a wide tonal range will show data distributed over the length of the horizontal axis, whereas a photo with limited dynamic range will show all the data clustered in one area of the graph.

The colors in the Histogram represent pixel values for each of the RGB channels and their complements: cyan, magenta and yellow. Gray represents areas of overlapping pixel values for all three channels.

As you move your cursor within the Histogram, tone ranges are illuminated that correspond with the Tone sliders in the Basic panel (which also become illuminated).

At the bottom of the Histogram is an information display. Its default state shows key settings of the capture. As you move your cursor over the photo the readout changes to show the values for each channel, in percentages. (In Lightroom's color model, pure white is 100% and pure black is 0%.)

The Histogram in Lightroom 3 is now "animated"; as you switch from one photo to another in Develop or Library, the Histogram dynamically updates as the photo is loaded. This helps evaluate minor differences in Histogram data between photos whose previews appear very similar.

4

Click and drag in the Histogram
To adjust the tones in the photo using the Lightroom-defined zones.

Clipping
Clipped highlights are pure white; clipped shadows are solid black. Both result in a loss of detail, so clipping should be identified and dealt with

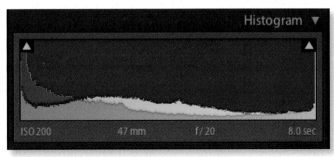

Figure 4-33

appropriately on each image. On the Histogram, clipping is shown by tall spikes at either end (see Figure 4–33).

J
Hide and show luminance clipping (Develop only)

The triangles at the top of each end of the Histogram activate *clipping indicators* overlaid on the image preview (see Figure 4–34). Place your cursor over a clipping indicator to temporarily see the clipping preview. Click an indicator to toggle it on and off. In the preview, blue indicates black point clipping; red shows white point clipping.

Figure 4-34

The red and blue displays are brightness (or *luminance*) clipping indicators. **They will appear even if clipping is only present in one channel.** To see clipping in individual channels, use the Option/Alt method, discussed later in this chapter.

You can use the Exposure, Blacks and/or Recovery sliders to reduce or eliminate clipping, as appropriate for each photo.

Keep checking for clipping and noise throughout processing
While processing your photos in Develop, periodically check for clipping and other artifacts, and as necessary, apply appropriate adjustments to remove them.

OPTIMIZING TONAL VALUES

Working with a raw capture, you may be very surprised at how much tonal data you can pull from what originally appears as an improperly exposed or low-contrast image. With just a few adjustments, you can maximize a photo's dynamic range and increase contrast with dramatic results.

Start by adjusting the black and white points (Blacks and Exposure, respectively) then focus on the midtones. Then fine tune smaller tone zones to your liking.

Lightroom provides controls on several panels to adjust the tones of a photo:

⌘+1 or
Ctrl+1
Open/close
the Basic
panel

Basic panel: Exposure, Blacks, Fill Light, Recovery, Brightness and Contrast sliders;

Tone Curve panel: adjust tones using sliders, direct manipulation of the curve and the targeted adjustment tool (see next section); and

HSL panel: allows you to adjust tones in the image based on color range.

Step 1. Set Exposure and Blacks (see Figure 4–35)
Use **Exposure** to adjust the white point and the range transitioning down toward the midtones. This will have a major effect on the overall brightness of your photo.

Then use **Blacks** adjustment to adjust the black point and shadows, which will add contrast to the photo. Typical Blacks values might fall between 5 and 10; for some images you may go higher or lower, and in some cases, zero.

Figure 4-35

Adjust the two back and forth, playing them against each other, to create the starting tone range for the image. Stretch out the tonal range to increase contrast and your photo will look better immediately. Periodically check the Histogram

4

and watch for clipping. I like to get as much contrast as I can using Exposure and Blacks before going on to the other adjustments.

Hold Option or Alt while dragging Exposure and Blacks sliders

While adjusting Exposure and Blacks, holding the Option or Alt key will display where clipping is present in individual channels (see Figure 4–36).

Figure 4-36

The most important step in successfully processing your photos

Spend a few minutes working both the Blacks and Exposure sliders before moving on. These two sliders make the biggest difference in the overall rendering of the image.

Step 2. Set midtones using Brightness

The **Brightness** slider (see Figure 4–37) adjusts a relatively wide range of tones in the image by manipulating the midpoint. Like Exposure, increasing or decreasing Brightness has a big impact on appearance of the overall image. However, it's important to keep in mind that the Brightness and Exposure are manipulating different sections of the tone range.

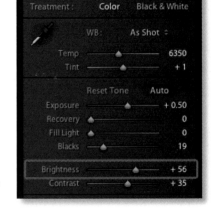

Figure 4-37

Whereas deciding on Exposure and Blacks can be relatively easy, correctly placing the midtones is somewhat trickier. For starters, black and white are absolute; the midtones span a range.

Fixing Over- and Under-Exposure

Go to the next adjustment in the active panel

Depending on the image, and whether it's over- or under-exposed, you should work the Blacks and Exposure, bit by bit, to gain the ideal tonal range. Don't expect to do everything with just one slider!

,
Go to the previous adjustment in the active panel

For overexposed images, try decreasing Exposure as the first step, then increase Blacks. Use Recovery to reduce white point clipping (see below).

For underexposed images, decrease Blacks (if possible) and increase Exposure. For some sliders, there is no negative value possible; for example, the lowest you can go on Blacks is 0.

-
Decrease the value of the active adjustment

Handling highlight and shadow detail

=
Increase the value of the active adjustment

Shift+= and Shift+=
Increase the adjustment amount

;
Reset the active slider

If your photo contains clipped highlights, you can often recover some tonal information using the **Recovery** adjustment on the Basic panel (see Figure 4–38). The Recovery slider instructs Lightroom to apply data values from channels that are not clipped into the channel(s) that is/are clipped. The exceptions are cases where all three channels are clipped to pure white, in which case Recovery won't help. The result of Recovery is most often a very

Figure 4-38

light, neutral gray replacing the pure white pixels, but at higher amounts, Recovery also affects a significant range of highlight values in addition to pure white (see below).

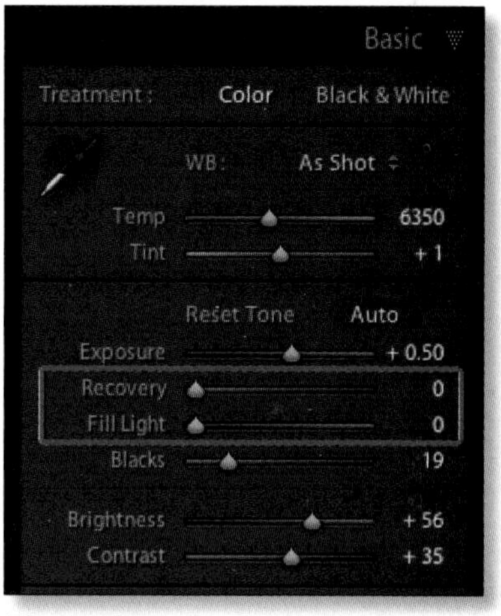

Fill Light brightens dark shadow areas but leaves the black point alone. Use Fill Light to "open up" shadows and reveal more detail. Higher values make the shadows lighter.

Don't overdo Recovery or Fill Light

Going too far with these controls is easy to do and causes a loss of overall contrast in the image. Except for extreme cases, or images you're stylizing for effect, you shouldn't usually use values over +20 on the Recovery or Fill Light sliders. Instead, try to use the Tone Curve to get more control over those tonal ranges (next section).

4

Fill Light and Highlight Recovery have been modified in the 2010 Process Version. You will probably need to adjust these sliders on which you upgrade the process version.

Step 3. Adjust Contrast

This simple slider on the Basic panel (see Figure 4–39) conceals a lot of power. Unlike the crude, old-school controls in programs like Photoshop, Lightroom's Contrast (and Brightness) adjustment has been programmed from scratch and can be used to great effect. The Lightroom default for Contrast is +25; my personal default starts with Contrast at +35 and I adjust up or down from there as appropriate for each photo.

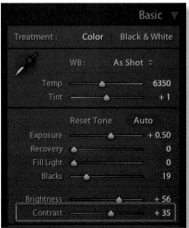

Figure 4-39

Step 4. Clarity

Also in the Basic panel, the Clarity slider adjusts contrast—but only in the midtones; see Figure 4–40. Increasing the Clarity value can enhance contrast and the appearance of sharpness, while negative amounts create a lower contrast, "softer" look. Some images benefit greatly by increasing the Clarity slider; others, not as much. Photos with strong edges and details containing relatively high contrast, such as buildings and architecture, are good candidates for increased Clarity amounts; see Figure 4–41 next page. Portraits may benefit from *negative* Clarity settings. Negative Clarity values create a softening effect that is beautiful for some images; see

Figure 4-40

Figure 4–42 next page. I particularly like to use negative Clarity on black and white photos.

Like Sharpening, setting Clarity too high can result in visible halos along edges, producing a cartoonish look; keep an eye out for this. I recommend that you try adding Clarity to your photos to determine the proper amounts and what kinds of images work best with this adjustment.

4

Figure 4-41: low Clarity, high Clarity

Figure 4-42: low Clarity, high Clarity

Keep working the Basic adjustments

Get as close as you can to your desired result with the controls on the Basic panel before moving on to settings in the other panels.

⌘+2 or Ctrl+2
Open/close the Tone Curve panel

TONE CURVE

After adjusting the settings on the Basic panel, you can further refine the photo's contrast by manipulating specific tone ranges with the Tone Curve panel (see Figure 4–43).

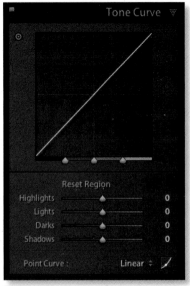

Figure 4-43

4

If you've used curves in Photoshop or other software, the Tone Curve panel will be familiar to you. The horizontal axis represents the original, unaltered values in the image, with the black point at the left and the white point at the right. The vertical axis represents the adjustments you make.

The background of the curve box shows a histogram and a highlighted area indicating (see Figure 4–44) the minimum and maximum range of curve adjustments based on the split controls in effect (see below).

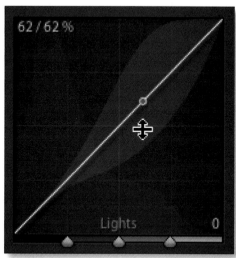

Figure 4-44

Lightroom 3 allows you to apply and save custom point curves; see below.

Parametric Curve

Lightroom's default Tone Curve is *parametric:* it adjusts sections of the tone scale, rather than from individual points. This provides smooth transitions between tone ranges and reduces the possibility of introducing undesirable hue shifts and posterization (banding).

Adjust the curve to increase or decrease contrast in specific areas of the tonal range. Positive values lighten tones and negative values darken them. The steeper the curve (or section of the curve), the higher the contrast. The flatter the curve, the lower the contrast. A typical example of this is the application of an "S" shaped curve, which increases contrast in the photo by lightening highlights and darkening shadows. Thus, the midtone section of the curve displays a steeper slope than before the adjustment. And viola—increased

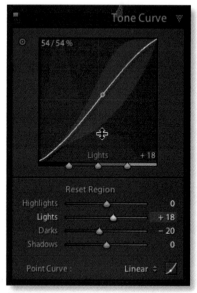

Figure 4-45

contrast; see Figure 4–45. I typically start with these custom default settings: Highlights: 0; Lights: +5; Darks: -5; Shadows: 0; and Point Curve: Linear.

4

Click on the Point Curve button to switch between the Point Curve and the Parametric Curve (see Figure 4–46).

You can adjust the Tone Curve in the following ways:

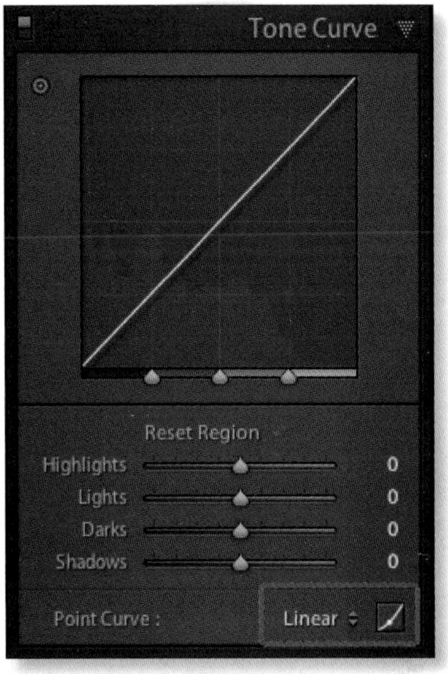

- **Select an option from the Point Curve menu:** Medium Contrast, Strong Contrast or Linear. (I always start with Linear.) Applying a point curve setting affects the same curve as parametric, but not the region slider values.

- **In the parametric curve, drag the sliders to adjust the four tone ranges independently:** Highlights, Lights, Darks, Shadows. The curve will be adjusted accordingly.

Figure 4-46

- **Click and drag on the curve itself:** up to lighten, down to darken. In the point curve, click to place points on the curve. Drag the points to change the tone values. In the Point Curve mode, the numeric values of point adjustments are shown at top left of the Tone Curve.

- **The Targeted Adjustment tool:** click the bull's-eye to activate it, then either click and drag up or down in the image, or use the up and down arrow keys. See the next section for more information about the Targeted Adjustment tool. There's more about the TAT coming up.

The *split point controls* on the bottom axis of the curve box define the range of adjustment for each of the four regions (see Figure 4–47). As you drag the split controls, the slider background adjusts to display the range of tones available for each region. Using the split controls you can achieve very precise control over the curve adjustment.

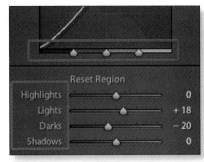

Figure 4-47

4

Double-click to reset sliders

If you change your mind after adjusting a slider, double click the name of the slider to reset it to its default value. To reset all the sliders in a section to their default values, either double-click the name of the section, or hold the Option or Alt key; the name of the panel section changes to Reset. Click to reset all the adjustments in that section.

More about point curves

Lightroom's point curve editor is similar to point curves in Photoshop and Adobe Camera Raw, with a couple of differences:

- No Input and Output text boxes (no numeric entry of point values)

- Percentages instead of 0-255 values

- Does not retain focus on a point after it's been edited (point does not stay "selected")

- Delete a point by right-click or double click

- Holding option/alt requires more mouse movement/finer control

- When saving presets, the point curve gets saved along with parametric values in the Tone Curve part of the preset, but not independently

- You can save point curve settings (as XMP files) in the Curves folder (which is shared with ACR curves).

Soft contrast

Some photos look best with a low range of contrast. Imagine a shot of a foggy morning at the lake. This kind of image naturally has a low range of contrast, and thus, probably shouldn't "pop". Always make your processing decisions based on the theme, subject and mood that you want to portray with the photo.

TARGETED ADJUSTMENT TOOL

The Tone Curve, HSL and B&W controls provide a *targeted adjustment* tool (or TAT) that you can use to edit the image interactively (see Figure 4–48). Click the

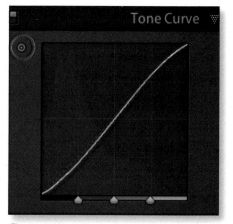

Figure 4-48

4

⌘+Option+Shift+T
or Ctrl+Alt+Shift+T
Activate the targeted
adjustment for the
Tone Curve

target to activate the tool. Position your cursor in an area of the image that you want to adjust. You can then use your mouse or the keyboard to modify the adjustment directly within the main preview. With the mouse, click and drag up or down to increase or decrease the adjustment, or use the up and down arrow keys (my preference).

When you're done, click the target again (or use the shortcut or press Esc) to deactivate the tool. Now in Lightroom 3, when you switch panels, any TAT that was in use on another panel becomes inactive.

Color adjustments

Do the colors in the photo look "correct"? Are the colors vivid and bright, or dull and lackluster? Would the image be stronger as black and white?

Evaluate global color first, and then consider adjustments to specific colors.

GLOBAL ADJUSTMENTS TO SATURATION AND VIBRANCE

Because these two adjustments are applied globally, it's very easy to overdo them with destructive effect on the appearance of the photo. (Set the Saturation and Vibrance sliders all the way to the right to see what I mean.) In this age of digital photography, in my opinion, there is a preponderance of over-saturated, garish images out there. Of course, sometimes this is the appropriate treatment for the photo, but more often, I believe, the photographer doesn't intend it. In critiquing images from my group classes and sessions with private students, over-saturation is the most common flaw I see in the processing. I recommend that as you're mastering Lightroom, and processing larger numbers of your own photos, you apply Saturation and Vibrance with a certain measure of restraint. Like all digital image processes, color saturation is a tool that must be wielded wisely.

Note: If you find that you're pushing Saturation or Vibrance over values of +20 or so, stop and think more about it. Unless you're looking for a certain effect, +20 is usually the maximum amount you should need. Choosing a different Camera Profile might be a better way to go.

Saturation

After setting white balance to adjust global color rendition, consider whether you want to increase or decrease saturation in the photo. Saturation refers to how vivid and pure a color is, as opposed to neutral gray; see Figure 4–49 next page). A photo that appears very bright and colorful could be called "highly saturated". Some images benefit from increasing the saturation; others may look better with decreased saturation.

4

Figure 4-49: high saturation, low saturation

In the Basic panel, drag the Saturation slider to the left for less saturation, and to the right for more, to see its effect on the photo. Stop where you like. See Figure 4–50.

Vibrance

The Vibrance control in Lightroom works similarly to Saturation, in that it makes colors more or less vivid, with a couple of important differences.

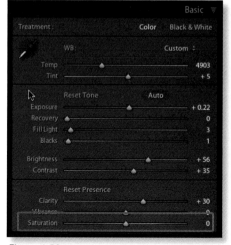

Figure 4-50

First, Vibrance will not affect colors that are already highly saturated. This non-linear behavior helps avoid that over-saturated, neon effect when Saturation is pushed too far. Second, the Vibrance control is designed to not affect skin tones—peachy, orangey or tan shades will not receive the increased saturation. For example, if you're processing a photo of a group of people outside in a park on a sunny day, increasing Vibrance will help push more color into the blue sky and green grass, without turning the people's faces pumpkin orange. Try Vibrance on a range of photos and you'll quickly get to know its personality.

Vibrance and Saturation are disabled for photos using black and white treatment.

4

SELECTIVE COLOR ADJUSTMENTS

In addition to the global Saturation and Vibrance settings, you can adjust colors in the image based on their named *hue* (orange, purple, aqua, etc.). These colors may seem arbitrary, but quite the opposite is true: Lightroom's color ranges are loosely based on the color wheel (as defined more practically by Mark Hamburg at Adobe) and divided into distinct hues that blend together in between. The defined colors are Red, Orange, Yellow, Green, Aqua, Blue, Purple and Magenta.

You may be surprised to find that all the colors in your photos fall primarily into one of these hues, sometimes with slight overlaps into neighboring colors. Lightroom provides controls for adjusting both specific color hues and blended combinations.

⌘+3 or Ctrl+3
Open/close the
HSL panel

With the HSL panel (see Figure 4–51) you can adjust the following components of individual color zones in the image.

- **Hue:** the named color. Adjust the sliders to "rotate" the hue around the color wheel by moving the slider toward either end.

Figure 4-51

- **Saturation:** the purity of the color as opposed to neutral gray. Adjust the sliders to increase or decrease saturation.

- **Luminance:** the brightness of the color. Adjust the sliders to lighten or darken.

The HSL panel is itself comprised of three distinct sets of controls; click the names in the panel header to access the various types of adjustments:

- **HSL:** this is the default set of controls in the panel for working on a color photo. The three color components are separated into groups; click each adjustment name to access the sliders for that set of controls (see Figure 4–52 next page). Click All to show all the controls on one (very long) panel.

- **Color:** these controls do the same things as the standard HSL sliders; they're just arranged differently. Adjusting the sliders in the Color mode also adjusts them in the HSL view, and vice versa. Click a color swatch to show

4

all three component sliders for that color (see Figure 4–53). Again, click the All button to see all the controls at once.

- **B&W:** when working on a black and white image you can adjust the brightness of the original color components of the photo here, resulting in different grayscale conversions (see Figure 4–54).

Figure 4-52

Figure 4-54

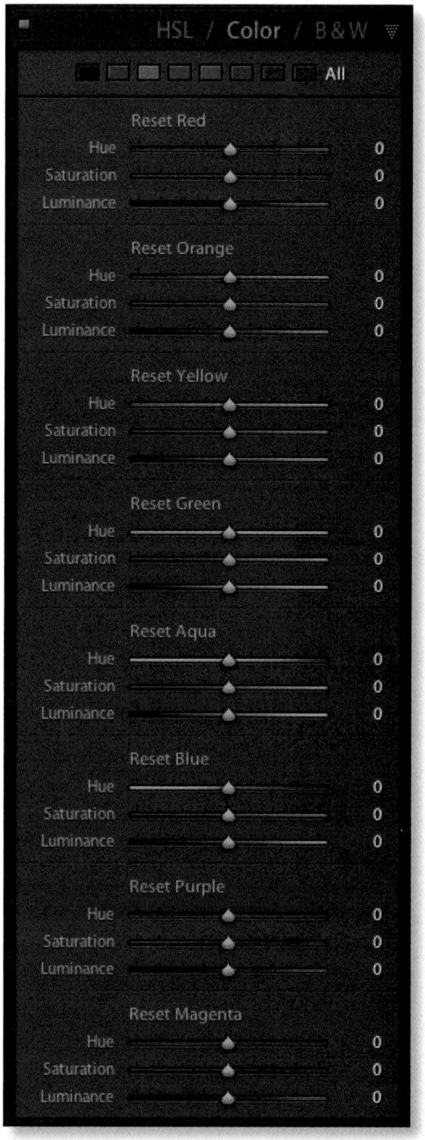

Figure 4-53

⌘+Option+Shift+H or
Ctrl+Alt+Shift+H
Activate the targeted
adjustment for Hue

⌘+Option+Shift+S or
Ctrl+Alt+Shift+S
Activate the targeted
adjustment for
Saturation

⌘+Option+Shift+L or
Ctrl+Alt+Shift+L
Activate the targeted
adjustment for
Luminance

⌘+Option+Shift+G or
Ctrl+Alt+Shift+G
Activate the targeted
adjustment for Black and
White Mix

⌘+Option+Shift+N or
Ctrl+Alt+Shift+N
To deactivate all targeted
adjustment tools.

Use targeted adjustments in HSL

You can quickly and easily adjust colors in the photo (including darkening and lightening them) with the target adjustment tool, available in each of the HSL panel sections. This is much easier than adjusting sliders directly. More importantly, when you use the targeted adjustment tool in HSL; several sliders are often adjusted at once. This provides much more accurate adjustments and allows you to fine-tune colors by directly manipulating them in the preview; see Figure 4–55.

Simulating a polarizing filter

One very useful application of the Luminance adjustment is darkening blue skies.

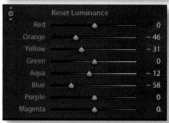

Figure 4-55

Watch for noise

When adjusting colors in the HSL panel, keep an eye out for the introduction of noise as a result. This especially applies when lowering Luminance, such as when darkening skies.

Hiding and showing panel adjustments

Most of the panels in the

HSL / Color / B & W

Figure 4-56

Develop module include a small button (like a switch; see Figure 4–56) to temporarily hide and show the effects of that panel's adjustments. Like a light switch, up is "on" and down is "off". Rather than Before and After or Undo/Redo, you can use this to show all the effects of *a single panel*. This is especially useful with the HSL panel. Turning on and off a panel's adjustments is tracked in history, is undoable, and can be saved as part of a preset.

4

The Detail panel

Lightroom 3 offers major improvements in noise reduction and sharpening for all types of files. The Detail panel contains Lightroom's controls for these adjustments (see Figure 4–57).

⌘+5 or
Ctrl+5
Open/close
the Detail
panel

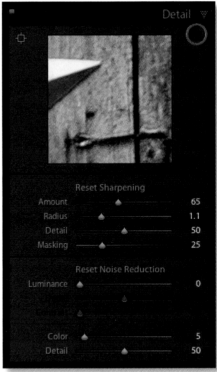

Detail previews

New in Lightroom 3, the effects of the Detail panel are visible at all zoom ratios in the main preview.

The Detail panel also includes a small preview where you can see the effects of adjustments independently from the Develop loupe preview (see Figure 4–57). If it's not showing, click the black triangle button to expand the preview section of the panel. To choose the area of the photo to use for the preview, click the target button at the

Figure 4-57

upper left of the panel, then click in the photo. The Detail preview window will then show the area clicked. You can also click and drag to pan in the preview box, or single-click to zoom in and out, just like in the main image preview area.

Zoom in and out when processing for small details

To effectively apply many of Develop's adjustments requires you to get in closer to really see what's happening, sometimes at the very high zoom ratios. Use the zoom functions to look closely at key areas of the photo.

NOISE REDUCTION

Digital *noise* (see Figure 4–58) is a common artifact that appears as small dark speckles and/or soft colored blobs in the image. Noise is typically introduced at high ISO settings, during long exposures and exposures made in low light and in captures that are underexposed. In these, noise is most common in the blue channel of an RGB image.) Lightroom 3 provides dramatically improved controls for noise removal.

Figure 4-58

A little noise here and there will not always present a problem; the main issue is whether or not the noise will be visible when the image is printed. Zoom into the image to check for noise.

Because other adjustments can affect the appearance of noise, you should check for it at several points during processing. To reduce or remove noise from photos in Lightroom, use the Noise Reduction controls on the Detail panel; see Figure 4–59.

⌘+S or Ctrl+S
As you're Developing photos, remember to frequently save out your metadata!

In most cases, noise reduction is best done before sharpening, as any noise present in the image will be increased when sharpening is applied.

To use the new noise reduction controls described below, you must be using the 2010 Process Version.

Figure 4-59

Luminance: reduces the appearance of gray/black speckles in the image. Be conservative applying Luminance noise reduction; fine detail can suffer. Applying a value other than 0 enables the Detail and Contrast sliders. Detail helps preserve areas of fine detail in the image, while Contrast increases edge definition in those areas.

Color: reduces the appearance of color noise, which shows itself as multicolored, soft blobs in the image, especially in shadows and solid-color midtones. Color noise reduction also provides a Detail slider.

There are no magic formulas for noise reduction here; work with the sliders at various zoom levels to get the look you want.

SHARPENING

Is the image in focus? If not, you might well choose to work with another capture. With very few exceptions, a photo captured out of focus can't be fixed with sharpening in post-processing. Conversely, the appearance of sharpness in a capture that was made in perfect focus can be enhanced dramatically.

4

Every digital image can benefit from some kind of sharpening. The ideal sharpening for any image is completely dependent on the resolution of the file and the medium in which it is viewed.

The appearance of sharpness in a photo is determined by edge contrast—the amount of contrast between the pixels defining edges and details in the photo.

The sharpening workflow

In today's digital image processing, it's better to sharpen an image in several steps rather than all at once. The late Bruce Fraser is credited with greatly advancing the art of digital image sharpening in recent years, and many of the principles he developed have been implemented in Lightroom's sharpening routines. The modern sharpening workflow is comprised of the following stages:

Capture sharpening: When the continuous-tone real world is mapped onto a grid of pixels in a digital image, some softening is introduced. The first pass of "gentle" sharpening is intended simply to overcome the loss of sharpness resulting from digital capture. **The sharpening controls on Lightroom's Detail panel are designed for capture sharpening only.**

Creative sharpening: Intermediate rounds of sharpening can be applied, as needed, to enhance all or part of an image, based on its characteristics. For example, areas of *high-frequency* information—those with lots of small, fine detail—require different sharpening treatments than do *low-frequency* areas with relatively little detail. Creative sharpening is also dependent on subjective considerations, such as the desire to emphasize or de-emphasize parts of the photo. Creative sharpening can be applied using Lightroom's local adjustment brushes (see next section).

Output sharpening: the final application of sharpening is dependent on the size and resolution of the file and the medium for which it is intended. For example, a low resolution image destined for display on a Web site requires different sharpening than does a high resolution file that's going to be printed. Lightroom's output sharpening is applied either when exporting (see Chapter 5) or printing (see Chapter 6).

Apply capture sharpening in the Detail panel

Use the sharpening controls on the Detail panel (see Figure 4–60, next page) to apply Lightroom's capture sharpening to your photos.

As you're adjusting the sliders, **Hold Option or Alt** while dragging the sliders to see the separate sharpening adjustments displayed as a grayscale preview the main Loupe preview and Detail panel (see Figure 4–61, next page).

Amount: the strength of sharpening to be applied. The default is 25; my typical range: 45-65.

Radius: the width of the edges on which to apply sharpening. Decimals are provided due to the feathered "falloff" of the sharpening. For images with fine, detailed edges, use lower amounts. Recommended range: .8 up to 1.2. As a general rule, to avoid visible halos from sharpening with higher Amounts, use lower radii. The default is 1.0.

Detail: set this based on the amount of fine detail in the image. Use higher Detail values for images containing lots of high-frequency detail. I find that nearly all images benefit from some amount of the Detail adjustment. Recommended range: 25-70.

Masking: keeps the sharpening from being applied to smooth, solid areas of the photo, such as skin and sky. With Masking at 0, sharpening will be applied to the entire image uniformly. At higher values, sharpening will only be applied to defined edges. The ideal masking varies by image. To determine this, preview an area of interest at 1:1 or greater and hold the Option or Alt key as you adjust the slider. This previews the areas where masking will be applied. On the mask, the areas in black will not be sharpened, and the white areas will, with gray levels in between, producing sharpening of varying amounts. See Figure 4–62, next page for an example.

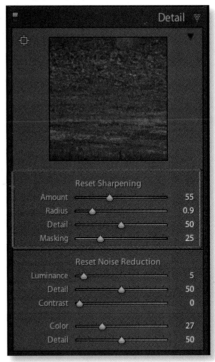

Figure 4-60

Figure 4-61

4

In the example at right, masking is being applied to keep the sharpening from being applied to the sky (see inset). These areas of smooth tones do not require sharpening; doing so may well introduce lots of noise. Masking provides the ability to restrict the sharpening to only the edges in the image that meet the minimum contrast level defined by the Masking slider.

Zoom in to various levels to check for sharpness in key areas and consider whether some parts of the image need more sharpening than others.

The suggested values are based on raw capture; if you shoot JPG then some sharpening is already applied in the camera, and the optimal settings would be different.

Figure 4-62

If you do as much of your work as possible in Lightroom, you may find that you never need to go into Photoshop, especially for sharpening. Though there may be special cases and images that benefit from the pixel-level editing that Photoshop provides, Lightroom's sharpening options, when properly used, may be all you need.

When to turn off Lightroom's sharpening altogether
If you're planning to do all of your sharpening in other software, set the Amount to 0 to turn off sharpening in Lightroom. (And if you're Exporting files for that purpose, make sure you don't apply any sharpening there, either; see Chapter 5.)

4

"Fake focus"

In some cases you can make the subject of a slightly soft photo appear sharper by slightly *blurring* other areas.

Smoothing

If there are areas of the image that show noise or include more sharp detail than is desired, you can smooth these areas using negative Clarity. For example, smoothing is effective for reducing the appearance of wrinkles in human skin. See the section on adjustment brushes for more about this.

⌘+6 or Ctrl+6
Open/close the
Lens Corrections
panel

Lens Corrections

In my opinion, this is one of the greatest new additions to Lightroom's toolset. The Lens Corrections panel (see Figure 4–63) allows you to correct for lens distortion, chromatic aberration and vignetting. The Lens Corrections panel provides two modes of operation: Profile and Manual.

PROFILE MODE

In Profile mode, Lightroom first reads the photo's EXIF metadata to identify what lens was used to make the picture. It then loads a corresponding *lens profile*, if one is available, and

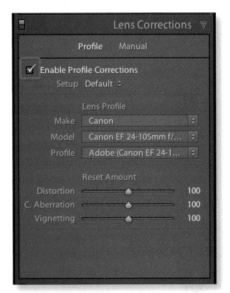

Figure 4-63

uses the profile to make automatic adjustments. Lightroom 3 ships with profiles for many popular lenses; if Lightroom can't find a profile for the lens that was used, a warning message is displayed at the bottom of the panel.

You can make your own lens profiles; information is at the Adobe Labs site http://labs.adobe.com.

Tick the checkbox for Enable Profile Corrections; the rest of the controls become active; see Figure 4–63. Lightroom loads the default setup based on the profile. In the Setup menu you can save a new Default or restore the Default to its original settings. This is useful in cases where you have multiple profiles for a lens and want to use a specific one. The Default applies to each camera and lens combination and also will include the values of the settings below.

4

At the bottom of the panel are sliders for Distortion, Chromatic Aberration and Vignetting, which allow you to further customize the adjustments beyond what's specified in the lens profile. The default values are all 100 and can be adjusted up or down. Setting a slider at 0 turns off that adjustment entirely. However, using these adjustments in Profile mode usually produces much less dramatic results than when in Manual mode, discussed in the next section.

MANUAL MODE

Manual mode offers much more control over Lens Corrections. Click the Manual text button at the top of the panel to switch modes; see Figure 4–64.

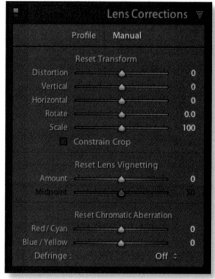

Figure 4-64

Transform

This section of the panel provides sliders to adjust for Distortion (pincushioning and barreling), Vertical and Horizontal warping, Rotation and Scale. (See examples at the end of this section.)

Checking the **Constrain Crop** box forces the crop rectangle inside the edges of any transformations applied.

Lens Vignetting

Vignetting is darkening (or lightening) around the corners of an image. A dark vignette can be caused by the camera lens, especially wide angle lenses, particularly with a filter attached. Depending on the photo and your preferences, vignettes can either be pleasing or altogether undesirable; vignetting has typically been considered an unwanted photographic artifact. These days, it's en vogue. Lightroom provides adjustments for removing or adding lens vignetting, applied to the full frame and/or the crop.

The adjustments in the Lens Vignetting section are designed to reduce or remove the effect of vignetting caused by the lens (or add it). It's applied at the corners of the full-frame image, regardless of crop. (Lightroom 3 also offers *Post-Crop Vignetting*, on the Effects panel, discussed later in this chapter.)

The Amount slider controls the strength of the adjustment; you can apply positive amounts to lighten the corners of the image or negative amounts to darken. The Midpoint slider determines how far from the corners the adjustment is applied; see Figure 4–65.

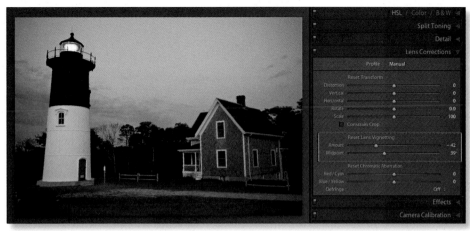

Figure 4-65

Chromatic Aberration

Chromatic aberration (CA) is caused by the camera lens (see Figure 4–66). Under certain lighting conditions, when the light comes through the lens, the light rays are scattered at the point where they hit the sensor, causing colored edges to appear in the image. CA is easiest to find near the corners of the image, along edges of high contrast.

Use the Chromatic Aberration adjustments in the Lens Corrections panel to remove CA. Zoom in very close (even up to 11:1 can be helpful). Drag the sliders to realign the color channels until the edges line up. Lightroom intelligently shrinks or enlarges the color channels accordingly. You may often need to adjust both sets of sliders.

Figure 4-66

Option or Alt while dragging the CA sliders

Temporarily press the Option or Alt key to hide the other colors not affected by the current CA slider adjustment.

Defringe

Fringing (also called *blooming*) is different from chromatic aberration; it's an artifact that occurs on the sensor itself. Fringing happens when a high amount of energy hits a photosite and some of its charge spills over onto adjacent

photosites. Fringing usually shows as purple outlines around very hot specular highlights, such as sunlight glinting on specular surfaces like water, chrome, etc.; see Figure 4–67.

Use the options on the Defringe popup menu (see Figure 4–68) to remove fringing. Choose from All Edges or Highlight Edges and see which produces better results. You may need to look closely at different areas of the image to be sure. Defringe can have a destructive effect on the appearance of the photo; if it doesn't produce an improvement, always leave it off.

Figure 4-67

Figure 4-68

Examples of Lens Corrections panel

Figure 4-69 on the facing page shows before and after Developing this raw capture with the Lens Correction tools along with Basic adjustments. Below are the settings used in Lens Correction.

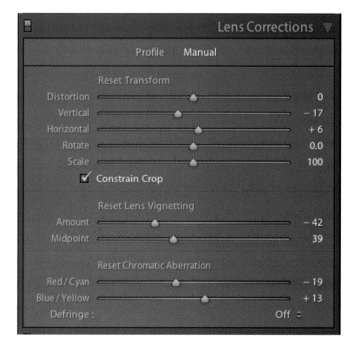

Figure 4-69

4

Local adjustments

Selectively lightening or darkening localized areas in the photo has traditionally been referred to as *dodging* (lightening) and *burning* (darkening). Most photos can benefit from some amount of dodging and/or burning; Figure 4–70 shows a subtle example.

Figure 4-70

Evaluate whether or not the photo could be enhanced with Lightroom's localized adjustments. For example, are there light or dark areas that distract from the subject? Could the appearance of depth and dimension be enhanced? Dodging and burning can help in these situations.

Some very general, suggested uses for dodging and burning include:

- Direct eye movement within the frame

- Remove distractions

- Enhance depth and dimension

- Increase contrast and "pop"

Lightroom offers local adjustment tools that can be used for dodging and burning:

- **Graduated filters:** linear gradients that can be applied anywhere in the image

- **Adjustment brushes:** "painted-on" adjustments

Using Lightroom's local adjustments, you can make skin appear smoother, hair glossier, skies bluer. In many cases, you will find you no longer need to use Photoshop for these tasks.

GRADUATED FILTER

M

Activate/
deactivate
the graduated
filter tool

On a camera lens, a split neutral density (ND) filter (or *graduated* ND) reduces the amount of light entering part of the lens in order to balance the exposure between bright highlights and dark shadows. The most common use for a split ND is to balance a bright sky and a darker foreground within a single exposure.

Invert the
direction of
the gradient

Similarly, Lightroom's *graduated filter* tool simulates the effect of a split ND filter and allows you to apply various adjustments in a smooth, gradual transition. It's accessed from the tool strip; see Figure 4–71.

Figure 4-71

The graduated filter creates *linear gradients* that are applied in a straight line between two points: start and end. (Unlike Photoshop, you can't add additional control points between the start and end of the gradient.) The graduated filter smoothly transitions from full effect to no effect. Put another way, the strength

4

of the adjustment at the start of the gradient is 100%, and at the end is 0%. The transition is always soft; you can't adjust the "hardness" of the gradient.

From each end of the gradient, the strength level of the adjustment continues to all edges of the photo in both directions; see Figure 4–72. You can't restrict the effect of the gradient to a specific area (use a local adjustment brush for that; see the next section).

Figure 4-72

Apply a graduated filter

**Return
or Enter**
When you're
done applying
the gradient

1. Click the graduated filter tool to activate it (or use the shortcut).

2. Place your cursor at the spot where you want the gradient to start.

3. Click and drag to the point where you want the gradient to end.

   To constrain the gradient to 90 degrees, hold the shift key while dragging.

   To create the gradient from its center, hold Option or Alt while dragging. (You can also use this along with Shift.)

4. Set the desired adjustments to be applied by the graduated filter.

Modify an existing graduated filter

You can change an existing graduated filter in the following ways:

- Click and drag the start or end points to reposition them (see Figure 4–73);

Figure 4-73

- Click and drag the center node point to move the entire graduated filter (see Figure 4–74);

Figure 4-74

- Click and drag the line extending from the node to rotate the graduated filter (see Figure 4–75)

Figure 4-75

- Change the adjustments being applied by the active graduated filter (see Figure 4–76).

Return or Enter
When you're done changing the gradient

Figure 4-76

You can't erase from graduated filters

However, to isolate areas of a graduated filter, you can use an adjustment brush to apply opposite adjustments (see next section).

4

Deleting a graduated filter

If you want to completely remove a graduated filter, select its node pin and press Delete.

GRADUATED FILTER AND ADJUSTMENT BRUSH CONTROLS

The graduated filter and local adjustment brush tools (see Figure 4–77) **use the same kinds of adjustments.** This is basically a subset of the main controls found on other Develop panels; see those sections earlier in this chapter for more about how the adjustments work.

Figure 4-77

Note the darkened background around the sliders. This indicates no graduated filter or brush is active. If you change settings with no instance of a tool active, these remain as the defaults until you change them again. Each new instance you apply with either tool will use these settings as the starting point. Otherwise, you can adjust settings while a tool is active, in which case the changes to settings apply only to that instance of the tool, and the background becomes lighter, as in Figure 4-76.

For graduated filters and local adjustment brushes, the adjustments all default at 0 so they can be adjusted up or down. You can use any combination of adjustments on each application of a graduated filter or adjustment brush.

To reset any slider double-click its name.

Exposure: dodge or burn parts of the image, with an emphasis on lighter tones

Brightness: dodge or burn parts of the image, with an emphasis on midtones

Contrast: increase or decrease contrast in local areas of the image

Saturation: increase or decrease saturation in local areas of the image

Clarity: increase or reduce clarity in local areas of the image

Sharpness: increase or reduce sharpness in local areas of the image

Color: apply a color tint; see below.

The color picker

You can apply a subtle color to the graduated filter or adjustment brush. (The color picker is also used in the output modules.)

For dodging and burning, a little color helps blend the adjustments into the image and makes them appear more natural and realistic. (In Lightroom, it's not possible to paint with a fully opaque, solid color.)

By default, when you apply any of the local adjustments, the color swatch is neutral gray with an X through it; see Figure 4–78.

Figure 4-78

To apply a color tint to the adjustment, click the color swatch to open the color picker; see Figure 4–79.

Figure 4-79

Then select a color from the palette, or click and hold your cursor while dragging outside the box to sample a color from the photo, or anywhere on your screen (see Figure 4–80).

Figure 4-80

In some instances of the color picker, such as the output modules, the color picker layout is a bit different. If the color currently selected is a shade of gray, white or black, and you want to pick a color, you first need to click somewhere in the vertical saturation slider (called the "elevator") at the right side of the color picker (see Figure 4–81). Then you'll see a full-color spectrum. Click inside the spectrum to choose the hue range you want, then use the saturation elevator to increase or decrease saturation.

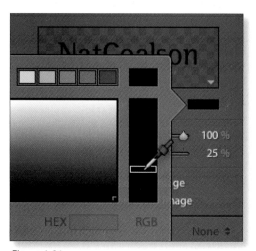

Figure 4-81

To change from color to grayscale, drag the elevator all the way down to the bottom. Then you can choose a brightness from within the gray spectrum.

4

While you're picking colors, notice the small color swatch at the top right of the color picker; see Figure 4–82. It constantly updates to show you the currently selected color. Next to it is the previous color; you can click it to reset the color picker to the previous color.

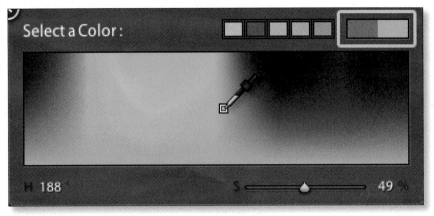

Figure 4-82

To the left of the current and previous color swatches are five additional swatches where you can store colors for later use. These five swatches are shared between all the modules. Click on a swatch to load it as the current color.

First, set the color that you want to save as a swatch. Then simply click and hold on a swatch to set it to the current color.

Setting swatches cannot be undone, so be careful about overwriting swatches you've previously saved, especially if you set those swatches using another module.

Also, note that it is possible to switch between modules and panels, using keyboard shortcuts, while leaving the color picker open.

Along the bottom of the color picker are readouts of numeric values for the current color. The default readout is HSL (Hue, Saturation and Lightness) and RGB (Red, Green and Blue). If you have the numeric values for a color you're trying to precisely match, you can double click to manually enter the numbers, or drag the scrubby sliders right and left to change the values.

In the output module pickers, you can also view and select colors using Hexadecimal ("Hex") color values. Hex colors are commonly used for Web graphics, because their values can be specified to conform to operating system color palettes. Many Web designers specify colors as Hex values and there are lots of online resources for color pickers in Hex and other color modes. (Adobe's very useful Kuler application, for example.)

To switch between Hex and RGB values click each respective text button in the palette (see Figure 4–83).

When you're done making changes in the color picker, click the X in the

Figure 4-83

upper left corner of the picker or simply press Return/Enter.

If you want to cancel any changes you just made in the color picker (except for changing swatches) press Esc.

Sample a color from anywhere on the screen

From within the color palette, click down with your mouse button, and while holding down, drag the eyedropper anywhere on your screen to sample a color. This is very useful for precisely matching colors from any other items visible on your monitor, such as an existing Web site, logo art, etc.

H
Toggle hide/
show node
pins or overlay

**⌘+Shift+H or
Control+Shift+H**
Toggle always
show/hide node
pins

Shift+H
Toggle show/
never show
the overlay for
selected tool

TOOL OVERLAYS

All the tools in the strip—Crop, Spot Removal, Red-Eye, Graduated Filter and Adjustment Brushes—provide a *tool overlay* when activated. The tool overlays provide controls for manipulating each instance of the tool application or deleting it. The overlays can also be hidden or shown while the tool is active.

Graduated filters and brushes provide a *node pin,* used for selecting each individual instance of the tool within the overlay. For brushes, you can click

4

Figure 4-84

and drag your cursor over the node pin to increase or decrease the intensity of the effect being applied; see Figure 4–84.

The Toolbar provides a menu for controlling how node pins are displayed, and in the case of adjustment brushes, the visibility of the mask overlay; see Figure 4–85.

Figure 4-85

K
Toggle the
adjustment
brush on/off

ADJUSTMENT BRUSHES

Using Lightroom's local adjustment brushes, you can perform precise dodging and burning, localized sharpening, color tinting and much more. The brushes allow you to "paint" adjustments with varying opacity, feathering and edge control. On a single photo, you can add as many instances of the brush as you like.

Activate the local adjustment brush tool by clicking it in the tool strip (see Figure 4–86), or use the shortcut. When the brush is active its controls are displayed in the tool drawer: the same adjustments as the graduated filter (see previous section) plus brush controls below.

Figure 4-86

With the brush active, the first thing you will likely want to do is change its size. Click the black triangle button (see Figure 4–87 next page) to adjust its settings at the bottom of the drawer. As with other settings, you can drag the sliders, enter numeric values or use shortcuts to change the brush settings.

[
Decrease brush size

]
Increase brush size

Shift+[
Decrease feather

Shift+]
Increase feather

Number Keys
Set flow amount. This is just like in Photoshop; 1 is 10%, 4 is 40%, etc. Press two numbers quickly for more precise amounts. For example, pressing 7 then 5 consecutively sets the flow to 75%.

A
Toggle Auto Mask on/off

/
Switch between A and B brushes

Size: the size of the current brush.

Feather: soft or hard edge for the brush. With Feather at 0, you see just a single circle for the brush. Higher amounts of Feather show two circles on the brush, indicating the range of the feathering. Similar to the start/end on the Graduated Filter, the inner brush circle is 100% (full effect) and the outer edge is 0% (no effect).

Flow: how fast the "paint" is applied while painting. Higher values apply the effect faster. You can "build up" an application of the adjustment brush by using a lesser Flow and gradually painting over the area again and again.

Figure 4-87

Density: opacity/transparency of the brush stroke. Density limits how strongly the adjustment settings are applied **for this instance** of the brush.

Auto Mask: when this box is checked, Lightroom will try to conform the edge of the painted mask to edges in the image. This can be useful if you need the adjustment to be applied within a specific area, such as whitening teeth in a smile.

Usually leave Auto Mask off

For general dodging and burning, you should usually leave Auto Mask off. For one thing, dodge and burn effects typically look more natural if they are soft and feathered, rather than hard-edged. Also, leaving Auto Mask on, especially when painting over large areas, can significantly degrade performance.

A and B brush settings

You can store two brush sets, each with different settings. Each brush set retains the most recently used settings until you change them. I usually use A for the soft, feathered brush and B for a harder edged brush. You could also use one for a large brush and the other for a small brush, etc.

Mouse wheel

If you have a mouse with a wheel, you can use it to change brush size.

4

Applying the local adjustment brushes

Click and drag your cursor to paint over areas of the image you want to adjust. Using a tablet and stylus is even better.

As you paint, a *mask* is applied to the image that constrains the adjustment to the painted area. A node pin is placed at the point of the mask where you started painting. When you're done, press Enter or Return to apply that brush, which also makes a new adjustment brush mask.

As with graduated filters, you can set the adjustments that are applied with the brush masks both before and after you create them.

Using a single mask, the adjustment can be applied in multiple spots, anywhere in the photo. You can also create additional masks and modify or delete existing masks. Each mask can have its own settings. Apply separate masks in different areas of the photo to apply unique adjustments in those areas.

A single mask can also have multiple brush applications using different brush settings, so some areas could be stronger than others, though I don't recommend this. I think it's better to use single applications of the brush for very specific settings. This gives you a lot more control.

Place your cursor over a node pin to temporarily show the mask overlay. To select a brush mask, click its node pin. A solid black center indicates a brush mask node is active; only one can be active at any given time (though none may be).

To change the values of the adjustments, click and drag left/right over the node pin. All adjustments for that mask will be increased or decreased simultaneously, relative to their starting values.

Hold Shift while painting

This will constrain the brush stroke to a straight line.

With the brushes active, press Return or Enter

… to make a new brush instance.

Be economical with the number of brush masks

… but use as many as necessary for the work you need to do. Just as with global adjustments, you should be economical with your application of localized adjustments. For example, if you want to dodge multiple areas of the photo using the same adjustment, use just one mask for all the areas, rather than separate masks for each of them. At minimum, though, you will need separate brush applications for dodging and burning.

O
Show/hide the
adjustment brush
mask overlay

Shift+O
Cycle through
mask overlay
colors

Option or Alt
(while painting)
Temporarily
switch to Erase
mode

Erasing from adjustment brush masks

You can refine brush masks by erasing from them. Like the A and B brushes, the eraser has its own settings.

To erase from a mask, first click its node point to activate it (see Figure 4–88). Show the overlay, if you like–this can make erasing lots easier. Make sure the eraser is active and set the eraser brush settings as necessary (size, feather, etc.).

Paint to erase from the selected mask (see Figure 4–89).

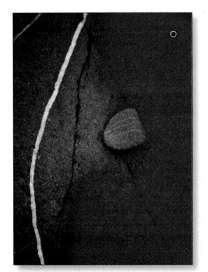

Figure 4-88

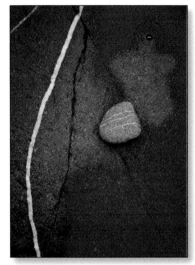

Figure 4-89

Hiding and showing local adjustments

Use the switch at the bottom left of the panel (see Figure 4–90) to temporarily hide or show all of the graduated filters or local adjustment brushes.

Figure 4-90

4

Deleting an adjustment brush

To completely remove a brush adjustment, select its node pin and press Delete.

RESETTING LOCAL ADJUSTMENTS

Click the Reset button near the bottom right of the panel (see Figure 4–91) to remove all graduated filters or brushes at once; there are separate Reset buttons for graduated filters and brushes.

Figure 4-91

LOCAL ADJUSTMENT PRESETS

You can save presets for graduated filters and local adjustment brushes. The presets simply contain values for the sliders and the list on the popup menu is shared by both tools. With the desired settings applied, click the Effect: menu (see Figure 4–92) and select Save Settings as New Preset.

Figure 4-92

Sharpening or smoothing with adjustment brushes

You can use graduated filters or adjustment brushes to sharpen or smooth local areas of the photo. To sharpen, increase the amount of the Sharpness slider. To smooth, use negative amounts of Clarity. These techniques are very handy for portrait retouching.

The Effects panel

Also new in Lightroom 3 is the Effects panel; see Figure 4–93. Post-Crop Vignette has been moved here, and there's now a Grain adjustment to simulate the look of film.

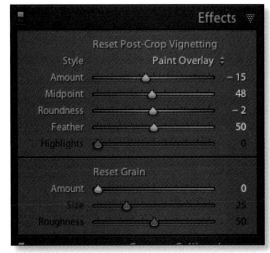

Figure 4-93

Post-Crop Vignette

These adjustments use a slightly different algorithm than the Lens Vignette and thus produce an effect that looks a bit different. In Lightroom 3 the behavior of Post-crop Vignette has been modified. As its name implies, the Post-crop Vignette is applied to the inside of the crop, not the outer edges of the full image.

There are now three types of vignettes, accessed from the Style popup menu; see Figure 4–94:

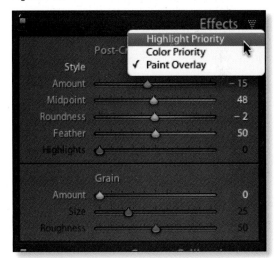

Figure 4-94

Highlight Priority: this is the default style and is most similar to the processing in the regular Lens Vignette adjustments.

Color Priority: similar to Highlight Priority but also attempts to avoid shifts in hue.

4

Paint Overlay: this is most similar to the Post-crop Vignette from Lightroom 2, whereby the adjustment applies black or white overlays to achieve the effect.

Along with Amount and Midpoint, controls are provided for Roundness and Feather; see Figure 4–95. Roundness makes the vignette more circular or square; Feather makes the vignette edges softer or harder. These controls are only available if the Amount is not 0.

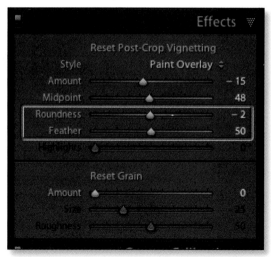

Figure 4-95

For Highlight and Color Priority, if the amount is set to a negative value (to add vignetting) the Highlights slider becomes active, which applies a different level of processing for lighter areas of the photo.

Grain

To apply a simulated film grain effect to the photo, first set an amount other than 0. You can then adjust the Size and Roughness of the grain; see Figure 4–96. (Zoom in close in the main preview to accurately see the effect.)

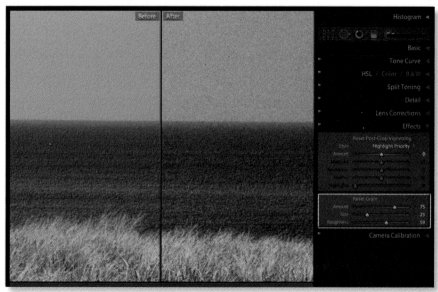

Figure 4-96

Spot removal

Are there elements in the image you'd like to remove or otherwise clean up? Examples are spots caused by dust on the sensor, a branch appearing to stick out from someone's head, red-eye from flash, etc. (see Figure 4–97). Determine what elements you want to remove from the photo, but plan to re-assess the need for retouching after completing all the other steps. As you work on the image, you're likely to discover artifacts and other flaws you didn't notice earlier, or find that your processing has reduced the need for retouching or eliminated it altogether.

Figure 4-97

Here, we're talking about removing what we don't like from the image—if something doesn't work with everything else, we want to get rid of it. Assessing the need for retouching is highly subjective, but most photos can follow some common criteria. Typical retouching tasks include removing dust spots, smoothing or removing wrinkles and blemishes from skin and generally eliminating distracting elements from the composition.

Lightroom's Spot Removal tool is used for getting rid of small- to medium-sized imperfections in the photo. There are two modes available: Heal and Clone. Each has its own strengths and best uses. Note that as a *Spot Removal* tool, it's best used for just that—if you have heavy-duty retouching to do, consider using Photoshop instead.

4

Step 1. To activate the Spot Removal tool, click its icon in the tool strip under the Histogram (see Figure 4–98) or use the shortcut. This enables the tool overlay and reveals the controls in the tool drawer, which shows any previous applications of the Spot Removal tool on the photo and the most recently used settings.

Figure 4-98

Step 2. Next, set the brush size using the slider or shortcuts (same as local adjustment brushes). As with the other sliders in Lightroom, there are several ways to adjust the value. You can click and drag the cursor in the preview area to set the size of the Spot Removal tool before applying each instance.

The Spot Removal tool works best when the size of the brush is just larger than the spot to be removed (see Figure 4–99).

You can also adjust the opacity of each instance of the Spot Removal tool, though I usually work with opacity set to 100.

Figure 4-99

Step 3. To remove spots, click once on each element to be retouched. Lightroom automatically finds a nearby point to sample for the new pixels necessary for the retouching. Each time you click, two circles are added to the tool overlay, connected by a line with an arrow at one end. The arrow shows the direction from the sample to the spot being retouched; see Figure 4–100.

Unlike the Healing Brush and Clone Stamp in Photoshop, you can't really "paint" with Lightroom's Spot Removal tool; each click applies a single, circular spot removal instance.

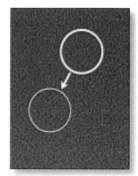

Figure 4-100

You can come back later to change all these settings after applying the Spot Removal tool.

N
Activate/
deactivate the
Spot Removal
tool

[
Reduce brush
size

]
Enlarge brush
size

Shift+[
Reduce feather
by 5

Shift+]
Increase feather
by 5

H
Hide the spot
removal tool
overlay

HEAL SPOTS AND BLEMISHES

After activating the tool, select Heal mode. Heal works best for retouching areas of solid color or smooth gradients, like sky and skin. Heal mode smoothly blends the sample into the spot.

CLONE TEXTURES AND PATTERNS

Clone is best used for replicating textures, patterns and hard lines in the photo. It makes exact copies of the sampled pixels and pastes them at the destination.

Whereas the Heal brush evaluates the surrounding areas when applying the new pixels to the destination, the Clone tool does not—it just copies pixels. If you need to retouch over the slats of a picket fence, replicate leaves and grass, or place a third eye on your mother-in-law, the Clone tool is the right tool for the job; see Figure 4–101.

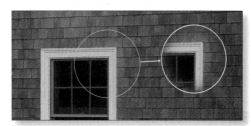

Figure 4-101

As you might expect, because it exactly copies pixels without blending, cloning requires you to work with more precision than Healing. After clicking to place your retouch spot, you may need to relocate the source.

Like the other tools, you can hide the spot removal overlay while you work. I find this really makes retouching easier.

Do your retouching late in the workflow

You may often be inclined to perform retouching at the beginning of your processing, such as blotting out annoying sensor dust spots evident in the blue sky or getting rid of the twig poking out of someone's head. But as troublesome as these elements may appear at first glance, most of the time it's best to wait until the end of the workflow to do your retouching—you might save lots of time.

For example, you wouldn't want to spend time retouching the edge of the image and then crop it. More importantly, you will often find that other processing reduces the need for retouching.

Bearing in mind the principle of working from large to small, global to local, it stands to reason that retouching is best done after the other stages of the Develop workflow.

4

Zoom in

It's usually difficult to accurately retouch a photo viewing the full image; zoom in to various magnification levels while doing your retouching.

Page Up and Page Down

To scroll the image uniformly, in vertical columns. As you reach the end of each column, the preview resets at the top of the next column. This ensures you cover the entire image.

Space bar

To temporarily enable the hand tool; click and drag to pan the image in any direction.

MODIFYING AN INSTANCE OF THE SPOT REMOVAL TOOL

After applying the Spot Removal tool, you can adjust each instance of it in the tool overlay. Start by clicking a circle to select it. The active circle has a heavier outline than the other; see Figure 4–102. With any instance of the Spot Removal tool selected, you can modify it in several ways:

- Click and drag the edge of the circle to change its size;

- Click and drag the center of the circle to move it. (This can be used to move the source circle to a different point for better results.);

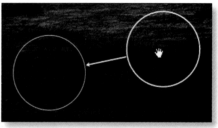

Figure 4-102

- Switch between Clone and Heal;

- Click and drag to change the source to a different location; or

- Delete it.

AUTO SPOTTING

To easily apply spot removal to multiple photos containing the same spots, just spot the first photo, making sure not to move any of the source circles. If you allow Lightroom to determine the source spots, you can then Sync that photo with others, and Lightroom will automatically clean up spots in those photos too, even if they have different compositions. This doesn't always work perfectly, but is a huge time saver when you've got lots of photos to clean up. You can then go back and fine tune spotting in individual photos. See the information about Syncing photos toward the end of this chapter.

When to use Photoshop for retouching

You can use Lightroom's retouching tools to remove many unwanted elements, but Photoshop's retouching capabilities far surpass those in Lightroom. One example is the replacement of any large section of a photo; Lightroom can't do this—it might better be considered compositing. Heavy-duty retouching is best done to exported files (Chapter 5), or using the Edit In command (Chapter 9).

RED EYE CORRECTION

Red-eye in photography is a phenomenon caused by light from a flash bouncing off the inside of a person's (or animal's) eyeball. Usually, it's an undesirable effect.

Lightroom's red-eye removal tool looks for red-colored pixels and changes them to neutral gray or black. Its application is similar to that of the Spot Removal tool.

Figure 4-103

To remove red-eye from a photo, zoom in close to see the affected eye; work on one at a time. Click to activate the red-eye tool; see Figure 4–103 (there is no shortcut). Click and drag to set the tool to just slightly larger than the pupil you're working on (or use the current size). Release the mouse button to apply (see Figure 4–104), and you're done!

Figure 4-104

Converting a photo to black and white

If you like black and white photographs, this can be one of the most fun and creatively rewarding aspects of working in Lightroom. Starting with a color original, it's possible to produce stunning black and white photos. And, no doubt, some images look much better in black and white than in color.

In Lightroom, a black and white image remains in RGB mode, even when exported. The colors in the image are simply converted to equal values in all three channels. (This is very different from the Grayscale mode in Photoshop, which only contains one channel.) Keep in mind that the color components are

4

being turned into gray levels, but Lightroom still processes them based on their original, named hue values (red, purple, aqua, etc.).

There are several ways to turn a color image into black and white in Lightroom. However, this is a case where the fastest method doesn't always produce the best results.

V

Convert a photo to Black and White

Fastest: click the Black and White button the Basic panel (see Figure 4–105), the HSL B&W panel header, or the Quick Develop panel in Library, or use the shortcut. You can then edit the sliders on the B&W panel to your liking (see Figure 4–106). This provides basic control for how the colors in the original photo are mapped to gray values.

Figure 4-105

Figure 4-106

Best: make the conversion by desaturating all the colors, individually, first. In the HSL panel, set all the Saturation values to -100. Then use the Luminance sliders to brighten or darken the converted grays. This gives you the maximum amount of control over the placement of tones in relation to their original color values (see Figure 4–107). You can tweak the Hue sliders a bit, too, for the most control over the conversion.

Figure 4-107

White balance effect on Black and White conversions Regardless of the initial method you use to convert your color original to black and white, **try adjusting white balance afterward.** As mentioned previously, white balance has a major effect on the rendering of the base raw capture, resulting in wide variation in the resulting tones.

Figure 4-108

Creative color processing

Trends and styles in photography have been heavily influenced by special ways of processing photos, and until very recently, these effects were all done in the wet darkroom. But Lightroom provides far more control and flexibility than any photographers working in the darkroom could have ever hoped for.

That said, there are certain photographic processing styles that have endured for decades; some since the earliest days of photography. These can be reproduced in Lightroom; instructions for simulating some of them are provided below.

Lightroom offers many options for processing your photos in unique ways. With such a wide range of controls, there are unlimited possible outcomes for the way an image will end up. I encourage you to experiment as you work—maybe you will invent the next popular photographic style!

⌘+4 or Ctrl+4
Open/close the
Split Toning
panel

SPLIT TONING

The term *split toning* refers to the application of different color tints to highlights and shadows. For example, you can warm the highlights and cool the shadows, or vice versa. A common "cross processing" effect applies warmth to the highlights and coolness to shadows; see Figure 4–109.

Figure 4-109

4

To apply split toning to a photo, open the Split Toning panel and make sure the controls are expanded with the black triangle buttons; see Figure 4–110.

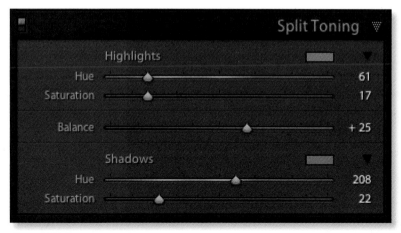

Figure 4-110

You can independently adjust the hue and saturation for Highlights and Shadows. You can set the hues with the sliders, or click the color swatches to open the color picker. The Balance slider adjusts the balance between the highlight and shadow tints. Hold Option or Alt while dragging a hue slider for a live preview of the color overlaid on the image; you can then fine tune the saturation.

Though split toning is usually applied to black and white photos, you can also achieve some interesting effects in Lightroom by split toning color photos.

COLOR TINTING

To give a photo a uniform color tint (see Figure 4–111), first convert it to black and white using one of the methods described earlier in this chapter. Then use the Split Tone panel to apply the color. For a uniform color tint, set the Highlights and Shadows sliders at the same values, and set the Balance at 0.

Figure 4-111

4

History

Everything you do to a photo in Lightroom is tracked in the History panel (see Figure 4–112). This is one of the great benefits of using a database-based image editor. You can go back to any point in time. (Unless you clear the history, which I generally don't recommend, since the textual history data being used to store each adjustment hardly takes up any disk space at all.)

Clicking any step in the History panel will return the image to that state. History is linear, however: if you make further adjustments after going back to that state, all the steps that were after it will be lost. History is most useful for recovering from mistakes or changing your mind. If you want to go back and forth, that's where Snapshots come in.

Note: a photo's History is *not* saved in its XMP metadata.

⌘+Control+3 or Ctrl+Shift+3
Open/close the History panel

⌘+Control+2 or Ctrl+Shift+2
Open/close the Snapshots panel

Snapshots

Unlike presets, Snapshots always include all the settings in effect when the Snapshot is made—you don't have the option to choose what settings are saved into the Snapshot. Snapshots are useful for saving various states of history for a single photo. Use Snapshots when you want to store all the photo's current settings to retrieve later; they are stored in the Snapshots panel (see Figure 4–113).

Figure 4-112

Figure 4-113

Note: Now, in Lightroom 3, Snapshots *are* stored in a photo's XMP metadata.

4

The on/off state of panels is included in Snapshots
If you have panels turned on or off using the switch in the panel header, that condition is also stored in the Snapshot.

Snapshots versus Virtual Copies
Given all the functionality provided for managing Develop settings, I don't find Snapshots very useful, and don't often use them. If you want to make different versions of a photo all at one time, use virtual copies instead of Snapshots. One advantage of Virtual Copies is that you can view multiple variations at once; this is not the case with Snapshots.

Creating multiple versions of a photo

While processing your photos in Lightroom, you can generate multiple versions of a photo in the catalog from a single, original file on disk. This is done using *virtual copies* ("vcs"). A virtual copy is indicated by a turned-corner icon on the thumbnail (see Figure 4–114).

In terms of adjustments, vcs are treated exactly like originals.

⌘+′ or Ctrl+′
Make a virtual copy of selected photo(s)

When you make a virtual copy, the current settings on the photo being copied (whether an original or another vc) are used as the base settings for the copy. But this is where the direct connection between settings ends; **further modifying the original will not affect the copy/copies, or vice versa.** However, you can sync the settings from a copy back to the original using the Sync Copies… command, discussed later in this chapter.

vcs can be useful in a number of ways. For example, you could try different crops and compare them side-by-side. Or Develop an image in both color and black and white. There are also some interesting and practical uses for vcs when working in the output modules. The possibilities are virtually endless!

You can also make a copy of a copy, which—unlike in the real world—does not degrade quality due to generation loss. With this method, virtual copies can be used to progressively process an image in a variety of ways, resulting in multiple versions that can then be compared to determine the best one, or used for different kinds of output.

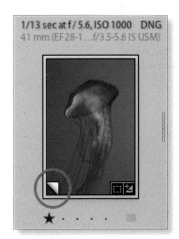

Figure 4-114

4

If you're not sure where you want to go in processing a photo, you might want to work on a VC first, then later sync the settings from the VC to back to the original. (Syncing is covered in the next few pages.)

By default, a virtual copy is stacked with its original. For more information about stacks, see Chapter 3.

To make a VC, right-click or Ctrl+click on a photo, and from the popup menu select Create Virtual Copy, or use the shortcut.

Deleting originals also deletes VCS

Virtual copies exist only in the Lightroom database. If the original file on disk is removed from Lightroom its VCs will also be removed.

Resetting adjustments

There will be times when you want to remove Lightroom adjustments from one or more photos. *Resetting* restores the default settings and removes any settings you've applied since the photo was imported (excluding any Develop presets applied during import, which would remain).

⌘+Shift+R or Ctrl+Shift+R
Reset all the adjustments on selected photo(s)

Resetting a virtual copy will revert its settings back to those in effect at the time it was created.

Resetting is undoable. Like most everything else in Lightroom, if you Reset a photo and then change your mind, simply Undo it (⌘+Z or Ctrl+Z).

There are several options for resetting some or all adjustments applied to a photo:

- Reset an adjustment slider by double-clicking its name;

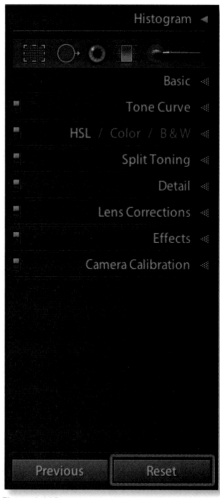

Figure 4-115

- Reset a group of sliders in a panel by double-clicking the name of the group; or

- Reset *all* adjustments on a photo with the Reset button on the bottom right of the right panel group (see Figure 4–115). Click the button to reset the photo to the state at which it came into the catalog.

Hold Shift while clicking Reset

To reset the photo to Adobe defaults (even if you've overridden them with Set Default Settings command; as discussed earlier in this chapter).

Comparing before and after

In Develop you can see left/right or top/bottom comparisons of the before and after states of the photo. You can also toggle the Develop loupe preview to show before/after.

To see both Before/After previews at one time, click the button on the toolbar (see Figure 4–116) or use the shortcut. The triangle button next to the Before/After button opens a popup menu with options for arranging the before and after views.

Figure 4-116

The Before state shows either:

- The image as it came into the catalog during import, including any Develop presets that were applied on import; or

- A Before state that you have applied yourself at some point.

The After state always shows the image with **all current settings** applied.

When the Before/After preview is active, you can use the buttons on the toolbar (see Figure 4–117, next page) to copy settings between the Before and After states, or use the shortcuts.

⌘+Option+Shift+Left Arrow or Ctrl+Alt+Shift+Left Arrow
To copy the After settings to Before

⌘+Option+Shift+Right Arrow or Ctrl+Alt+Shift+Right Arrow
To copy the Before settings to After

⌘+Option+Shift+Up Arrow or Ctrl+Alt+Shift+Up Arrow
To swap the Before and After settings

****
Toggle before/ after in the main preview

Y
Cycle between Loupe and Before/After views (left-right)

Shift+Y
Activate before and after previews and toggle between side by side or top/ bottom and split image views (based on which was selected before)

Option+Y or Alt+Y
Cycle between Loupe and Before/After views (up-down)

4

Figure 4-117

- Copy Before's Settings to After;

- Copy After's Settings to Before; or

- Swap Before and After Settings.

(Hover your cursor over the buttons to see tooltips.)

Progressively Developing a photo using Before/After
If you get to a point in processing where you want to take all the current settings and make that the Before state, simply **drag and drop any history state onto the Before preview.** You can then continue processing, using the newly-created Before state as your reference.

Come back later
Sometimes it's helpful to work an image up to the point where you can't seem to make it any better, then stop. Come back later, with "fresh eyes", to confirm your previous processing decisions and make additional changes if needed.

Applying settings to multiple photos

Lightroom—a batch processing application at heart—allows you to very easily apply Develop adjustment settings to many photos at one time using a variety of methods. Any Develop setting on one photo can also be applied to other photos; for example, you could replicate your application of Spot Removal or dodging and burning to multiple images.

Select photos from the Filmstrip or collections
While working in Develop, you don't need to go back to Library to load different images.

COPY/PASTE

You can copy and paste Develop adjustment settings from one photo to another.

To copy the settings from the active photo, use the command under the Settings menu (see Figure 4–118, next page) or the shortcut. A dialog box will be presented for you to choose which settings are being copied; see Figure 4–119. Make your selections then click the Copy button.

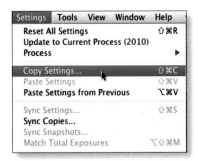

Figure 4-118

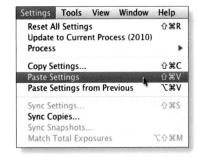

Figure 4-120

⌘+Shift+C
or
Ctrl+Shift+C
Copy settings
from the
active photo

⌘+Shift+V
or
Ctrl+Shift+V
Paste the
copied
settings to
other photos

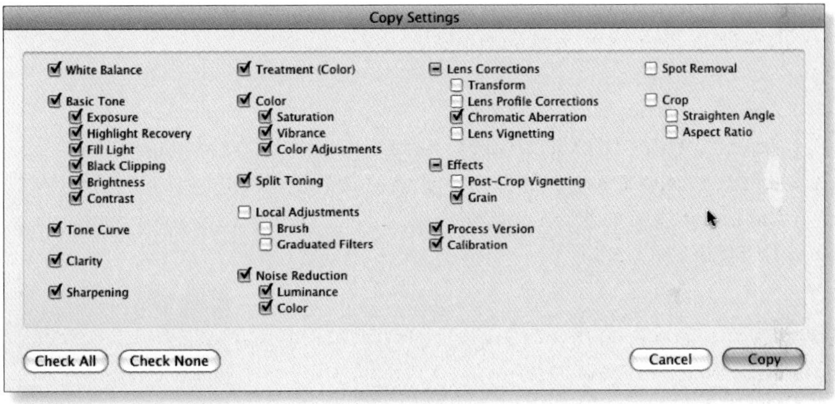

Figure 4-119

To paste the copied settings to other photos, select them, then use the Paste Settings command (see Figure 4–120) or shortcut.

When you paste, all settings you chose in the copy dialog will be pasted to the selected photo(s).

Paste from Previous

This command, also under the Settings menu, will instantly copy and paste *all* the settings from the previously active photo to any selected photos.

4

SYNC SETTINGS

You can *synchronize* Develop settings between multiple files in Lightroom. This produces the same results as Copy/Paste—the settings from the active photo will be applied to the other selected photos. It's just another way of applying one batch of settings to multiple photos. You can also sync settings from a VC back to the original.

With multiple photos selected (pay attention to which is the active photo), click the Sync... button on the right panel group, or use the shortcut. A window appears allowing you to choose what settings to sync; see Figure 4–121.

⌘+Shift+S or Ctrl+Shift+S
Sync settings from the active photo to other selected photos

Synchronize Settings

☐ White Balance	☐ Treatment (Color)	☑ Lens Corrections	☑ Spot Removal
		☑ Transform	
☐ Basic Tone	☐ Color	☑ Lens Profile Corrections	☑ Crop
☐ Exposure	☐ Saturation	☑ Chromatic Aberration	☑ Straighten Angle
☐ Highlight Recovery	☐ Vibrance	☑ Lens Vignetting	☑ Aspect Ratio
☐ Fill Light	☐ Color Adjustments		
☐ Black Clipping		☑ Effects	
☐ Brightness	☐ Split Toning	☑ Post–Crop Vignetting	
☐ Contrast		☑ Grain	
	☑ Local Adjustments		
☐ Tone Curve	☑ Brush	☐ Process Version	
	☑ Graduated Filters	☐ Calibration	
☐ Clarity			
	☐ Noise Reduction		
☐ Sharpening	☐ Luminance		
	☐ Color		

(Check All) (Check None)   (Cancel) (Synchronize)

Figure 4-121

Auto Sync

Next to the Sync button at the bottom of the right panel group is a switch that toggles between Sync and Auto Sync; see Figure 4–122.

When active, Auto Sync will continually apply any adjustments made to the active image to all the other selected images.

When done, click the switch to go back to the standard Sync.

Figure 4-122

Sync white balance

One very useful application of Sync Settings is adjusting white balance. To accurately set white balance for a batch of photos, begin a photo shoot by making an initial capture containing a target reference, such as the X-Rite Passport. In Lightroom, use the reference shot to set the white balance with the eyedropper. Then simply use Sync Settings on the rest of the files to match the white balance from the reference image.

Copy/paste vs Sync

The end result of copying/pasting settings and syncing settings is the same. However, when you copy settings, they remain in memory and thus could be pasted to other photos later. A sync operation does not store the synced settings anywhere.

MATCH TOTAL EXPOSURES

With multiple photos selected, this command (under the Settings menu) applies a relative Exposure setting from the active photo to the other selected photos. (Only the Exposure adjustment is applied.)

DEVELOP PRESETS

Using Develop presets can save you lots of time processing files. With them you can quickly apply any previously saved settings to large numbers of images all at once. Lightroom also offers many built-in Develop presets; see Figure 4–123.

You can make your own presets or use presets made by other people—there is a growing number of Web sites where photographers share presets, a few of which are listed at the end of this section.

After you've worked with Lightroom a while you will begin to identify settings that you frequently apply as a basis

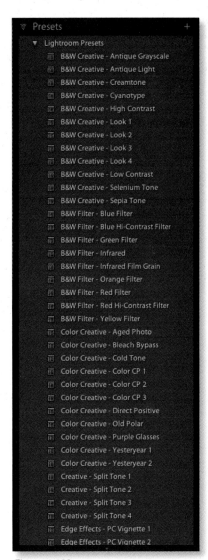

Figure 4-123

4

for your "starting point" in processing. When you find that you are repeatedly applying the same settings to many photos, you should save a Develop preset with those settings. For example, you can save a preset for your preferred sharpening settings, or one for Blacks, Brightness and Contrast adjustments. Or, one that just applies a linear point curve. Or all of them at once. In general, though, it's usually most convenient to save presets with fewer settings rather than more.

Preview presets in Navigator

With an image loaded in Develop loupe view, move your cursor over the presets in the left panel of the Develop module. The Navigator preview automatically updates to show the effect of the adjustments in that preset; see Figure 4–124. This is an easy way to preview presets without actually needing to apply them.

See the contents of presets

You can open Lightroom presets in a text editor. This will show you how they are structured. (Just to be safe, I recommend you make a copy of any presets or other metadata XML files before you open them.)

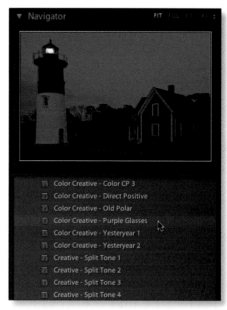

Figure 4-124

Making your own presets

To make your own Develop preset, first make sure the active photo has the exact adjustment settings that you want to store. Then click the + button on the Presets panel header; see Figure 4–125. A dialog box opens asking you to select the settings that you want to save into the preset; see Figure 4–126, next page. The Develop settings shown are very similar to those in Copy/Paste and Sync dialogs.

Figure 4-125

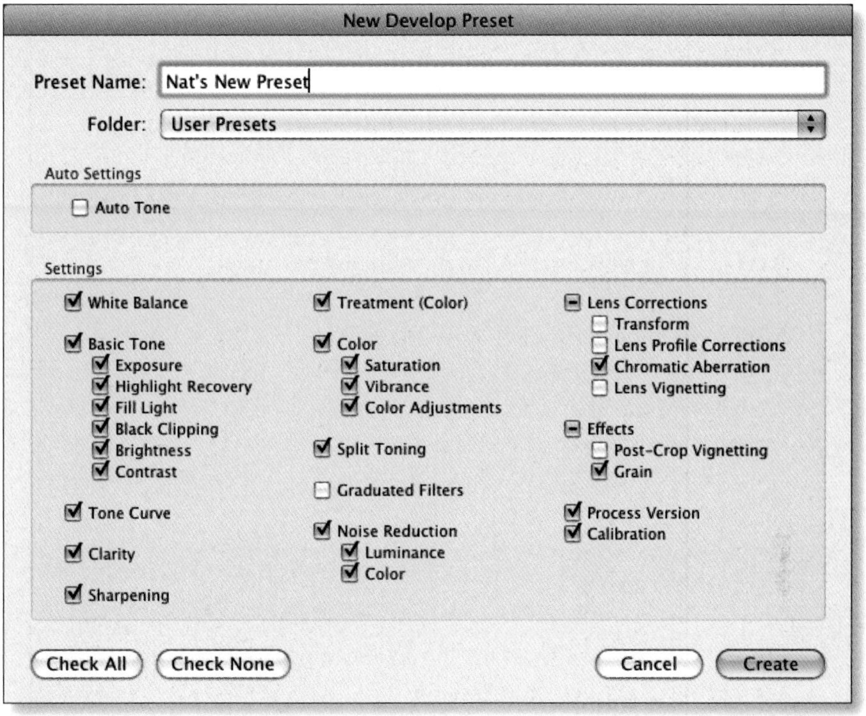

Figure 4-126

This choice is important. Remember that Develop settings are *absolute*. Thus, a preset that contains a value for a given adjustment will override the current setting when the preset is applied. Any adjustment that *isn't* included in the preset will not be changed when the preset is applied.

For example, if you have a photo with a Contrast setting of +25 and you apply a preset that contains a Contrast setting of +35, the resulting value will be +35 (not +60). But if you apply a preset that doesn't contain a setting for Contrast, it will remain +25, regardless of the other adjustments that are changed.

Since each adjustment checked in the dialog box will be saved into the preset using the current value, you should carefully consider which settings to include, and in most cases, it's best to include as few adjustments as possible within each individual preset so you can apply them progressively.

Eventually, you'll likely make some presets with lots of settings included, and others that include only a single adjustment. It all depends on the purpose of the preset.

4

Give your presets meaningful names

Name your presets according to their settings or purpose.

Apply a Develop preset during import

When you've established the baseline settings that can be applied to the majority of your photos, save them as a Develop preset. Then, during future imports, apply the preset to photos in the Import dialog box. Your images will come into the catalog looking much closer to the way you like them.

Using presets made by someone else

A good way to learn the effects of the Develop adjustments is to use presets from someone else and then evaluate the results. To use presets from an outside source, you need to copy them into the presets folder and restart Lightroom. Any preset with a valid format will then appear in the list; you can organize them as you see fit; use the + button on the panel header for options or right-click/Ctrl+click to open the presets popup menu. You can also drag and drop to rearrange presets and presets folders.

To show the Lightroom presets folder in Finder or Explorer, go to Preferences➔Presets➔Show Lightroom Presets Folder

Here are a couple of good resources for Lightroom presets:

http://www.presetsheaven.com/
http://lightroompresets.com/
http://www.ononesoftware.com/detail.php?prodLine_id=33

Google "Lightroom presets" for bunches more.

(Note that presets made for earlier versions of Lightroom may produce unexpected results—or may not work at all— in Lightroom 3.)

4

Modifying and Removing Presets

You can update the settings contained in a preset or remove it from the list entirely.

Right-click or Ctrl+click on a preset or folder to open the presets contextual menu (see Figure 4–127).

Select an option from the menu:

Update with Current Settings: replaces *all* the settings in the selected preset with *all* the current Develop settings.

Delete or Delete Folder: immediately removes the preset from the list and deletes it from the Lightroom presets folder.

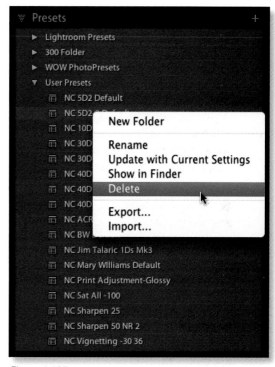

No confirmation when deleting presets and preset folders

Figure 4-127

Be forewarned that when you select Delete or Delete Folder from the presets contextual menu you will not get a confirmation dialog—the preset files will be deleted from disk immediately. They do not go to the trash or recycle bin! **(However, deleting presets or preset folders is undoable within the current program session.)**

Save an alias or shortcut to the Lightroom folder on your desktop

If you frequently add, remove or otherwise maintain presets, you may want to save some shortcuts in your file system to make finding the Lightroom folders easier. This way, you can update Lightroom folder contents without needing to launch the program first. (This tip applies for all types of Lightroom presets and templates; not just Develop.)

4

SETTING YOUR OWN DEFAULT

As described toward the beginning of this chapter, beyond just applying Develop adjustments using presets, you can also override the main Lightroom default settings, which are applied to all raw images that haven't otherwise had settings applied.

To change the default, first make sure all the Develop settings are the way you want them; you will need to have a representative image loaded in Develop for this.

Then select Develop menu→Set Default Settings; see Figure 4–128. A dialog box will appear asking you to confirm your choice; see Figure 4–129. Note that by running this command again later you can restore the original Lightroom defaults.

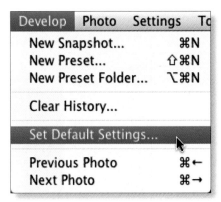

Figure 4-128

Now, if you *don't* apply a Develop preset during import, these default settings will still be applied to all newly imported images as they come into the catalog.

Figure 4-129

You'll notice the message stating that the changes are not undoable; this means just what it says—you won't be able to use Undo to reverse your action here. However, you could always just save a new default, or revert to the Adobe defaults.

Default settings by camera or by camera and ISO

In Lightroom preferences (see Figure 4–130) you can specify to have defaults applied based on camera serial number or a specific camera and ISO setting. This way you can use a wide range of defaults without needing to apply different presets to each and every image from different cameras or ISO settings.

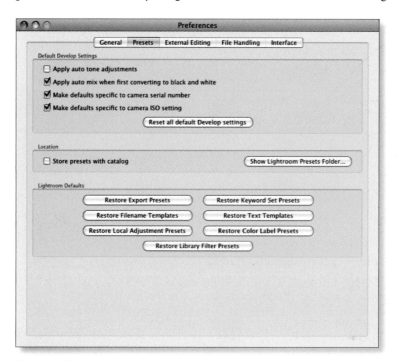

Figure 4-130

Save your work!

As you Develop photos, remember to frequently Save Metadata to File, as described in Chapter 3 and shortcuts throughout the book.

And back up your hard drives often!

Before and after examples

Every one of the photos used in this book, including the cover and chapter openers, were Developed entirely within Lightroom. Photoshop was used only for the final conversion to CMYK for offset printing.

The following pages show a few more examples of my photos processed only with Lightroom. See if you can figure out what adjustments, tools and techniques were used for each... or at least, how you might do it.

4

Before

Figure 4-131
Greve in Chianti, Italy
Canon EOS 5D Mark II
EF 28-135mm f/3.5-5.6 IS USM
1/2 sec at f/11
ISO 100

After

4

Before

Figure 4-132
West Wanaka, New Zealand
Canon EOS 5D
EF 24-105mm f/4L IS USM
2.5 sec at f/22
ISO 200

After

4

Before

Figure 4-133
Seal Rock, Oregon
Canon EOS 5D
EF 28-135mm 3.5-5.6 IS USM
1/13 sec at f/11
ISO 200

After

4

Before

Figure 4-134
Kawainui, Hawai'i
Canon EOS 30D
Tamron XR Di II 18-200mm
1/200 sec at f/7.1
ISO 200

After

4

Before

Figure 4-135
Ecola State Park, Oregon
Canon EOS 5D
EF 24-105mm f/4L IS USM
1/25 sec at f/8
ISO 200

After

CHAPTER 5
EXPORT

5

Exporting photos from Lightroom

By now you've worked all the way through importing, editing and developing your photos in Lightroom. What's next? Maybe you want to email someone a photo, upload images to a photo-sharing Web site, or burn a set of low resolution files to DVD for a client to proof. Other times, you'll want to process a photo further using different imaging software.

Unlike other programs, Lightroom doesn't have a "Save As…" command. So whether you're distributing finished photos or need to get working image files out of Lightroom and into other software, you will very often *export* those files from Lightroom.

Lightroom exports can also help you feed your image files into more extended, automated workflows: using plug-ins and post-processing actions, Lightroom can trigger all kinds of automated processes on the exported photos. These procedures are discussed further in Chapter 9.

Exporting photos from Lightroom *always* generates new image files. But depending on the purpose of the export, the new files are not always saved to your hard disk following the completion of the export. For example, if you're burning a DVD to copy or back up some files, maybe you don't need to save another set of local copies on your machine after the disc is burned.

In cases where you do save the newly exported files to your hard disk, you have the option to also add those images into the current Lightroom catalog.

Generally speaking, the Lightroom export process is straightforward:

1. Select the file(s) to export

2. Open the Export dialog box

3. Configure the settings in the Export dialog box

4. Click the Export button

However, due to the infinite range of possible uses and outcomes, exporting can be confusing at times. In this chapter, I'll do my best to simplify the process and help you understand the situations you will likely encounter.

EXPORT VERSUS OTHER METHODS

Keep in mind that using the Export command is just one of several ways to save new image files out of Lightroom. For example, if you need to process photos in

Photoshop, you may not need to (and probably shouldn't) export them. Instead, it's more efficient to use the Edit in… command, discussed in Chapter 9. In general, if you're just working with a single photo, Edit In… might be your best bet. In cases where you're batch processing multiple photos, Export is the way to go.

Also, before exporting final files for a particular use, consider that using Lightroom's output modules—Slideshow, Print and Web—might produce the files you need more efficiently. The functions of those modules provide capabilities that make some tasks easier than doing it through an Export, though the end results may be identical. One example is the "Print to JPG File" option in the Print module; see Chapter 6 for more on this.

Converting files to DNG

You can use an Export to save new DNG files from photos in your catalog, but this usually isn't the easiest way. Instead, use Library→Convert Photo(s) to DNG, as described in Chapter 3.

What to do with original JPGS

If you have photos in your catalog that were originally captured as JPG and not raw, you need to take special precautions with them.

Remember that in Lightroom, JPG files are processed non-destructively just like all other file types. You can edit and develop them in Lightroom with no loss of quality, because the original file on disk is never directly altered. And most often, you can safely export new files from those JPGS without problems.

But in Photoshop and other programs, you should *never* work on a JPG and then save over the same file as a JPG again—you will lose significant amounts of quality with each save.

If you have original JPGS in your Lightroom catalog that you want to edit in other software, I recommend you first export them from Lightroom as TIFS, then use those TIFS as your new working masters.

ORIGINAL AND DERIVATIVE FILES

When you export photos from Lightroom, the *original* is the photo from which the new files are being made. An original can be any photo or virtual copy in your catalog. For this reason, you might have more than one "original" version of a photo in your catalog, *all made from a single file on the hard disk.* In this case, each variation could be considered an original in terms of exporting. For example, if you use virtual copies (VCs) to produce three versions of a photo with different crops, each VC would be considered an original.

5

Derivatives, then, are copies of the original, made for specific purposes, and with file settings based on those purposes .

A couple of examples:

- You have a native camera raw file in your catalog that you need to export and send to a print lab in TIF format. The raw file is the original, the TIF is the derivative.

- You have a layered PSD file in your catalog from which you export a JPG file to email to your client. The PSD is the original; the JPG is the derivative.

Making files on disk from virtual copies
Remember that a virtual copy does not exist anywhere on your hard disk. It's just another instance of the file within the Lightroom catalog. So if you delete the original, or your catalog becomes corrupt, etc. and you don't have a backup (shame, shame), those VCs will be gone along with the work you put into them. So it can often be safest to export new TIFS or DNGS from those vcs, in which case you can also back up those photos as actual files on disk. (Exporting a VC made from a raw or DNG file as a *new* DNG is especially clever.)

Don't keep what you don't need
Some derivative files don't need to be kept around after you're done using them for their immediate purpose. For example, I usually don't keep derivative JPGS, since they're always made to a certain size and for a specific purpose and remaking them later, if necessary, doesn't take much effort. I don't like cluttering up my hard drive with files that will only be used once, so I delete these derivatives when I'm done with them.

Overwriting the original
Be careful when you export from Lightroom that you don't unintentionally overwrite your original image. Lightroom will prompt you if it encounters a file with an identical name, which we'll look at in a few moments.

PLANNING THE EXPORT
Like other parts of the workflow, exporting from Lightroom requires some thinking ahead. Before exporting, determine the requirements for the files that will be produced. Be as specific as you can. Write it out if it helps. Ask yourself:

- How are the files to be used?

- Do you have a set of specifications to follow?

5

- How will you name the exported files?

- Will you store them in your file system? If so, where?

- Following the export, what additional tasks need to be performed on the files?

- Do you want these new files to be added to the current Lightroom catalog?

When you've got the export requirements figured out, make sure to have the correct file(s) selected. Like Import and Develop, Lightroom exports provide powerful batch-processing capabilities. You can export a single photo or many photos at the same time. Select any number of photos, from any image source in the catalog, and the current export will process all the selected files using the same settings.

And, unlike an Import, of which can only have one going at a time, **you can start a new export while a previous one is still going.** This way, you could initiate multiple exports, and Lightroom will process them all simultaneously.

Batch JPG exports

One case where batch exporting really comes in handy is when exporting many JPG files from high resolution originals, which can be quite time consuming. If you have a large number of files to export as JPG, rather than queuing them up all at once, break them into smaller batches. For example, exporting four sets of twenty-five photos is much faster than exporting one set of one hundred. This is due to Lightroom's multi-threaded processing capabilities.

Export options on the contextual popup menu

When you right-click or Ctrl+Click on a photo anywhere in Lightroom, the popup menu provides export commands using presets and an "Export with Previous" option. These options bypass the Export dialog box altogether, and thus require you to have your settings worked out ahead of time.

⌘+Shift+E or
Ctrl+Shift+E
Opens the
Export dialog
box

The Export window

When you're ready to export you can click the Export button in Library; see Figure 5–1. Or, from anywhere in Lightroom, use the File➔Export menu command, or the keyboard shortcut, or the contextual menu, which

Export...

Figure 5-1

is discussed below. After opening the window, click and drag the bottom right corner to expand it (see Figure 5–2 next page).

5

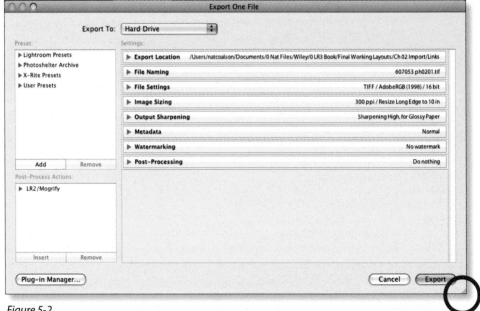

Figure 5-2

Next, work through each panel to carefully enter the settings in the Export screen. If you botch the settings, you may have a mess of files to clean up. Start at the top of the Export window and work your way methodically through the settings, making sure everything is correct before you click the all-powerful button.

(However, if you start the export and change your mind or realize you made a mistake, you can click the "X" to the right of the status indicator to cancel the export).

You can work in the Export dialog box without exporting

With any photo(s) selected, executing the standard Export command will simply open the Export dialog box. However, you don't necessarily have to *complete* an export at this point. You can view and change settings, create and modify presets, etc. and when you're done just click Cancel to close the box without performing an export. All the work you did in the dialog box will be retained.

Open the Export screen panels

Each of the panels of the Export dialog box (see Figure 5–2) can be closed if not needed. Click to open and close them. You don't need to click the arrow; just click anywhere on the panel title bar. When closed, a panel's header shows its current settings.

Following is an in-depth look at the settings in the Export window.

EXPORT TO:

Within the default Lightroom installation, you have two simple choices for the destination of the exported derivatives: Hard Drive or CD/DVD. (When you install other Export plug-ins, as explained later, more options may show here.)

The Export To: menu at the top of the dialog box shows which option has been selected (see Figure 5–3). **This selection determines the options available in the rest of the dialog box.**

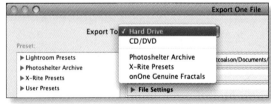

Figure 5-3

EXPORT LOCATION

The first panel in the main section of the dialog box is Export Location. The important decisions to make here are:

1. Where to save the exported file(s); and

2. Whether or not to add the new file(s) into the current Lightroom catalog.

Export To

This section of the Export window is only relevant if your Export To: menu selection (above) is set to Hard Drive; if it's set to CD/DVD, the files will not be saved anywhere on the disk.

Lightroom 3 has some very useful new options here. Use the popup menu to specify one of the following:

Specific folder: If you want to save the exported files in a location other than the original folder, specify it here; see Figure 5–4. Click the Choose button and navigate to the target folder on your hard drive. During this step, you can also create a new folder for the exported files. When you make new folders during an export and you add the exported files to the catalog (discussed below), the new folders are added, too.

Figure 5-4

5

Choose folder later: lets you specify the destination after the export is initiated. As noted in the tip in the Export window, this is particularly useful when creating Export presets.

Home folder: this refers to your User folder in your operating system.

Documents folder: within your User folder.

Pictures folder: within your User folder.

Desktop: the Desktop folder for your User account.

Same folder as original photo: this will create the newly exported files within the same folder as the original photo on your hard drive.

(If I'm keeping the exported files, I almost always save them into the same folder containing the originals. If I don't plan to keep the derivatives, I often save them to a folder on my desktop that is routinely emptied.)

Recent folders menu

Click the small black triangle to the left of the Choose button to select a recently used folder from the popup menu; see Figure 5–5.

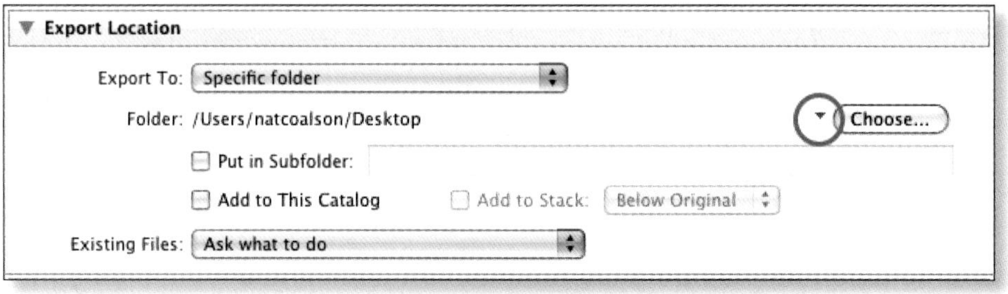

▼ **Export Location**			
Export To:	Specific folder		
Folder:	/Users/natcoalson/Desktop		▼ Choose...
	☐ Put in Subfolder:		
	☐ Add to This Catalog	☐ Add to Stack:	Below Original
Existing Files:	Ask what to do		

Figure 5-5

Put in Subfolder

By entering a folder name in this field, you can create another folder inside the one specified above. Tick the box to enable the option, then type the name for the subfolder in the text field.

Add to This Catalog

Enabling this option will automatically import the newly exported file(s) into the current Lightroom catalog. I always do this for derivatives I intend to keep, and usually don't for temporary ones.

Add to Stack

If your destination folder location is Same as Original Photo, and you enable Add to This Catalog, you can stack the exported derivatives with the original masters. (Stacking is discussed in Chapter 3.) I frequently enable this option; if you export derivatives that you want to add to the catalog, stacking them with the originals can help keep your image sources neat and tidy. Use the popup menu to choose where in the stack the exported files will be inserted.

Existing Files

This setting tells Lightroom what to do if files with the same names are already in the destination folder. I usually keep this on "Ask what to do" unless I'm doing a large batch and/or just want to overwrite everything in the target folder, in which case the other options come in handy.

Choose a new name for the exported file: when Lightroom comes to a file with the same name, a number will automatically be added to the end of the new file's name.

Overwrite files WITHOUT WARNING: the older file with the duplicate name will be overwritten by the new file. (Be careful with this.)

Skip: the export process will ignore the file with the name conflict; the new file will not be exported and you will not see a warning.

FILE NAMING

Exported files can use the same or different filenames as their originals; see Figure 5–6. Keep in mind that every file in the catalog must have a unique name, but the names can be differentiated by the file type extension only. For example, Cape_Cod_April_100422_106.dng and Cape_Cod_April_100422_106.jpg are different file names.

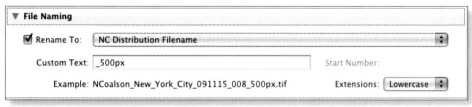

Figure 5-6

Carefully consider the names for your exported files. Think of this like a "Save As…" in other programs: you're starting with one file and creating a new file from it. Just as with Save As… you should be deliberate about how you name the new file. As with other stages in the workflow, practical naming of exported derivatives makes your work much easier.

5

You have two options:

- Keep the same filename as the original; or

- Use a different name.

For example, exporting

> Death_Valley_080412_044.dng

could create a derivative file named

> Death_Valley_080412_044.jpg

or, it could become

> NCoalson_DeathValley2008_420px_srgb.jpg

I almost always apply new names to derivative files to indicate their settings and/or what they are to be used for. But there are times when keeping the original filename is more appropriate, such as when exporting derivatives to be used as new masters and further processed in other software.

To name the exported files differently from the originals, tick the checkbox and choose a file naming template from the menu. To create a new template, choose Edit…. File naming templates are explained in detail in Chapter 3. If you don't check the box, the exported file will use the same base file name as the original.

An option in Lightroom Preferences➔File Handling➔File Name Generation controls Lightroom's automated file naming behavior (see Figure 5–7). This is intended to assist in ensuring file names are Internet-friendly. The preferences give you options for how to handle "illegal" characters and spaces in the name. They can be replaced with dashes or underscores, or left as is. During an export, if you create a file name that breaks the rules you've set, Lightroom will automatically change the name to reflect your preference settings.

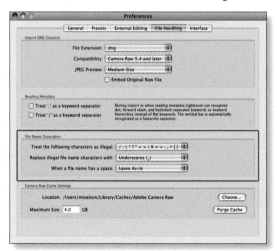

Figure 5-7

Back in the Export screen, use the popup menu to choose the case for the file extensions.

An example of how the current file naming template and preferences will affect the names for the files being exported is shown at the bottom of the File Naming panel.

FILE SETTINGS

In this section of the export dialog box (see Figure 5–8), enter the file settings for the exported photos. If you're doing a batch export, all the files will be exported using the same settings, unless the output file format is set to Original, in which case each exported file will be in the same format as the original from which it was made.

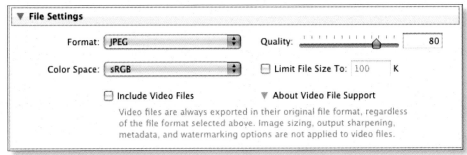

Figure 5-8

Format

First, select the file format, each which will present different options. Apply the other settings specific to that format. File formats are also discussed in Chapters 1 and 2; here's a list and descriptions of the formats available in the popup menu:

JPG: Joint Photographic Experts Group. Use for Web and email. Exporting as JPG allows you to specify a quality level in numeric values from 0 to 100. The quality setting determines the amount of compression to be applied to the files. Higher quality numbers will apply less compression and thus produce better looking files. With lower quality settings, more compression is applied, resulting in degraded image quality. The higher the quality, the larger the size of the resulting file will be, but keep in mind that JPG compression is *always* lossy—data is discarded during compression, even at the highest quality setting. For Web use, I usually keep JPG quality between 70 and 80 unless I need to adhere to provided specifications or other uses. For example, if you're exporting JPG files to send to a lab for printing, set the Quality at 100.

PSD: Photoshop Document. Can be used to create files to work with in Photoshop or Elements. Exporting as PSD allows you to set the bit depth; if you are planning to work on the file in other software, usually it's best to use 16 bit for the highest quality possible. Exporting as .PSD also allows you to choose a color space, and whether or not to include video files in the export. (See the next page for more about these topics.)

5

Don't use .PSD

From this point forward, I recommend that you don't use PSD files for any of your Photoshop work. Use TIF instead. It provides all the same saving capabilities as PSD (layers, type, alpha channels, etc.), with a distinct advantage: TIF offers much more long-term, archival viability than PSD.

The TIF format is an open source, industry standard. PSD is proprietary, and in my opinion, outdated, with a number of programmatic disadvantages to TIF. It's highly likely that more software, many years in the future, will be able to read TIF files than will read PSD. You might currently have many files in your image archives in the PSD format. Consider the benefits of re-saving all of them as TIF.

TIFF (.TIF): Tagged Image File format. TIF can be used for virtually any purpose except posting to the Web. When exporting TIFs you can also specify bit depth and apply compression. In all cases, compression on TIF files is *lossless*—no data is discarded during compression. Exporting as .tif allows you to set bit depth and color space, (see below) and whether or not to include video files in the export.

Use 16-bit for the highest quality

When exporting TIF files I recommend you usually use 16-bit depth, especially if you're going to continue processing the image(s) in other software. One exception might be if you're sending exported TIFs to a service bureau for printing, in which case 8-bit is usually adequate. (Ask your vendor for details on how they want files prepared.) Depending on your circumstances, 16-bit might not be worth the additional file size.

DNG: Digital Negative. Use to re-encode raw captures. I always work with my raw captures in DNG format and I don't save the original raw files from the camera after they've been converted. However, I do the DNG conversion on import, or at least, using the menu command in Library. I recommend using the default settings for DNG conversions in Lightroom. DNG is also discussed in Chapters 1, 2, 3 and 4.

Original: You can export derivative files in the same format as the original. In a batch with multiple file types selected, each derivative will be saved in the same format as its own original. If virtual copies are being exported, the resulting files will be in the same formats as the originals from which they were made; this can be a good way to generate "real" files from VCs. You can't change any file settings when exporting to Original format.

Video files: If you have video files selected for export, Lightroom will include them in the export, but the only processing Lightroom will do on the exported video files is renaming. All other export settings will be ignored for video files.

Exporting layered originals produces flattened derivatives

Though Lightroom will respect and preserve layers in TIF and PSD files when they are imported, if you export them (to any format), the resulting derivative will be a flattened file.

Color space

When you choose a color space in the Export screen, you need to do so based on how the file will be used. During the export, Lightroom will convert the photo's colors to the selected color space and embed the ICC profile for it.

To recap the fundamentals of color management from Chapter 1: the color space of an image determines colors possible and helps the color management system translate those colors to different devices. The image's color space is indicated to the CMS by an embedded ICC profile.

For the most part, when you're working on a photo in Lightroom, you don't need to worry about color spaces. Lightroom respects and preserves all color profiles embedded in image files. For images that don't have an embedded profile, sRGB is automatically assigned.

However, when you export a photo from Lightroom in any format other than Original, you *must* choose a color space for the new file, even if the original photo already has a profile embedded. (There are currently no options to automatically use the same profile as the original, or to export a file *without* embedding a profile.)

Example: if you work on a TIF file in Lightroom that has the ProPhoto profile embedded, you would still need to choose ProPhoto again when exporting if you want to keep the derivative file in that space.

The Lightroom default (and most common) color spaces/profiles are:

sRGB: "Standard RGB"; Developed by Microsoft and Hewlett-Packard around the turn of the 21st century; often referred to as "small RGB" due to its relatively small gamut. Of the three main working spaces, sRGB most closely resembles the output spaces of computer monitors and laser imaging devices (LightJet, Frontier, Chromira, etc.) sRGB excels in producing vivid greens and blues. If you're preparing files for viewing on screen (e.g. a Web site) or having prints made by a lab, use sRGB. For our purposes, think of it as the "small" color space.

Adobe RGB (1998): Also sometimes called "aRGB" or "RGB98", this is the most flexible of the color spaces supported by Lightroom. Some examples: aRGB

5

translates well to CMYK for offset printing and can also work very well for inkjet printing. Also, converting aRGB files to sRGB produces only minor shifts in color. It's capable of producing rich reds and oranges while maintaining dense blacks. Use aRGB if you're preparing the file for printing with ink, or if you don't yet know the ultimate destination of the file. Think of aRGB as the "medium" color space.

ProPhoto: While not the largest color space ever developed (Google EktaSpace and Bruce RGB, for example), ProPhoto is the largest of the three standard color spaces included in Lightroom (though you can use your own color space; see below). ProPhoto maintains the most vivid saturation of the three popular spaces. and contains some colors that can't (yet) be reproduced in print, particularly super-saturated yellows, oranges and reds. ProPhoto encompasses all the colors that can be captured by a digital camera sensor, plus some colors in the infrared spectrum that can't be seen by the human eye. In Lightroom, this is the "large" color space.

Choosing color space
If you're exporting to make a master file to work on in other software use ProPhoto or Adobe RGB (1998). If exporting for final delivery, use the appropriate color space for that destination.

Using a custom profile
You can also select your own Export color space by selecting "Other…" from the popup menu; see Figure 5–9. This allows you to export files in any color space available on your computer and is especially useful when preparing files for printing by an outside vendor. If someone provides a custom profile for you to use, you can add it to the list here and thus export files from Lightroom directly to that color space.

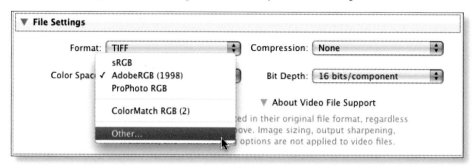

Figure 5-9

Ask vendors for their profiles
When sending an image to a lab or service bureau, you need to know how your file will be reproduced. Ask them if there is a specific color space that they want the file saved in.

Rendering intent

Lightroom exports use the Perceptual rendering intent (and Black Point Compensation) to perform color space conversions; you can't change this setting. Sometimes this produces color conversions with less than optimal results. If you're exporting to JPG, you can use the Print module instead, which allows you to choose Relative rending intent. Many images will print best using Relative; see Chapter 6 for more information.

(For the most control over color space conversions use Photoshop, where you can choose the rendering intent and many other conversion settings.)

Maintaining the most possible data

When exporting files from Lightroom to be processed in other software, I always use ProPhoto and 16-bit. This ensures the maximum amount of data from the raw capture will be preserved in the rendered file.

IMAGE SIZING

When you're working on photos in Lightroom you're always working at the files' *native resolution*. During an export, you have the option to resize the exported file. The Export dialog box provides several controls for this; see Figure 5–10. (Note that you can't resize files being exported as Original or DNG; you can only resize for TIF, PSD or JPG.)

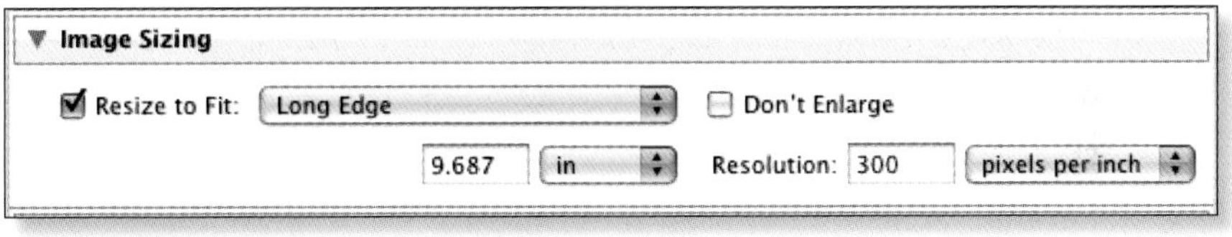

Figure 5-10

Remember that resizing a photographic image always requires *resampling*: pixels must either be created or discarded. (This is also referred to as *interpolation*.) Resizing in either direction will result in some loss of image data, insignificant as it may be for the circumstances.

For enlargements (*upsampling*), new pixels are synthesized from the existing ones. In reductions (*downsampling*), pixels are eliminated and the values of the remaining pixels are averaged to produce the final image.

Lightroom uses resampling algorithms similar to Photoshop's, usually with equivalent quality in the results. (Actually, in my tests, I've found that Lightroom's resampling is often superior to Photoshop's.)

5

Resize at the end of the workflow

Always resize your photos after all other post-processing has been completed, and only resize as necessary for the intended purpose. **If you're planning to do more processing on the files after the export, leave them at the native resolution.**

Resize to Fit

In this section of the export dialog box you can specify a different size for the new files. Check the box to resize them, otherwise the derivatives will be the same size/resolution as the originals.

All the numeric entries represent maximum constraints: the numbers entered here are always the *largest* possible size that would be output.

Also, regardless of how you specify the output size, no distortion of the exported images will result—all the resizing controls in Lightroom export produce images that retain the proportions of the original.

The choices for resizing are:

- **Width and Height:** enter the maximum size(s) for width and/or height. (You can leave one or the other blank.) The photo(s) will be scaled so that both dimensions fit within the specified measurements.

- **Dimensions:** the images will be scaled to fit within the specified dimensions without regard to which is width and which is height. The smaller of the two numbers will determine how much the image is scaled.

- **Long edge:** set the size for the long side of the photo; the short edge will be scaled proportionately.

- **Short edge:** set the size for the short side of the photo; the long edge will be scaled proportionately.

- **Megapixels:** this will proportionally scale the photo to fit within the target file size.

Don't Enlarge

Check this box to prevent Lightroom from enlarging any images whose originals are already equal to or smaller than the specified output size.

Limit file size

With this box checked, Lightroom will attempt to create an exported file(s) that fits within the specified size limit. However, be aware that other settings on the

Export screen could interfere with this, especially if you don't use Minimize Metadata. (If you just can't seem to get files under the limit, look at Minimize Metadata first.)

Resolution

The concept of *resolution* is consistently one of the most difficult for my students to grasp. This is most likely because the term is commonly used in two different ways.

One meaning refers to the actual pixel dimensions of a file (*x* pixels by *y* pixels). A "high resolution" file contains lots of pixels; a "low resolution" file contains relatively fewer pixels. **Bear in mind that an image pixel does not have a fixed size.**

The second meaning for resolution, and the one used in Lightroom Export, refers specifically to printed output. Measured in pixels per inch or pixels per cm, this "resolution" determines how the pixels in the image will be mapped to the physical measurements of a print. **The resolution setting in Lightroom Export—and its equivalent in Photoshop—is only relevant for printing.**

With printed output, besides the actual pixel dimensions, you have another issue to consider—real world, physical measurements such as inches or centimeters. On a printed photo, the pixels in the image need to be discreetly mapped to these real world measurements. Which raises the question, "how many pixels in an inch?" That's where the Resolution setting comes in: it determines how the pixels in the image will translate to the printed output. For example, an image with 240 ppi will use 240 pixels per inch on the printed output. This resolution determines the amount of detail possible in the print.

If the export is intended to produce print-ready files, set the sizes for the exported files to the final dimensions and resolution for the type of printing being used. A few examples: For inkjet printing, resolution anywhere between 180 and 480 will work. For offset printing at 150 lpi (lines per inch) 300 ppi is good. For lab prints, 300 ppi is also common. However, laser imaging devices actually support a wide range of print resolutions; ask your service provider.

To specify a resolution for the exported files, enter a value in the text field and choose pixels per inch or pixels per cm from the menu. The resolution setting will be saved as metadata value embedded in the exported file.

For screen-based media, such as a monitor, projector etc., the actual pixel dimensions are all that matters, and typically one image pixel will be displayed as one screen pixel. This applies to Web browsers, email readers, television,

5

handheld devices, etc. **If you're exporting files for any kind of screen output, don't worry at all about the Resolution setting: it will have absolutely no effect on the final output of screen-based media.**

In the past, you may have been told to use 72 ppi or 96 ppi for Web images. I'm here to tell you that this is a myth. It doesn't matter one iota whether an image being projected on a monitor is 72 ppi or 300 ppi; the output will only be based on the pixel dimensions (*x* by *y*) and the size shown on the screen will not be any different. That said, if you want to enter 72 or 96 ppi here, that's fine.

OUTPUT SHARPENING

In modern digital photo workflows, we usually use three types of sharpening: *capture sharpening, creative sharpening* and *output sharpening.* In Lightroom, the first two are applied in the Develop module (see Chapter 4).

At export time, Lightroom provides the capability to automatically apply output sharpening; see Figure 5–11. With this method, the new files are sharpened at the ideal point in the processing and at the proper amount for the image size and intended media.

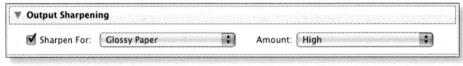

Figure 5-11

To enable output sharpening, tick the "Sharpen For:" box, then choose the type of sharpening and the amount to apply.

- **Screen:** use this if you're exporting files for display on a computer or television monitor.

- **Matte Paper:** use this for printing on matte paper, such as cotton rag art papers like Hahnemühle Photo Rag and Epson Somerset Velvet. Sharpening for Matte is stronger than for Glossy.

- **Glossy Paper:** use this for printing on glossy, luster and semi-gloss photo papers like Fuji Crystal Archive, Harman Glossy FB AL, Epson Premium Luster and Ilford Galerie Gold Fibre Silk.

These paper types apply equally to inkjet prints and lab prints.

After choosing the type of sharpening, set the amount: Low, Standard or High. Because sharpening routines are image-specific and dependent on file size, finding the ideal amount may require you to do some testing. Try the standard amount first, evaluate the results and adjust as needed. I usually use High for all media types.

When NOT to sharpen

If you're going to resize the image, apply noise reduction and/or sharpen it in another program (such as Photoshop), turn off all sharpening in the Lightroom export settings and do your final sharpening later in the workflow.

METADATA

This section of the Export window provides controls for how each file's metadata is handled during the export; see Figure 5–12.

▼ **Metadata**	
☐ Minimize Embedded Metadata	
☐ Write Keywords as Lightroom Hierarchy	

Figure 5-12

Minimize Embedded Metadata

Ticking this checkbox will limit the amount of metadata from the original files that will be copied into the newly exported files (all except the copyright notice). The purpose for this is to allow you to create smaller files: depending on how much other metadata you've applied, this can result in significant savings in file size. If you need to export files at the smallest possible size, enable this option. Just be aware that any other metadata—including keywords—will not carry over to the new files.

Write Keywords as Lightroom Hierarchy

If you use keyword hierarchies in Lightroom, checking this box will preserve these parent/child relationships when the keywords are written into the exported files. Note that this keyword structure may not be respected by other software; the only real benefit here is when you're going to import the files into another Lightroom catalog, in which case you will retain the hierarchies you've previously created. I typically leave this off.

WATERMARKING

Lightroom 3's watermarking is one of the most useful new tools. A "watermark" is a text or graphical overlay that appears on your photo(s). You've no doubt seen countless photos with watermarks on the Web—they are most often used to identify the creator or copyright owner of the image.

5

It's important to note that a copyright watermark is very different from the copyright metadata embedded in a photo. The watermark is visible on the photo itself; the metadata is plain text embedded in a special part of the computer file. However, you can use metadata copyright info as a basis for creating a watermark.

Lightroom's watermarking offers incredible power beyond just copyright notices. If you're familiar with Photoshop, this is "Layers" in Lightroom, albeit basic. Bring in any kind of graphic file containing transparency, and you can place it on top of your photos. Especially when combined with identity plates, watermarks enable exciting new ways to create complex graphic composites straight out of Lightroom.

The Export screen also provides access to Lightroom's Watermark Editor, which is also available from the output modules (Slideshow, Print and Web). All these use the same set of watermarks; if you create a custom watermark in any of the modules or the Export screen, you'll be able to use it anywhere else within Lightroom.

You can also open Lightroom's Watermark Editor using the Edit Watermarks command, under the Lightroom Menu on Mac and the Edit menu on Windows.

To apply a watermark to exported files, first check the box to enable the function; see Figure 5–13.

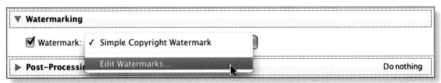

Figure 5-13

Select a saved watermark from the menu, or, to make a new one, choose Edit Watermarks. The default is Simple Copyright Watermark, which will place your metadata copyright notice over the photo in the lower left corner. (If the photo does not contain copyright metadata, nothing will appear.) You can use this as a starting point and customize the watermark how you like.

Clicking Edit Watermarks opens the Watermark Editor window; see Figure 5–14 next page. At the top left is a menu to select a watermark preset; you can also save new presets here.

To the right of that menu, above the preview, are left and right arrows. If you have multiple photos selected for the export, these buttons allow you to cycle through them to see how your watermark will look on different photos.

Figure 5-14

Next, you need to choose between a text or graphic watermark; you can't have both. Regardless of which you choose, the following panels are visible, though with a graphic some controls will be unavailable:

Image Options

Click the Choose… button to load an image from your hard drive; it doesn't need to be in the catalog. Clicking this will switch from Text to Graphic mode in the watermark; see Figure 5–15. As the informational text below the option explains, this must be a PNG or JPG image. And as with Identity Plates, Watermarks containing a PNG will provide transparency support.

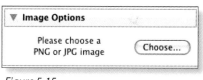

Figure 5-15

Text Options

If you're using a text watermark, type the text into the box below the preview. Then style the text with the following options; see Figure 5–16 next page:

- **Font:** from the menu, choose from one of the fonts installed on your computer.

- **Style:** depending on the font, other styles might be available. Bold, italic, small caps, etc. These can go a long way in styling text for all kinds of purposes.

5

- **Align:** left, center, right.

- **Color:** click the swatch to choose a color for the text. Click Return or Enter to apply, or Esc to cancel. For more about using the color picker see Chapter 3.

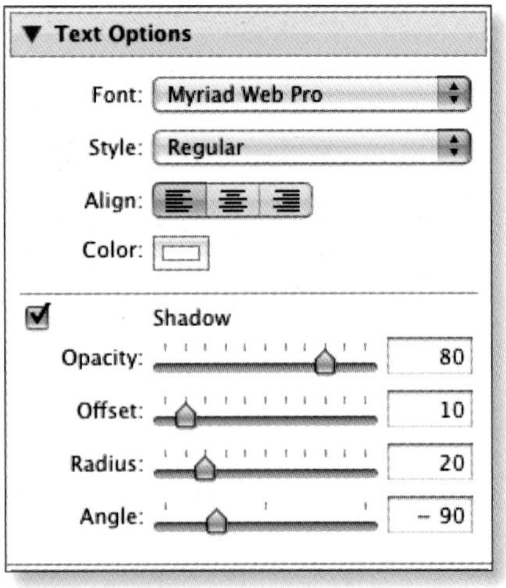

Shadow

- **On or off:** check the box to turn the text watermark shadow on or off.

- **Opacity:** this sets how strongly the shadow appears behind the watermark. At 100%, the shadow is fully solid on the photo. At lower opacity values, the photo shows through. Drag the slider to see the effect.

Figure 5-16

- **Offset:** this determines how far from the text or graphic element the shadow is placed.

- **Radius:** the width of the shadow.

- **Angle:** adjusts the direction of the shadow as it falls on the background. Try this in conjunction with the Offset slider.

Watermark Effects

Opacity: sets the opacity/transparency of the watermark as it's overlaid on the photo. Drag the slider or type a number to set the opacity; see Figure 5–17.

Size: sets the size of the watermark on the photo. Choose between Proportional, Fit, and Fill. If you choose proportional, you can drag the slider or type a number to scale the watermark in the photo.

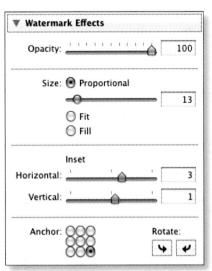

Figure 5-17

Inset: drag the sliders or type numbers to set the spacing between the watermark and the horizontal and vertical edges.

Anchor: determines the point from which the watermark is placed on the photo. The other controls will work relative to the anchor point, unless it's set to the center.

Rotate: click the buttons to rotate the watermark clockwise or counterclockwise in 90 degree increments.

When you're done setting up your watermark, click the Save button at the bottom right and give your watermark preset a name, or click Cancel to leave the Watermark Editor without saving. To update an existing watermark with the current settings, choose that option from the menu.

Applying multiple watermarks

You can use Lightroom's watermarking feature to apply multiple watermarks. Simply do a series of progressive exports generating multiple TIF files. Apply the first watermark during the export from the original. Then re-export that new, derivative TIF with a second watermark, etc. During each successive export you can add another watermark. During the last export, save to your final delivery format, such as JPG.

POST-PROCESSING

Lightroom can integrate its export operations with those of other software applications. When Lightroom is done with the export, the files are handed off to the other program(s) for further processing, often which themselves can also be automated, such as with Photoshop actions. Use the controls in the Post-Processing panel of the Export screen (see Figure 5–18) to set options for this. More about post-processing can be found in Chapter 9.

Figure 5-18

5

Export presets

As with the other areas in Lightroom, whenever you customize the settings, you should consider saving export presets for later use.

First, you need to have your desired settings applied in the Export screen—saving a new preset will store all the current settings.

Next, click the Add button at the bottom of the presets list on the left side of the Export dialog box (see Figure 5-19). Choose where to store the new preset and give it a name. (I prefer to put them in the default location, but you can make more folders or use special naming to group export presets for specific purposes.) Click Return or Enter to finish.

Updating and deleting presets

You can update presets in the list: right-click or Ctrl+click on a preset, and from the popup menu, select Update with Current Settings.

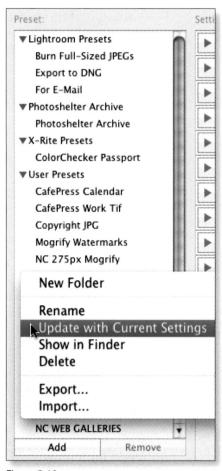

Figure 5-19

Or, delete presets from the list by clicking the present and then the Remove button.

Start with a preset

Often, the easiest way to set up an export is to select a preset and then customize the settings from there. The left side of the Export dialog box lists all the export presets that have been saved. Under Lightroom Presets, there are a few built-in presets for some common tasks. (When you're just starting with a new installation of Lightroom, there won't be any User Presets.)

Export plug-ins

There are many specialized export plug-ins available for Lightroom. These add-on extensions provide enhanced integration and functionality with other applications and Web services. To find plug-ins,

Figure 5-20

click the Plug-in Manager button at the bottom left of the Export screen; see Figure 5–20. In the Plug-in Manager, click the button for Plug-in Exchange see Figure 5–21. This will take you to the Adobe Web site, where you'll find many Lightroom plug-ins for export as well as other functions. There are also some Lightroom plug-ins available that for one reason or another are not on the Adobe site; Google "Lightroom plug-ins" to find them. Export plug-ins are discussed in more detail in Chapter 9.

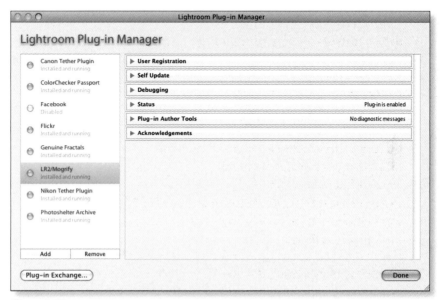

Figure 5-21

Example export scenarios

Bearing in mind the unlimited possibilities for handling your photos outside of Lightroom, I've put together the following few workflows based on some of the most common uses for exporting.

If, at this point, you're still unsure of how this whole exporting business fits into your particular workflow, I strongly suggest that you perform lots and lots of exports, even just for practice, so you get a handle on the settings. You can export files to your heart's content into a special folder from which you simply delete the derivative files every so often.

There is no inherent risk in exporting any original file an infinite number of times. Sometimes the best way to master a process is to play with it for a while. Just be careful that your exported files are stored and handled with the most possible efficiency.

5

Junk files clog the system

Since exporting generates new files, it introduces the likelihood that you will produce files that serve no further purpose and only waste space on your hard disk. It's easy to wind up with a host of unneeded image files strewn all over your hard drives. Try to avoid this by being careful and conservative with your exports, unless you're just practicing, in which case it's best to do your exports into a folder whose contents are routinely trashed.

BURNING A DVD

You can burn your exported photos to a CD or DVD straight out of Lightroom. During the export operation you can also apply any of the file conversion options, but post-processing options are not available.

After Lightroom generates the derivatives, they will be burned to the disc using your operating system's built-in functions. With a few exceptions (based on operating system and disc burner), Lightroom works with your OS to complete the entire process automatically.

Step 1. In Library, select all the photos to be exported and open the Export dialog box.

Step 2. Select a disc burning preset from the left pane of the window (see Figure 5–22), or, with any preset or previous settings selected, choose "CD/DVD" from the Export To: popup menu at the top of the Export window.

Figure 5-22

Step 3. Configure the remaining options for the files to be exported and burned, taking even more care than usual, because a disc will be burned even if your file settings are incorrect!

Step 4. Click the Export button, or press Return/Enter. If you don't already have a blank, writable CD/DVD in the writer, Lightroom will prompt you when it's time to insert one.

EMAILING PHOTOS

When you want to send photos to someone by email, you have a few options:

1. Do a regular export of JPG files, saving them somewhere on your hard disk, then attach them to the message in your email program; or

2. Use Lightroom to help streamline the process through plug-ins or post-processing actions. In this case, you don't need to export the files separately; the post-processing script will handle that. There are a couple of email plug-ins for Windows: MapiMailer and Export to Email (both can be found on the Plug-In Exchange Web site). They both create JPGs and attach them to your message. MapiMailer opens a new message in your email client; with Export to Email you can enter your SMTP mail information and your message within the program. When installed, both plug-ins show up in the "Export to" menu.

Lightroom provides a built-in export preset for emailing files. However, in my opinion, this preset is not very useful as-is; it serves best as an example starting point for how you might configure your own settings for this purpose. (For example, the built-in email preset doesn't include an email program as a post-processing function; you need to add your email program yourself.)

USING LIGHTROOM FOR FILE COPIES

One of the most basic applications for Lightroom's capabilities might be copying batches of files. There are likely to be many occasions where you need to make copies of image files, whether for yourself or someone else. Lightroom exports are very good for this.

EXPORT IMAGES FOR COPYRIGHT SUBMISSION

For most photographers, registering photographs with the U.S. Library of Congress is an essential activity. I recommend that at least once per year you export finished photos from Lightroom to submit to the copyright office. The easiest way to do this is to export small JPGs and burn them to disc—you can submit many files to the copyright office using just one form. You can also use the online registration system at http://www.copyright.gov.

CHAPTER 6
PRINT

6

Printing photos from Lightroom

I believe a photograph is never truly finished until it's printed. You can make all the Web galleries you want, present slideshows, share photos by email… but for generations, the intrinsic nature of viewing a *photograph* has meant viewing a *print*.

Of course, in this digital age, many more photos are shared electronically than are viewed as prints. I think this is unfortunate, for several reasons. First, color management: send ten people your photo to view on their computer monitors; ten people will see different colors in the photo. Today, this is an inescapable fact. Second, resolution: transmitting photos electronically requires lower resolution than can be achieved in a fine print, and thus, a loss of detail.

Nothing can take the place of standing in person before a great print, illuminated by good light. It can take your breath away. Call me "old school" if you will, but sharing snaps from your cell phone's camera on Facebook isn't *true* photography. These quick, often temporary, digital images certainly have their place—especially online— but the real art of photography remains in deference to the final print.

I realize that as times change, so will this standard. There's no escaping digital, and maybe there will come a time that photos won't often be printed on paper (maybe because paper is no longer available). But I hope even a century from now a photo printed on fine paper will still have special significance.

The content of this chapter assumes you want to have your photos printed, either by printing them yourself or having someone print them. We'll cover both scenarios.

If you're a wedding or portrait photographer, you'll be concerned with presenting many proof images to clients prior to making the final prints. Lightroom excels at this. If you're a nature or landscape photographer, you may be most interested in the perfect reproduction of fine detail and subtle tones within a single image. Lightroom handles this with grace. Whether you need to print one photo or lots of them, Lightroom's printing capabilities are up to the task.

Lightroom's Print module provides some of the most modern, sophisticated, automated controls available for resizing, sharpening and color management. And, of course, you can save templates for repeated use. We'll go through all the features of the Print module and explore some of the really creative and fun things you can do with printing in Lightroom. I'll do my best to explain all the controls and give you some ideas for how this all applies to your own situations.

Making your own prints

With the recent advances in affordable inkjet printers, many photographers are now making their own high quality prints. If you've been printing your own work using other software, I think you'll find Lightroom's solutions elegant and powerful. If you've been wanting to print for yourself but have been holding off, I encourage you to take the leap. Making a final print from your photo is one of the most rewarding aspects of photography, and Lightroom gives you all the control you need to make great prints yourself.

Having someone else make your prints

Many photographers, including seasoned pros, have perfectly valid reasons to send the bulk of their digital images to a lab or other service provider for printing. Lightroom can assist with this by giving you complete control for setting up the final files that you will provide to the lab. One of the most essential features of Lightroom's Print module is the ability to lay out all kinds of different print jobs. You can use Lightroom to set up contact sheets and proofs, picture packages containing prints at various sizes, and fine art enlargements.

Like everything else in Lightroom, printing takes some getting used to. Lightroom's printing procedures are very different from those of other software. But regardless of whether you're making your own prints or having a lab do it, setting up your prints in Lightroom is faster, easier and offers more capabilities than ever before.

LIGHTROOM PRINTING WORKFLOW

⌘+P or Ctrl+P
Switch to the
Print module

Lightroom's Print workflow has been thoughtfully engineered and often is the simplest, most straightforward way to make great digital prints. Here are the essential steps, which are explained in more detail throughout the rest of this chapter:

1. Get the printer ready: check ink, load paper, etc.

2. Organize and collect the photo(s) that you want to print.

3. In Lightroom's Print module, apply Page Setup options for paper size and orientation.

4. Select a layout style or template.

5. Modify the print layout to arrange the image(s) how you want them on the paper.

6. Add overlays for identity plates, text information, cut lines, etc. (optional)

7. Set the output options in the Print Job panel.

8. Print the job on your printer or output the layout as a JPG file.

6

Before setting up your print job, give some thought to the optimal process and the settings you will use. Are you printing just one photo, or multiple photos? What size and kind of paper will you use? Will all the photos be printed at the same size, or different sizes? Do you need to print textual information or graphics along with the images?

SETTING UP THE PRINTER AND CHOOSING A PAPER

When printing your own photos, everything you can do starts with the printer you'll use. These days, the average minimum cost for a printer capable of high quality output is around $500. At this point, you really can expect to get beautiful, long-lasting prints. Below that price... not so much. (This "entry level" price point continues to decline; just a few years ago, comparable technology would cost twice as much.)

The primary shortcoming with printers below this price point is that the manufacturers provide no support for color management, including the use of ICC profiles. With lots of effort, you *might* be able to get great color from a $150 printer, but don't hold your breath.

Also, the longevity of prints made from low-end printers is much less than those from high quality machines. The inks used in cheap models are not designed to retain their color for very long. On the other hand, archival inks in good printers can often be expected to last 100 years or more under typical conditions.

If you're in the market for your own printer, the current crop of printers from Epson and Canon are capable of the highest quality results; I've been very pleased using both brands.

Besides the printer, the second important factor in print quality is the paper you use. In most cases, papers branded by your printer manufacturer will provide the most predictable results. Note that this doesn't necessarily mean the *best* results: independent paper manufacturers are making papers often far superior to what your printer manufacturer offers. Companies such as Ilford, Harman, Hahnemühle and Premier manufacture excellent inkjet papers designed to work with a wide range of digital printers. If you're just getting started in printing, I recommend you use papers from your printer manufacturer. When you're comfortable with the printing workflow, you can invest in more expensive, higher quality papers. (There's more about paper at the end of this chapter.)

To make your own prints, you'll first need to choose a paper, get it loaded, check ink levels, print a nozzle test, etc. Having your printer ready when you hit the print button in Lightroom may seem obvious, but with so many options it's easy to overlook something. As you've heard me say... think it through before you commit.

COLLECTING PHOTOS FOR THE PRINT JOB

Whether you're making your own prints or preparing files for a lab, you'll want to spend a little time in Library organizing the photos you want to print. You can use a collection (which I normally do), or a Folder.

The Print module includes the Collections panel on the left panel group. You can make a new Print Collection by selecting photos from the Filmstrip, clicking the + button on the Collections panel header, and selecting "Create Print" from the popup menu. This creates a new Print Collection that displays a special icon and is accessible also from the other modules (see Figure 6–1).

Figure 6-1

Also, in the Filmstrip you can choose images for printing by selecting or deselecting them. In the Toolbar, you then have the option to print all the images in the chosen source, or just the selected ones, by choosing the appropriate option from the Use: popup menu (see Figure 6–2).

Figure 6-2

Use virtual copies for printing

When you need to adjust a photo to meet the criteria of a particular print job, using a virtual copy (vc) is a good idea. There are many print situations where using vcs can streamline your process. And in general, once you have "finished" a master photo and applied all the adjustments to make it look the way you want, any further modifications for specific purposes (such as printing) should be done using vcs. From your finished master files, make virtual copies for different print jobs. You can adjust the size or cropping of the photos differently, apply adjustments specifically for the printing conditions, add unique identity plates, etc.

Using vcs, your work can be economically retained for future use, or you can delete it when you're done. Through it all, your master file is never altered. You can return to it to make new derivative vcs later as needed.

6

For example: many printer/paper combinations produce printed output that is darker and less saturated that what you see on screen. You can make a VC with adjustments to compensate for this. For example, you might increase Brightness, Fill Light and Saturation to improve the printed output. You can also use VCs for alternate crops/aspect ratios, making triptychs and multi-image layouts, etc., all without affecting your original master photos. There's lots more about VCs in Chapter 4.

Use Quick Develop for Print adjustments

On your VCs, use Quick Develop in the Library module to apply adjustments for print. Quick Develop adjustments are relative, meaning they are applied *on top of* the values of any existing adjustments. See Chapter 3 for information about working in Quick Develop.

The Print module panels

Print is set up similarly to the other output modules: templates, previews and collections are on the left side, and all the controls for customizing the print job are on the right.

PAGE SETUP

The most important control for specifying the size of the printed pages, and thus the size of the photos that can fit on them, is Page Setup. You need to apply a Page Setup as one of the first steps in the printing workflow; all the other measurements will be determined based on the Page Setup. Click the Page Setup button at the bottom of the left panel group (see Figure 6–3).

In the Page Setup dialog box, choose the correct paper size and orientation for the current print job. Depending on your operating system, the controls for this may vary, but the common goal is to precisely specify the size of the paper and the direction the images will be placed on the page.

Figure 6-3

After selecting your printer, you can then choose from preset paper sizes provided by the printer driver software, or set up a custom page size. You also need to specify whether the paper source is sheet or roll (see Figure 6–4).

6

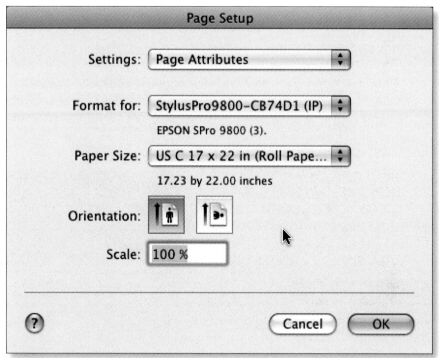

Figure 6-4

Borderless printing

If you want to print borderless, you need to apply a borderless page setup first. Otherwise, Lightroom will not allow you to use a layout with margins set at zero.

If you're framing the print, don't print borderless

Be sure to leave an inch or two of blank paper around all the outside margins.

⌘+Control+1
or Ctrl+Shift+1
Open and close
the Template
Browser panel

TEMPLATE BROWSER

Like the other output modules, preparing a job in the Print module requires the selection and customization of a template. Lightroom comes with several print layout templates, some of which are more useful than others depending on the printing needs you have. You can preview the templates in the Preview panel as you move your mouse over them; see Figure 6–5.

Choose a template from the Template Browser panel. Clicking a template loads it with its

Figure 6-5

6

associated Layout Style (see below). Choose the template that is closest to your intended layout. You'll usually need to make changes to the built-in template settings for them to meet your needs.

Note that templates include the paper size and orientation specified in Page Setup. If you're starting from a built-in template, this is one of the settings you will frequently need to change.

⌘+1 or Ctrl+1
Open/close the Layout Styles panel

LAYOUT STYLE

In some cases, before you choose a template, you will select an option from the Layout Style panel at the top right of the Print module; see Figure 6–6. The selection of a Layout Style determines the options available for the print job. Lightroom 3 offers the following built-in Layout Styles, each providing different controls for a particular purpose.

Figure 6-6

Single Image/Contact Sheet

Use the Single Image/Contact Sheet layout when you want to print a single photo or multiple photos all at the same size. This places photos in *layout cells* of the same size, in a fixed-grid layout. You can rotate photos and/or scale them to fit into the grid cells differently, but all the grid cells remain the same size (see Figure 6–7).

The order of the photos placed in the rows and columns of the grid is based on the current sort order, which can be set either in the Layout Toolbar or by dragging photos to rearrange them.

Figure 6-7

Picture Package

Use the Picture Package layout to print one photo per page in multiple sizes. With Picture Package you have more control over the size and positioning of the printed photos on the paper than with Single Image/Contact Sheet; see Figure 6–8.

Custom Package

Custom Package allows you to totally customize the photos and their sizes and placement on each page of the print job; see Figure 6–9. With a Custom Package you can print different photos at different sizes on any number of pages.

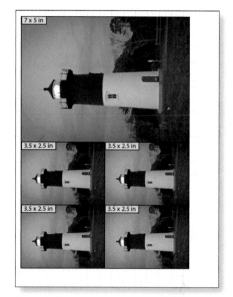

Figure 6-8

Following are descriptions of example uses for each Layout Style.

Single Image/ Contact Sheet

Use a Contact Sheet/Grid when you want all the photos to be printed in the same size cells. This determines the maximum possible size for the longest side of the

Figure 6-9

photo(s). This style is also ideal for printing one single image, including making fine art prints.

(The term *contact sheet* comes from the old days of film and photo paper. Strips of processed film were placed in rows on the photo paper, which was then exposed. This produced a sheet of thumbnail images for proofing and client selection.)

6

Image Settings panel

The settings on this panel configure how the photos are placed within the grid cells; see Figure 6–10.

Figure 6-10

⌘+2 or Ctrl+2
Open/close the Image Settings panel

Zoom to Fill: enlarges each photo to fill the entire grid cell. Depending on the size and aspect ratio of the cell, this can result in cropping the photo within the cell (but the original Develop cropping for the photo doesn't change); see Figure 6–11.

Rotate to Fit: rotates photos as necessary to use the most available space in the cell. Individual photos are rotated so their longest edge corresponds with the longest side of the cell; see Figure 6–12.

Repeat One Photo Per Page: with multiple images selected, enabling this option will force Lightroom to place only one photo on each page of the print job. Depending on the number of rows and columns you specify, this could result in just one photo on the page, or multiple copies of the same photo repeated at the same size in all the cells; see Figure 6–13.

Figure 6-11

Figure 6-12

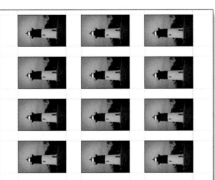

Figure 6-13

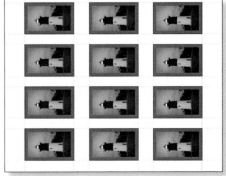

Figure 6-14

6

Stroke Border: enable this option to add a solid, outline border to the printed photos; see Figure 6–14. Use the slider or type in a numeric value to set the width of the border. Click the rectangular color swatch to open the color picker and set a color. (The color picker is explained in detail in Chapter 4.)

Enable Solo Mode

Right-click or Ctrl+click on any panel header and click the popup menu option to enable Solo Mode.

⌘+3 or Ctrl+3
Open/close the
Layout panel

Layout panel

The Layout panel contains settings for adjusting the grid layout (see Figure 6–15). These measurement settings all work in conjunction: changing one setting will usually also change the others, and sometimes it's impossible to get everything you want if the numbers don't add up. This is one area in Lightroom that often requires doing some math, and you'll likely need to work the settings back and forth until you get the precise measurements you're looking for.

Figure 6-15

Ruler Units: use the popup menu to specify inches, centimeters, millimeters, points or picas.

Margins: sets the outer page margins using the specified units. The minimum allowable margins are determined by the Page Setup settings.

Page Grid: specifies the number of rows and columns used to place the photos on the page. Along with the other measurements, the number of rows and columns in the grid determines the allowable size of the cells.

Cell Spacing: if there is more than one cell on the page, this sets the amount of vertical and horizontal space between the cells. If the Page Grid is set to one row and one column, these settings will be dimmed and unavailable.

Cell Size: sets the size of the cells in which the photos are placed. The cell sizes possible are determined by the other measurements. If you have a specific size you want the cell(s) to be, type to enter a numeric value. Cell spacing will be adjusted accordingly. If you enter a number and Lightroom refuses to accept it, you will need to adjust one or more of the other measurements. You can tick the checkbox to force the cells to Keep Square.

6

⌘+4 or Ctrl+4
Open/close the
Guides panel

⌘+R or Ctrl+R
Hide/show rulers

Guides panel

Check or uncheck the boxes on this panel to show or hide the available guides and measurement indicators (see Figure 6–16). **When guides are visible, you can click and drag them to modify the layout.**

Rulers: turns rulers on and off in the top and left sides of the main preview.

Figure 6-16

Page Bleed: in traditional lithographic printing, bleed refers to the amount that an image(s) extends beyond the edges of the page. Bleeds are used to provide "wiggle-room" for misalignment when printing full-page images on the paper, so that the image is ensured to go all the way to the edge when the page is trimmed. In Lightroom, this "Page Bleed" is really a "page margin"; however, with the other use of the term "margin" in the Print module this could become confusing.

If this box is checked, the "page bleed" is shown as a gray margin on the page, which actually is showing the margins of the maximum printable area, based on the Page Setup; see Figure 6–17. It's not possible to place a photo to extend beyond this area.

Figure 6-17

Margins and Gutters: these guides show the effect of the settings in the Layout panel. Margins are the spaces around the outer edges of the paper; gutters are the spaces between cells on the page. With this box checked, lines are displayed in the preview to show the edges of margins and guides, as visible in Figure 6–17.

Image Cells: show and hide the cell borders in the preview, which appear as solid black outlines but do not print. Toggle the checkbox on and off to see how cells are shown.

Dimensions: enable this option to display the sizes of the photos as they are placed within the cells. If Print Resolution is unchecked in the Print Job panel, (discussed later in this chapter) this will also display the print resolution of each photo at its current size; see Figure 6–18.

Hide/show the information overlay in the preview area

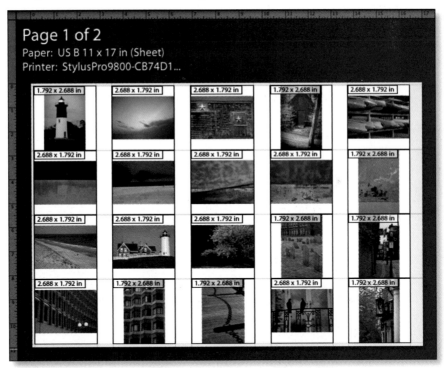

Figure 6-18

None of the elements in the Guides panel will appear on a print.

6

Figure 6-20

⌘+5 or Ctrl+5
Open and
close the Page
panel

Page panel

With the settings on the Page panel you can add other elements to the printed page along with the photos; see Figure 6–20.

Page Background Color: new in Lightroom 3, you can specify a solid color to print on the page background around the photos. Tick the box to enable the feature, then click the color swatch to set the color using the color picker; see Figure 6–21.

Figure 6-21

Identity Plate: as in Slideshow and Web, you can add a graphical or textual overlay, such as a logo, your studio name, etc. to your prints. First, check the box to enable the Identity Plate, then click the preview to choose one from the dropdown list, or to make a new one. The Identity Plate in the Print module works exactly the same as in Slideshow and Web, where the Identity Plate is covered further. Also see the tip below for a cool way to add custom borders and graphics to your photos using Identity Plates.

- **Angle:** the default is 0 degrees; click the number for a popup menu with preset rotation values; see Figure 6–22.

Figure 6-22

- **Override Color:** enabling this option will fill your identity plate with the specified color, regardless of the colors originally used.

- **Opacity:** sets the level of transparency for the identity plate. This is useful when you're using the identity plate as a watermark.

- **Scale:** enter a value to enlarge or reduce the Identity Plate. You can also click and drag in the main preview to reposition and/or resize your Identity Plate.

Note that you can't do this if you have multiples of the same image on the page and have Render on Every Image selected; see below.

- **Render Behind Image:** when checked, the Identity Plate will be placed behind the photo(s).

- **Render on Every Image:** applies the selected Identity Plate to every photo in the layout. Enable this if you're applying logos/watermarks, borders or other graphics on the photos (see the tip that follows this section).

Printing custom borders or graphics on your photos

In addition to the main identity plate, in the Print module (and Slideshow and Web) you can make unlimited, additional identity plates. You can use Identity Plates to overlay customized borders or other graphical elements on your photos. Design your border or other artwork in Photoshop, making sure to leave areas transparent so the photo can show through. Save the file from Photoshop as a PNG and bring it into Lightroom as an identity plate. On the Page panel, you can specify your border as the active Identity Plate.

Watermarking: also new in Lightroom 3 is a customizable watermarking feature. Tick the box to turn on the watermark, then select one from the list. Setting up watermarks is discussed in detail in Chapter 5.

Page Options

- **Page Numbers:** with this option enabled, the Print module will add a number to the bottom right corner of each page in a multi-page job.

- **Page Info:** shows print job information such as sharpening, color management settings and printer.

- **Crop Marks:** places crop marks outside the corners of the cell(s).

Photo Info: this is text displayed below each photo in the layout. The text is placed within each cell, so adding Photo Info slightly reduces the size of the photo. If you need an exact photo size and are also using Photo Info, you'll need to compensate accordingly. To apply Photo Info, check the box, then choose the kind of information to show using the popup menu; see Figure 6–23 next page.

To make your own style of Photo Info, choose Edit… from the popup menu. This opens the Text Template Editor (see Figure 6–24). Here you can configure any kind of information to show with each photo. When you're done setting up your text template, be sure to save it by clicking the Preset menu at the top of

Figure 6-23

the window and choose "Save Current Settings As New Preset…" (Note that this "Save…" option may be disabled in some cases if you are storing presets within the catalog, instead of the Lightroom Presets folder on disk; check your Preferences setting for this.)

Font Size: this sets the size of the type for the text elements in points. All type options use the same size, and you currently can't choose the font.

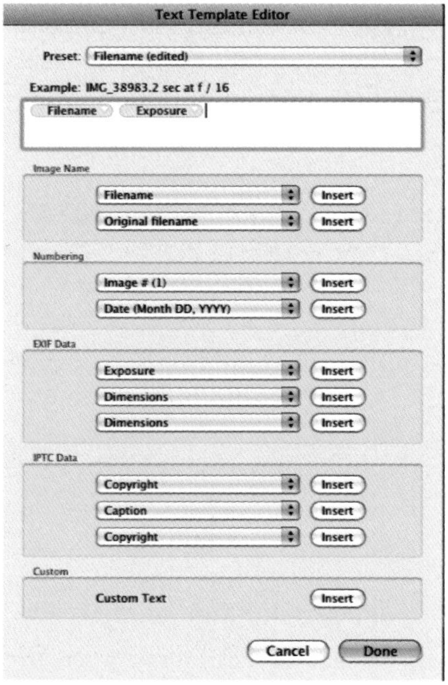

Figure 6-24

Multi-page jobs

Depending on the number of photos and the layout options used, you may often end up with a print job comprised of multiple pages. All Layout Styles provide support for multi-page jobs.

The Toolbar shows how many pages are in the current job (see Figure 6–25) and indicates which page you're previewing. There are arrow buttons for moving forward and back in the multi-page print job. Click the square button to go to the first page.

Figure 6-25

If the Info Overlay is enabled (as shown on Figure 6–16) it will also display page information.

Picture Package

Use a Picture Package when you want to print multiple copies of a photo(s) at different sizes; see Figure 6–26. With Picture Package, each individual photo in the print job will go on a separate page. (Each photo can have multiple pages using different layouts, but to put multiple photos at different sizes *all on one page* you should use Custom Package instead; see next section.)

Figure 6-26

Picture Package is a good solution for wedding, portrait and event photographers who need to lay out pages for printing client photos in a variety of sizes. The panels and settings for Picture Package are similar to those of Single Image/Contact Sheet, with a couple of important differences.

To start, make sure you have the photos organized the way you want. Then apply a Page Setup for the paper size you'll be using. Next, choose a template or a the Picture Package Layout Style. Then customize the layout for your print job.

Keep in mind that if you have, say, six pictures to print, Picture Package will start by making six pages of identical layouts, each for one photo. The number of pages in the job is shown on the Toolbar.

6

Manual layout in Picture Package

In Picture Package, you can click and drag to rearrange or scale the photos on the page. Click within the picture and drag it around to reposition it; you will feel it "snap" to positions within the page grid. Click and drag one of the control handles to change the size of the cells, which also scales the photos; see Figure 6–27. This is the easiest way to put together your rough layout, but for more precision you'll probably need to go to the right-side panels to fine tune the numeric settings.

Figure 6-27

Right-click or Ctrl+Click on a photo on the page
Select from the contextual menu to rotate or delete the cell

Also, in a Picture Package, if any cells are overlapping, a warning triangle is shown at the top right of the page preview; see Figure 6–28. However, Picture Package *will* allow you to print with photos overlapping. (Think about the creative possibilities here.)

⌘+Z or Ctrl+Z
Undo the last operation. Continue pressing to undo further back

To duplicate a cell within a Picture Package layout, hold Option or Alt and click and drag the cell. A copy will be placed in the position where you release the mouse. You can then change the settings for that cell if needed.

Figure 6-28

⌘+Shift+Z or Ctrl+Shift+Z
Redo the last operation. Continue pressing to redo further forward

You can drag and drop photos from within the filmstrip to add them to the layout. In Picture Package, doing this will change all the photos on the current page(s).

Image Settings panel

Use these settings to configure how each photo is placed within the cells (see Figure 6–29). **All the photos in the Picture Package will use the same settings.**

Zoom to Fill and **Rotate to Fit** function the same as in Single Image/Contact Sheet, discussed earlier in this chapter.

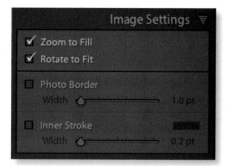

Figure 6-29

Photo Border: you can set the width of an outer, white border around each photo (but you can't change the color). Uncheck the box if you don't want an outer border.

Inner Stroke: this is an additional border that's placed along the edge of the photo, inside the Photo Border described above. Tick the box to enable it, then drag the slider or enter a numeric value to set the width. Click the swatch to pick a color for the Inner Stroke.

Rulers, Grid & Guides panel

These settings provide visual aids to help you position the photos on the page. Tick the checkbox for Show Guides to enable them; see Figure 6–30.

Rulers: tick the box to show the rulers, or use the shortcut. Use the popup menu above to select the ruler units.

Figure 6-30

Page Bleed: this turns on and off the visual preview for the live area of the page. If your Page Setup supports a bleed, you'll see it shown in the preview. If not, the bleed will show as a gray area around the margins of the page.

Page Grid: this checkbox enables or disables the Grid, which is displayed in light blue lines behind the photos. The Grid Snap popup menu (see Figure 6–30) allows you to choose whether to snap photos to other cells or to the grid as you drag to reposition them, or to turn snapping off. If you're manually adjusting the layout and you need precise positioning, the snapping feature really helps.

Image Cells: when this is enabled, outlines will show around the cells on each page. (These will not print.)

Dimensions: when enabled, this displays the size (and resolution, if applicable) for each photo on the page, in ppi. If Print Resolution is enabled on the Print Job panel (covered later in this chapter) the resolution ppi will not be displayed.

Cells panel

This panel provides controls for adding and removing cells and pages to and from the Picture Package, and for adjusting the size of selected cells; see Figure 6–31.

Figure 6-31

6

The top section of the panel is labeled "Add to Package". There are six buttons showing size dimensions. Click a button to place a new cell, using the size shown, on the current page. To the right of each button is a popup menu (see Figure 6–32) where you can choose a different size to assign to that button. From the popup menu, click Edit… to make a new size of your own.

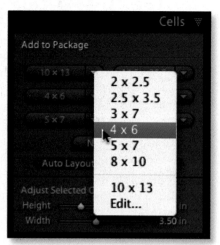

Figure 6-32

You can click a button multiple times to add more cells of that size to the page. If the new cell you're adding won't fit on the current page, a new page is automatically added.

To create a new, blank page in the current template click the **New Page** button (see Figure 6–33). All the page layouts in the current package are shown together in the preview area, but the layout shows the pages for only one photo at a time. The maximum number of pages you can use for each photo is six; this applies whether you use New Page or by auto-adding cells. To navigate between pages, use the forward and back buttons on the Toolbar.

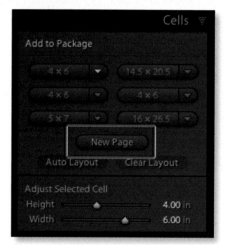

Figure 6-33

To delete a page from the layout, place your cursor over it, then click the red X at the top left of the page (see Figure 6–34).

Clicking the Auto Layout button to the left and below New Page tells Lightroom to arrange the existing photos/cells in the most economical manner possible. **This will affect all cells and all pages;** if you do this and then change your mind, you can Undo using the command under the Edit menu or the shortcut.

Figure 6-34

Clear Layout, below and to the right of New Page, will remove all the cells from all pages. This will also delete all but the first page in the current layout.

The Adjust Selected Cell sliders in the bottom section of the panel allow you to resize the currently selected cell. It's often difficult, if not impossible, to set the sliders to an exact number by dragging them. Double-click the value and then you can type in a number. Remember to press Return or Enter when you're done typing.

Page panel

This panel offers most of the same controls as Single Image/Contact Sheet covered earlier in this chapter: Page Background Color, Identity Plate, and Watermarking.

Using a Picture Package, you can also check the box to apply Cut Guides. When Cut Guides are enabled, you can use the adjacent popup menu to choose either solid lines or corner crop marks.

Custom Package

For total control over the photos and their position on each page, use a Custom Package. This works essentially the same as the Picture Package style, but you can use multiple photos on any number of pages. The controls in Picture Package that are *not* available in Custom Package are Zoom to Fit and Auto Layout; these functions are irrelevant in the Custom Package.

Don't forget to do your Page Setup first. Then choose Custom Package from the Layout Styles panel.

The easiest way to start laying out a Custom Package is to simply drag and drop photos on the page, then resize and position them where you want them. You can also place cells first (using the controls on the Cells panel as described in Picture Package), then drag and drop your photos into them.

Like Picture Package, in Custom package it's possible to have photos overlapping. However, in Custom Package you can right-

Figure 6-35

click or Ctrl+click for a contextual popup menu with many additional options. From this menu, for example, you can change the stacking order of the pictures by sending them forward or back, rotate or delete the cell, automatically match the cell to the photo aspect ratio, or *anchor* the cell (see Figure 6–35).

6

Anchoring a cell places it and the photo it contains in the same position on all pages. With this feature, along with the fact that you can overlap images, you can create all kinds of elaborate layouts, including customized background, logo or branding elements, etc. that extend far beyond what you can do with identity plates or watermarks.

Note that the option for Lock to Photo Aspect Ratio is not available in Custom Package. You can, however, Rotate to Fit and Rotate Cells in Custom Package.

I hope the functionality offered by the addition of the Custom Package inspires you to put together all kinds of creative print layouts that were difficult or impossible before. Instead of simply having photos in your catalog, imagine having a set of additional graphics, created in Photoshop, that you use to combine with your photos to make exciting print layouts.

Save a template
Particularly with Print layouts, if you spend any significant amount of time working on a layout, be sure to save a template when you're done. If you make changes to the layout and want to update the template with the new settings, use the Template Browser menu options to Update with Current Settings.

The Print Job panel
After laying out your page(s), configure the options on the Print Job panel (see Figure 6–36). The choices you make here will determine the destination and quality of the printed output.

Figure 6-36

Print To:
This popup menu allows you to spool the job to your printer or to generate a JPG file. (Printing JPG files from Lightroom is very useful when preparing files to be printed by a lab or service bureau, which is explained in detail at the end of this Print section.) Changing the Print To: setting will determine the options available below.

Draft Mode Printing
When Draft Mode Printing is enabled, Lightroom outputs the image data from the photo previews, not from the full-resolution files on disk. This can

6

dramatically speed print time but, of course, produces lower quality output. With Draft Mode enabled, the rest of the Print Job options become disabled. Use Draft Mode Printing if you only need a very rough print of the photos. This can be handy sometimes, such as when you just need a quick contact sheet to compare comps. Otherwise, for the best quality prints, leave Draft Mode Printing unchecked.

Print Resolution

When Print Resolution is checked, you can specify an output resolution in pixels per inch (ppi). Regardless of their native resolutions, all the photos in the print job will be resampled to the specified resolution as they are output from Lightroom. Depending on the size and native resolutions of the photos you're printing and their output sizes, this usually results in either *upsampling* or *downsampling*. During upsampling, Lightroom interpolates the original image data to make new pixels for the output. In downsampling, the reverse occurs: pixel data is discarded to match the output to the specified resolution. The maximum Print Resolution you can set in Lightroom is 720 ppi; the minimum is 72 ppi.

As mentioned earlier, the importance of higher resolution determines the ability to resolve more detail and make larger prints. The resolution that an image can be made to different print sizes is based entirely on the requirements of the printing medium, and the intended viewing distance determines the necessary resolution for high-quality output. Depending entirely on the final size and the detail in the original photo, it's safe to assume that most photos should be printed between 180 and 480 ppi.

For example, to reproduce high-quality photographs in a book like this one, the image file must be somewhere around 300 ppi at final print size. A high quality inkjet print most often requires resolution between 180 and 240 ppi at final print size. A very large print, one that a viewer needs to stand several feet from to view, can be printed at 180 ppi (or less) with good results. Huge, building-size billboards can be successfully printed using files of 100 ppi and less.

It's usually OK to print multiple photos that have different native resolutions all at once, as long as they are all within the specified tolerance. However, this can be impractical, and sometimes resampling is necessary to produce the best possible quality. For example, if you're printing a group of photos that at their final print size will have different resolutions, you may want to resample all of them to the same resolution so that the printed results appear similar.

Example A: A 10 x 10 inch file at 100 ppi is the same as a 1 x 1 inch file at 1000 ppi.

6

Example B: A photo with a resolution of 1000 x 3000 pixels is:

- 10 x 30 inches at 100 ppi

- 5 x 15 inches at 200 ppi

- 2 x 6 inches at 500 ppi

Resolution is also discussed in Chapter 5.

Whenever possible, leave the Print Resolution option unchecked
If a photo, when scaled to final print size, falls anywhere between 180 ppi and 480 ppi, it's usually best to leave it at its native resolution. The negative effects of resampling may produce worse results than leaving the file at a lower resolution.

Print Sharpening
Tick the checkbox to have Lightroom apply output sharpening during the print job. Like the capture Sharpening controls in Develop and Export, Lightroom's Print Sharpening is based on modern algorithms developed by Bruce Fraser and his colleagues at Pixel Genius, LLC.

Choose an amount (Low, Standard or High) and a media type (Matte or Glossy paper; Matte applies stronger sharpening). If you're printing to glossy or semi-gloss paper, use Glossy. For art papers and canvas, use Matte. Using these simple menu selections, Lightroom is often capable of applying the ideal sharpening for print. Make a few test prints using different settings to determine what works best for certain photos. If you have Photoshop, you might also make test prints using different sharpening methods in both Lightroom and Photoshop.

Lightroom can apply auto-sharpening for any file between 180 and 720 ppi. If your file falls outside this range, and you're not resampling, you'll need to consider alternatives.

Don't over-sharpen
If you've used Photoshop to resize or sharpen your files for printing, leave Lightroom's Print Sharpening off.

Color management
You have two options for Color Management when printing from Lightroom.

1. Have Lightroom do the color output using an ICC profile; or

2. Let the printer do the color management.

For accurate color, in nearly all cases I recommend using ICC profiles and having Lightroom handle the color management. I always use this method, unless I'm printing black and white; see the next section.

Click the black triangle button at the top right of the panel to show additional information about the settings; see Figure 6–37.

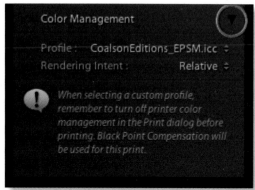

Figure 6-37

To do this, select a profile from the popup menu; see Figure 6–38. If none are listed in the menu, select Other... A dialog box appears that allows you to add profiles into Lightroom. All the available profiles on your computer are shown here. Choose the ICC profile made for your printer and the type of paper(s) you are using.

If no printer profiles are listed, you can download them from your printer and/or paper manufacturer's Web site. For example, if you're using an Epson printer and Epson paper, you can get the profile from the Epson Web site. If you're using an Epson printer and Ilford paper, you will need to look on the Ilford site for the correct profile. Make sure to use the profile made specifically for your model of printer. Unfortunately, in rare cases, none will be available, and you'll need to use the closest alternative or use Printer Color Management (discussed momentarily).

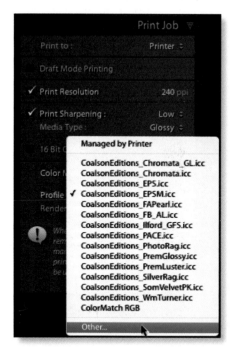

Figure 6-38

6

In the Choose Profiles window, check the box(es) for the printer/paper profile(s) you want to add to Lightroom and click ок; see Figure 6–39. When added, they will remain in the Profile popup for future use.

○ ○ ○	**Choose Profiles**	

Choose profiles to appear in Custom Profile popup:

☐ Pro9800 7800 Canva...	/Library/Printers/EPSON/InkjetPrinter/ICCProfiles/Pro9800 ...
☐ Pro9800 7800 Canva...	/Library/Printers/EPSON/InkjetPrinter/ICCProfiles/Pro9800 ...
☐ Pro9800 7800 DWMP...	/Library/Printers/EPSON/InkjetPrinter/ICCProfiles/Pro9800 ...
☐ Pro9800 7800 DWMP_PK	/Library/Printers/EPSON/InkjetPrinter/ICCProfiles/Pro9800 ...
☐ Pro9800 7800 EMPB_MK	/Library/Printers/EPSON/InkjetPrinter/ICCProfiles/Pro9800 ...
☑ Pro9800 7800 EMPB_PK	/Library/Printers/EPSON/InkjetPrinter/ICCProfiles/Pro9800 ...
☐ Pro9800 7800 EMP_MK	/Library/Printers/EPSON/InkjetPrinter/ICCProfiles/Pro9800 ...
☐ Pro9800 7800 EMP_PK	/Library/Printers/EPSON/InkjetPrinter/ICCProfiles/Pro9800 ...
☐ Pro9800 7800 PGP	/Library/Printers/EPSON/InkjetPrinter/ICCProfiles/Pro9800 ...
☐ Pro9800 7800 PGPP	/Library/Printers/EPSON/InkjetPrinter/ICCProfiles/Pro9800 ...
☐ Pro9800 7800 PGPP170	/Library/Printers/EPSON/InkjetPrinter/ICCProfiles/Pro9800 ...
☐ Pro9800 7800 PGPP250	/Library/Printers/EPSON/InkjetPrinter/ICCProfiles/Pro9800 ...
☐ Pro9800 7800 PLPP	/Library/Printers/EPSON/InkjetPrinter/ICCProfiles/Pro9800 ...
☐ Pro9800 7800 PLPP250	/Library/Printers/EPSON/InkjetPrinter/ICCProfiles/Pro9800 ...
☐ Pro9800 7800 PLPP260	/Library/Printers/EPSON/InkjetPrinter/ICCProfiles/Pro9800 ...
☐ Pro9800 7800 PPG250	/Library/Printers/EPSON/InkjetPrinter/ICCProfiles/Pro9800 ...
☐ Pro9800 7800 PPSmC	/Library/Printers/EPSON/InkjetPrinter/ICCProfiles/Pro9800 ...
☐ Pro9800 7800 PQIJP_MK	/Library/Printers/EPSON/InkjetPrinter/ICCProfiles/Pro9800 ...
☐ Pro9800 7800 PQIJP_PK	/Library/Printers/EPSON/InkjetPrinter/ICCProfiles/Pro9800 ...
☐ Pro9800 7800 PSP	/Library/Printers/EPSON/InkjetPrinter/ICCProfiles/Pro9800 ...
☐ Pro9800 7800 PSPP	/Library/Printers/EPSON/InkjetPrinter/ICCProfiles/Pro9800 ...

☐ Include Display Profiles

(Cancel) (OK)

Figure 6-39

Next, choose the Rendering Intent; see Figure 6–40. This setting determines how the colors in the photo are translated to the printer"s color space. The two available rendering intents in Lightroom are *Perceptual* and *Relative*.

Figure 6-40

There's more about color management and rendering intents in Chapters 1 and 5.

Your printer (and the printer at the lab) has a specific range of colors it can print, called its *color gamut*. Perceptual rendering compresses the range of colors in the photo to preserve their visual appearance on the print. Relative keeps all the colors in the photo that the printer can reproduce as-is, and clips the *out-of-gamut* colors to their nearest equivalent.

If I want to match most of the colors in the photo as closely as possible, I will use Relative. Relative preserves the tonal relationships in the photo. However, for photos with very saturated colors, especially blues, oranges and greens, Perceptual sometimes gives a nicer overall appearance, even though some of the colors may shift a bit. Perceptual better preserves the color relationships. Only testing will tell you which is the better rendering intent for a given photo, but in general, if you want your photos to look nice but don't care if they are totally accurate, use Perceptual. If you're really trying to match exact colors and tones, you must use Relative.

It's critical that if you use Lightroom's color management with an ICC profile and rendering intent, that you disable all color management in the printer driver; see the "Printing the Job" section below.

Get custom profiles

If you have a device like the X-Rite ColorMunki or EyeOne Pro, you can make your own printer profiles. If not, you can use a service to do it. It's simple; you download and print a set of test targets using the provided instructions, let them cure, and mail them in. The service bureau makes your own custom profile from the targets you printed and typically sends them to you by email. For this service, I highly recommend http://www.cathysprofiles.com. You can also Google "custom printer profiles" for more options.

Using printer color management

If you can't, or don't want to, have Lightroom handle color management, set the popup menu to *Managed by Printer.* Lightroom's color management controls become disabled. You then make all your color management settings in the printer driver screens.

One example of when this might apply: I use Epson's Advanced Black and White driver options for making black and white prints and have been very pleased with the results. In this case, I turn *off* Lightroom's color management altogether and use only the driver settings to handle the output.

You should also set the menu to Managed by Printer if you're sending the files to a raster image processor (or "RIP", such as ImagePrint, Qimage, ColorBurst, etc.) and want color management handled there.

Soft proofing in Photoshop

It's important to remember that because a monitor is a *transmissive* device (transmitting light to generate color on the screen) and a print is a *reflective* image (made visible by light reflecting from the surface of the paper and ink) it is physically impossible to have a print look *exactly* like what you see on screen.

However, in Photoshop, *soft proofing* provides a reasonable simulation of the printed output on-screen, and with practice, you can train your eye to accurately predict how your prints will look.

As of this writing, soft proofing is not available in the current version of Lightroom. If you need this capability, you can open the file from Lightroom into Photoshop, do your soft proof and make any necessary adjustments, then return the file to Lightroom as a TIF file to print.

Save or update your template

All the settings described above can be stored within a Lightroom Print template. After you've configured everything the way you want (and presumably, tested the results) you should, in most cases, save a template for later, or update a template you've previously saved. It's a good idea to name your print templates with text indicators describing what conditions for which the print template was made.

Printing the job to your own printer

Click the Print button at the bottom of the right panel group (see Figure 6–41). The printer driver dialog box appears. Because printer driver dialog boxes vary in the extreme, I can't go into further detail on this here, but general settings to check include paper size, media type and color management settings. I've included screenshots for Epson 9800 on Mac and Canon ipf6100 on Windows (see Figure 6–42 and 6–43); consult your printer documentation for more about its specific settings.

Figure 6-41

Apply the appropriate settings for the print job. **If you're using Lightroom's color management, you need to take special precautions to make sure that color management is completely turned off in the printer driver.** The vast majority of color problems on prints are due to "double color management". Depending on your printer and driver software, this will be found in different places. While working in the dialog boxes, most printer drivers allow you to save

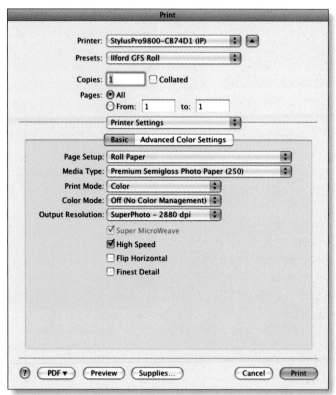

Figure 6-42

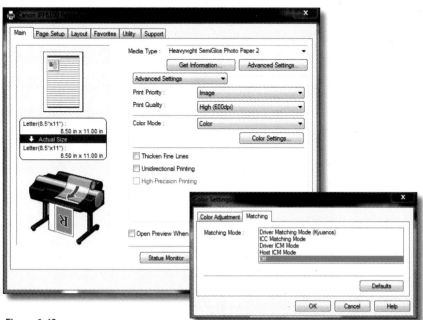

Figure 6-43

6

your custom settings for the driver. Along with saving a Lightroom template, saving your printer driver settings will make the process faster on future jobs.

Finally, you'll need to click Print in the printer driver one more time to spool the job to the printer (or file).

The Print One button (see Figure 6–44) allows you to quickly send a print job, bypassing the driver dialog box and using the most recent settings. This can be a real time saver, just make sure you have the correct settings in place before clicking.

Figure 6-44

Update your template!
All the printer driver settings also get stored with the print template when it's saved, so be sure to save/update your template when you're done with your print settings.

Preparing print files to send to a lab

You can very effectively use Lightroom to generate print-ready files for printing by a lab.

All photographic print labs accept JPG files for output. Lightroom's Print module has controls for you to save out JPG files using the current print layout and settings, instead of spooling the job to your own printer.

Perform the workflow steps as usual, up to the point where you are setting the options in the Print Job panel.

Figure 6-45

Then, set the popup menu for **Print To: jpeg File;** see Figure 6–45.

The Print Job panel options will change to let you specify:

File Resolution: the resolution in ppi for the output file. Use the info provided by your lab for this.

Print Sharpening: check the box to enable output sharpening, and use the popup menu to select the amount of sharpening to apply.

Media Type: choose the kind of paper to be used: Glossy or Matte. (If you're printing on semi-gloss, satin or "luster" paper, choose Glossy.)

JPEG Quality: I strongly recommend you always use Quality set at 100 for making JPG print files.

Custom File Dimensions: this lets you specify a size for the print file. This option provides the ability to produce print files at different sizes from a single print layout, but in practice, this is rare. If you've done your layout carefully, you most often won't need to enable this. Otherwise, type to enter the new dimensions here, and Lightroom will resize your printed output as the JPG files are being created.

Color Management: try to get a printer profile from your lab. Select the Edit… option to add it to the list using the instructions above. You need to know what kind of machine the lab is using to make your prints. If you are having laser prints made (Lambda, LightJet, Frontier, Chromira, etc.) you can safely use SRGB. If you are having inkjet prints made, it's OK to use Adobe RGB.

Ask your print vendor for a list of specifications to guide your decisions when making these settings.

When the correct settings have been entered, click the Print to File button. Lightroom will prompt you to choose a location to save the files. When you're ready, click Save. Lightroom will output JPG file(s) for each page of your print job After you get the prints back from the lab, you can decide for yourself whether it's worth saving these files for future use. (Because it's so easy to make print files from Lightroom, I usually don't.)

Getting the best possible printed output

The printer and paper you use will make a big difference in the quality of your prints. Most mid- to high-end printers, when using good quality papers, are

6

capable of making very accurate, beautiful prints straight from Lightroom, or from JPG files made by Lightroom. Here are a few tips to help you get good prints.

Use good paper

You really do get what you pay for. When you're printing your photos for display, don't skimp. For inkjet, I highly recommend papers from Hahnemühle, Harman, Premier and Ilford. For laser imagers, Fuji Crystal Archive is usually the way to go, and the Kodak metallic papers are really nice, too.

Photo papers (gloss, luster, semi-gloss, etc.) provide the widest gamuts and the deepest blacks. This results in prints that look vivid, clear and show the most "depth".

Art papers (matte, cotton rag, etc.) provide a more artsy look. Prints on art papers may lack the three-dimensional characteristics of those on photo papers and thus appear more "painterly". The range of colors possible with art papers is significantly smaller than with photo papers, and most art papers are available only for inkjet.

Choose the right paper for each image: photos with large, solid-color areas will look better on smooth papers. Photos with lots of fine detail look great on textured paper or canvas.

Use good profiles

For the most part, the profiles you download from a printer or paper manufacturer can get close to optimal color, but they weren't made using *your* printer. Don't expect perfect color from "canned" profiles. A custom printer profile, made specifically for your printer and paper combination, will produce the best possible results. (See the tips earlier in this chapter, or search the Web for "custom printer profiles".)

Adjust derivative photos to match the printer/paper gamut

Different papers have widely varying color gamuts. It's highly likely that you won't get equally good results printing the same photo on a variety of substrates by only using different profiles and driver settings. Sometimes it's necessary to adjust the image prior to output to compensate for the destination gamut. It depends on the printer, the paper and the ink.

For example, Ilford Galerie Gold Fibre Silk has an extremely wide gamut on an Epson Stylus Pro 9800. The colors in most photos translate well to the print, with not much shifting of color or tone (using my custom profile). Still, I usually lighten the shadows a bit (Fill Light is good for this), and bump the Saturation by +4 to +7.

On art papers (and especially canvas) it's necessary to tweak the file settings more dramatically in order to produce similar appearances in tone and/or color.

Use vcs to make different versions, with different adjustments, for the various printing conditions you encounter. This procedure is described in detail earlier in this chapter.

Print anomalies

Some users have reported seeing differences in prints made from Lightroom versus those from Photoshop or other software. Problems have been reported on a few printers from Epson, HP and Canon.

There are several possible reasons for this. First, as Lightroom is still a relatively new program, some printer drivers have trouble with Lightroom's color-managed output. In cases where the problem lies with Lightroom's printing pipeline, Adobe has worked diligently to iron out the bugs. Unfortunately, this hasn't always been the case with problems in printer drivers. Printer manufacturers notoriously blame the operating system (and vice versa), so these kinds of problems are resolved slowly, if ever.

It's important to note that true software bugs related to printing from Lightroom are rare; the vast majority of prosumer and professional printers are capable of producing excellent prints from Lightroom. **Problems with printed output are most often due to incorrect settings in Lightroom, the printer driver, or both.**

Google the name of your printer model along with "Lightroom printing" etc. to see if people are discussing problems with your particular printer.

Test, test, test

If you're planning to do a lot of printing from Lightroom, I recommend you do your own tests to see the results on paper. Lightroom won't preview settings such as resolution and sharpening in the Print module, and there's no substitute for an actual print.

Print the same photos using different settings, and you will quickly get a feel for how those settings affect the final output. Get the hang of Lightroom's printing workflow and identify key variables before you're up against a deadline or an important print job.

CHAPTER 7

WEB

7

Lightroom Web Galleries

In Chapter 3, we looked briefly at Library's Publish Services, which you can use to upload image files to photo sharing services like Flickr. (There's a lot more about Publish Services in Chapter 9.)

But going far beyond Publish Services, which only publish image files, you can use Lightroom's Web module to build complete photo galleries for your own Web site. Lightroom outputs all the required HTML, CSS and images used for each gallery. You don't need to know anything about coding to make galleries with the Web module.

Like the other output modules, Web galleries are usually started with templates. These are based on the *Layout Styles* installed with Lightroom. (In previous versions of Lightroom, Layouts were called *Engines*.) Lightroom comes with some built-in Layout Styles, and you can find more online. You can see which Layout Styles are installed in the top right panel; see Figure 7–1. The

Figure 7-1

functionality and design of your Web gallery depends entirely on the Layout Style selected. We'll look at Layout Styles in more detail later in this chapter.

Before you start making a Web gallery, it's a good idea to do some organizing in Library first. Decide which photos to use and put them in Collections or Smart Collections. This makes it easier to choose which images are included, plus you can rearrange the photos as you like for each gallery. Depending on your organizational system, you might need to go back and forth between Web and Library a few times to get all the photos collected.

With the photos all chosen and sorted, you then use the Web module controls to customize the gallery. When you're done, if you want to use Lightroom to transfer your Web gallery files to your Web site's hosting server you will need the FTP account information. Otherwise, you can just save the gallery on your hard drive; you'll still be able to view the pages in a browser with full functionality. These options are discussed in detail toward the end of this chapter.

Here's the quick overview of the workflow to make a Web gallery:

1. In Library, organize the photos that will go into the gallery

2. In Web module, show all the panels

3. Make sure the correct photos are showing in the filmstrip

4. Check the Toolbar options and change as necessary

5. Choose a template and/or Layout Style

6. Configure the look-and-feel of the gallery: colors, type, fonts, etc.

7. Preview your gallery pages and make changes if necessary

8. Have Lightroom render the final Web gallery files, and either

   a. Upload them to your Web server, or

   b. Export the Web gallery to your hard disk

CHOOSING THE PHOTOS FOR YOUR WEB GALLERY

As with Slideshow and Print, in Web you can use folders and collections as sources for the gallery. Put simply, you have two basic options: use a folder with filters applied to only show the photos that will go into the gallery and hide the rest, or create a collection specifically for this gallery.

Using a collection as the basis for your Web gallery has some distinct advantages. I most often recommend making a smart collection using workflow keywords (as described in Chapter 3) but you could manually make a regular collection instead and use that as the source for your gallery, which I also do. All types of collections (and folder sources) will remember the latest settings applied in the Web module.

Smart collections would need to be created in the Library module before you start working with them in the Web gallery; you can modify the settings for smart collections from within the Web module, but keep in mind this will also affect those smart collections elsewhere. Also, you can't apply keywords to photos from within the Web module; if you're using workflow keywords to manage your smart collections for Web galleries, you'd need to apply those keywords in Library first. You can, however, apply or change attributes such as ratings and labels using the keyboard shortcuts also described in Chapter 3 and use these as criteria for the smart collection.

7

You can also make Web Collections from within the Web module. These are essentially the same as regular collections made in Library, with a special icon. With photos selected in the Filmstrip, click the + button on the Collections panel and select "Create Web Gallery". The new Web Collection will then be listed in the Collections panel in all the modules.

The main point of all this is that, one way or another, you should collect a unique set of photos for each new Web gallery. This will allow you to add and remove photos later if you wish, as well as tweaking the gallery layout settings, and easily regenerating the gallery, without having to worry about losing your selection of photos.

Obviously, your decisions for creating and organizing your galleries needs to be based on how you want to organize your photos on your Web site. On my Web site I have distinct portfolio sets that are organized and maintained in Lightroom. On the Web site, each portfolio is a direct representation of how the photos are organized in my Lightroom catalog. This makes it easy to add or remove photos from each individual gallery, and updating entire portfolios on my site just takes a few clicks and very little time.

SHOWING ALL THE WEB MODULE PANELS AND CONTROLS

The Web module is one of the areas in Lightroom where having all the panels open helps speed the workflow. Either click to expand each of the panels, or use the Tab and Shift+Tab. Also make sure the Toolbar is showing (T).

USING THE FILMSTRIP

Since you've already created a collection or smart collection, fine-tuning your selected photos will be easy. You can simply drag to rearrange photos in the Filmstrip or remove photos you don't want. Make sure that what you see in the Filmstrip reflects your final selections for this particular gallery.

SETTING TOOLBAR OPTIONS

The Toolbar has a setting for Use: All Filmstrip Photos, Selected Photos or Flagged photos; see Figure 7–2. If the Collection you're using only

Figure 7-2

contains photos that you intend to include in the gallery, make sure the Toolbar option is set to All Filmstrip Photos. If for some reason you have photos in the Filmstrip that you don't want to include, you can modify your Collection, or just click to select the photos you want to include and use the Selected Photos source. (However, as explained previously, using these temporary selections will likely mean more work later if you should change your mind or need to rebuild the gallery.)

The Toolbar also has buttons for "Go to First Page of Gallery" (see Figure 7–3), and for selecting previous and next photos. These can be useful for navigating through your gallery previews.

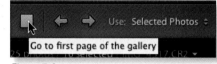

Figure 7-3

Use a small set of photos for setup

If you're building a Web gallery with lots of photos, changing templates and settings can result in slow performance. For the fastest response from the Web module, consider using a small, temporary set of photos to create your layouts. You can easily do this with Use: Selected Photos and just select a few of your photos from the full collection using the Filmstrip. Then, when you've finished your setup, change Use: back to All Filmstrip Photos.

SELECTING A TEMPLATE AND LAYOUT STYLE

To make a Web gallery, you'll first choose a template (or Layout Style) and then customize it to your liking. Whenever you switch to the Web module, the most-recently used settings are loaded for you.

Let's take a closer look at the relationship between Layout Styles and templates.

In Lightroom, a Web **Layout Style** (historically called the "Layout Engine") determines the layout and format to be used for the gallery. Different Layout Styles will offer different options. Lightroom comes with some preinstalled Flash and plain HTML layouts, which as their names imply, will use different programming technologies to construct and display your gallery.

Templates are listed in the Template Browser panel (see Figure 7–4) and are used to store presaved settings. By default, the templates you see in the Template Browser are from Lightroom's built-in HTML and Flash Layout Styles. Lightroom 3 comes with a whole bunch of new built-in templates. (After you've customized a Layout Style, you'll want to save your own template for later use, which we'll cover later in this chapter.)

Figure 7-4

7

As you move your mouse over the list of installed templates, you can see them in the Preview panel at the top left; see Figure 7-5. Also, the bottom left of the preview displays either "HTML" or an "*f*" for Flash.

Figure 7-5

Click on the name of a template to load it into the main preview area. When you click a template, Lightroom will also will switch to the Layout Style from which that template was made. Conversely, if you click a Layout Style, Lightroom will load the default template for that style.

Flash layouts can offer more visual appeal and customization of the design elements, transitions between photos, etc. The main disadvantage of a Flash gallery is that, although it may look nice, it's not well suited for search engine indexing. This is due to the programming code being embedded within the Flash file that displays the photos. Your photo metadata, including keywords and captions, is not visible to search engines. Secondarily, some people still resist using Flash, or have browser problems with Flash versions. Finally, in most cases, Flash galleries will take longer to load than HTML galleries. Besides these performance issues, I also think most Flash designs are generally too elaborate, and can easily distract from the photos themselves.

HTML galleries are very "search engine friendly": a search engine crawling the Web can find your HTML pages and read through their content, allowing the search engine to index the pages *and the photos themselves.* **If you have keywords embedded in your photos, the search engines will read them and index your photos accordingly.** Not so with Flash galleries. The potential drawback to pure HTML photo galleries is that you might not like the way they look, and you can't always include fancy transitions like fades, wipes, etc. However, I think this is outweighed by the speed and compatibility that straight HTML offers. If you want to have your photos found by people searching the Web, and you want a simple, clean layout, stick with HTML. (I almost always prefer HTML galleries over Flash; the exceptions may be situations where I don't care if the gallery is publicly visible, and I want to make a nice presentation for a specific client. In these cases, a Flash gallery may have more impact.)

Third-party layouts

There is a growing number of third-party Web gallery layouts available for Lightroom. You can greatly expand your range of options by installing additional Layout Styles. I've listed some of the best below, in no particular order:

- Slideshow Pro http://slideshowpro.net/products/slideshowpro

- LRG (Lightroom Galleries) http://www.lightroomgalleries.com

- LRB Portfolio http://lrbportfolio.com/

- Timothy Armes has produced several very nice looking (and functioning) layouts http://www.photographers-toolbox.com/

- TTG - The Turning Gate http://lr.theturninggate.net/html-galleries/

Also, the Adobe's Lightroom Exchange has all kinds of new plug-ins, presets and Web layouts:

http://www.adobe.com/cfusion/exchange/index.cfm?event=productHome&exc=25

Configuring gallery settings

After choosing a template or Layout Style as a starting point, you'll work through the controls on the right-side panels to customize your gallery design.

I usually start by styling the thumbnail pages. Most HTML templates use "index" pages for thumbnails, which link to individual pages that show each full-size photo. (Flash templates often have the thumbnails on the same page as the full-size photo.)

In both cases, using Lightroom's built-in templates, you can't change the size of the thumbnails, but you usually can change how many thumbnails will show on a single page. Some third-party Layout Styles allow you to adjust the size and presentation of thumbnails. (The add-on Web layouts will provide documentation for their controls.)

The available layout options depend on the Layout Style you use, and they vary widely. The following example is based on Lightroom's default HTML gallery, which is the one I use most often.

SITE INFO PANEL

The Site Info panel (see Figure 7–6, next page) provides controls for setting text on the page. In most built-in templates, each line of text is styled differently. Although you don't always have direct control over the text styles from within Lightroom, with some knowledge of CSS, you can change styles after you render the gallery files.

The top section of the Site Info panel includes:

- Site Title, such as "Nat Coalson Photography"

7

- Collection Title, something like "New Zealand, Spring 2009"

- Collection Description – you can enter more details about the photo gallery here, like "The Most Beautiful Place in the World". etc.

Note: this reference to "Collection" in the Web module has no relationship to Lightroom's collections image source. You can use whatever text you want here, regardless of how the photo collection itself may be named.

Click triangle buttons at the right of the text fields for quick access to recently used text values; see circled area.

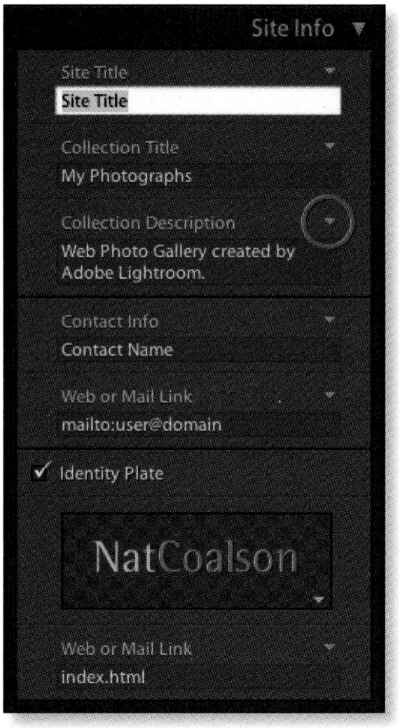

Edit type in the preview

When setting the Site Info type, instead of using the text entry fields on the panel, you can select the text in the preview and type directly on the page.

Figure 7-6

The middle section of the Site Info panel shows:

- Contact Info: this is the text used for the link at the bottom of each page. For example, you could enter text like "Email Me" and insert an email link, or use "Home Page" and provide a link to your Web site's main page.

- Web or Mail Link: this must be a correctly formatted URL. If you're using an email link, use the format *mailto:myemailaddress@mydomain.com.* If a link to a Web page, use the full address (including http://) such as http://mywebsiteaddress.com.

To remove any type element from the layout, leave the text field blank (select any text in the field and delete it).

Identity Plate

In the default HTML template, the bottom part of the Site Info panel allows you to apply and customize an Identity Plate. In other Layout Styles the Identity Plate may be in a different location, but the controls essentially work the same.

First, tick the box to enable the Identity Plate. Then click on the small preview to see a list of saved Identity Plates. If you want to make a new one, click Edit….

Then, in the Identity Plate Editor, choose whether to use a text or graphical Identity Plate. To use a graphic, you must first create an image file in other software such as Photoshop. Lightroom 3 now supports Identity Plate graphics using JPG, PNG, GIF, BMP and TIF. Click the Locate… button to find a file on your hard drive, or drag and drop a file from your desktop into the window.

(I keep all my Identity Plate files in my Lightroom Presets folder, but the file can physically be located anywhere on your hard drive. Note that if you move the original graphic file after using it in an Identity Plate, you will need to relink it.)

If you select the text option for your Identity Plate, type the text you want to use, then use the controls provided to style the text. The text must be selected to apply the styling.

Multiple font styles in one identity plate

By selecting different parts of the text, you can apply multiple text styles within a single text Identity Plate.

When you're done setting up your new Identity Plate, click the button at the bottom left that says Custom, then choose Save As…. Give your new Identity Plate a meaningful name, like "My Web Gallery ID plate", click Save, then click OK to apply the new Identity Plate to your Web gallery.

Your new Identity Plate will become available in all areas in Lightroom where you can specify an Identity Plate for a layout, including Print and Slideshow.

After applying the Identity Plate, you can enter a link to a Web page or email address that will be loaded when it's clicked. If you don't want to include a link on your Identity Plate, leave this field blank.

Provide a link to your Home Page

In the Site Info panel, the default HTML Lightroom Web templates provide the two places just described to create links to other Web pages or email. If you are adding Web galleries to an existing site, I recommend you be sure to use either the Identity Plate or the Web or Mail Link to include a link to the home page of the site. Otherwise, the Web gallery will be isolated from the rest of your Web site, offering users no way to get anywhere outside that specific Web gallery. This condition varies in other Layout Styles; some provide other ways to add outbound links from your gallery.

7

Color Palette

This panel allows you to specify colors for various elements within your layout; see Figure 7–7. The main elements to which you can apply color are listed down the left side of the panel. You can specify colors for the following items:

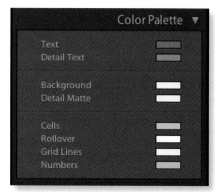

Figure 7-7

- **Text:** entered in the Site Info panel

- **Detail Text:** links and text on the large image pages

- **Background:** the main page background

- **Detail Matte:** the area surrounding the large image

- **Cells:** thumbnail backgrounds

- **Rollover:** the color to use for "highlighting" thumbnail cells as the user moves their cursor over each cell

- **Grid Lines:** lines separating thumbnail grid cells

- **Numbers:** numbers in the background of grid cells

Next to each element is a rectangular color swatch. (If you're using the HTML default template these will all be varying shades of gray and are easy to overlook.)

Hiding page elements

You can't actually "turn off" or remove any of these page elements using the Color Palette panel. However, you can easily hide elements by making them the same color as their backgrounds. These elements will still be included in the HTML code, even though they are invisible.

To change the color of an element, click its swatch. A color picker box appears with the name of the selected element along the top (see Figure 7–8).

Figure 7-8

⌘+R or Ctrl+R
Reloads/ refreshes the Web module preview.

If the color currently selected is a shade of gray, or white or black, and you want to apply a color, you will first need to click somewhere in the vertical saturation slider (called the "elevator") at the right side of the color picker. Then you'll see a full-color spectrum. Click inside the spectrum to choose the hue range you want, then use the saturation elevator to increase or decrease saturation.

The color picker is covered in detail in Chapter 4.

When you're done making changes in the color picker, click the X in the upper left corner of the picker or press Return/Enter.

If you want to cancel any changes you just made in the color picker (except for changing swatches) press Esc.

PREVIEWING THE WEB GALLERY

Though we've only worked through half of the panel settings, I want to switch gears and talk briefly about previewing your gallery. You've already been doing this; as you make changes to the settings you see the gallery preview continually updated in the main preview area. There will be times when you need to force Lightroom to make a new preview, or to preview the Web gallery in a browser.

Using our HTML gallery example, you can click the photos to navigate through the gallery and see all the pages and photos and adjust settings accordingly. Click a thumbnail to see the large image; click the large image to go back to thumbnails. Simple. If you're adjusting settings for the thumbnails, make sure you're looking at a thumbnail preview page; same goes for the large image pages. Otherwise you won't immediately see your changes.

In addition to previewing the Web gallery within Lightroom's image display area, you can also test it in the default Web browser on your computer. On the bottom of the left panel track is a button labeled "Preview in Browser…" (see Figure 7-9). Clicking this will render your gallery and load it into the default browser on your computer.

Figure 7-9

7

Previewing in a browser requires Lightroom to render temporary files for all the photos and can be quite slow. I recommend that you instead use the Web module's built-in preview whenever possible, or use a limited number of photos for your test previews.

If you want to test the gallery in multiple browsers, you should Export the gallery to disk and open the gallery files in any number of browsers of your choosing. Exporting Web galleries is discussed later in this chapter.

OK, back to styling your gallery.

Appearance panel

The Appearance panel is split into three sections; see Figure 7–10.

Common Settings are applied to all photos within this gallery. Tick the box to add drop shadows behind all photos. In the html default gallery you don't have any options for controlling drop shadows. Section borders are placed between the different areas of the page and can also be turned on and off. You can change the colors of the Section Borders by clicking the swatch.

The middle section of the Appearance panel contains options for Grid Pages within the Web gallery. (Of course, this is totally different than the Grid View in Library.) If you see a warning triangle to the right of the Grid Pages text, it's because you're looking at a large image page, not the thumbnails. The warning is telling you that if you make changes to those settings, you won't see the changes in the preview until you switch back to the Grid Page.

Figure 7-10

The grid you see in the panel represents rows and columns on your thumbnail pages. Click in the grid to change the number of rows and columns and the preview is updated immediately. (Don't click and drag; just click.)

If you have more images than can fit on one page of thumbnails, Lightroom will automatically add more pages—and links to them—in the bottom right corner of thepage footer; see Figure 7–11. (Make sure you can see the bottom of the page in the main preview area.)

Figure 7-11

One trick to setting up the thumbnail index page is deciding the right number of rows and columns for the number of photos you're showing. And though you have the option to use eight columns, I recommend that you refrain from doing this, because it's likely that people will need to scroll sideways to see all the photos. Most people aren't used to scrolling sideways and may not ever know there are more photos hiding over there. When possible, try to stick with thumbnails arranged in three or four columns.

Below the grid is a checkbox that turns the thumbnail numbers on and off. You can't change the type style for these numbers.

Finally, Photo Borders can be applied to thumbnails, or not. Click the swatch to change the color.

The bottom area of the Appearance panel is for Image Pages. These settings control the styles for the pages containing a single, large image. Again, if you see a warning triangle, it's because you're not looking at a large image page; click a thumbnail and the warning goes away.

The size of the large image can be set by dragging the slider or manually entering a value. This size shown here will be used for the size for the *longest side* of each photo in the gallery. This has several implications. First, if you have both horizontal and vertical photos in the gallery, you might be inclined to make the images really big so they fill up the screen. This works great for horizontal photos, but not as well for verticals, because people might not be able to see the whole photo at once. Having to scroll over a large photo can significantly degrade the user experience. The difficulties of choosing the size here are compounded if you have very wide panoramic images, square images, etc. You'll need to decide whether or not to present images with widely varying aspect ratios within a single gallery.

On the large image pages, Photo Borders can improve the overall presentation. I like to use very wide, white borders to set off the photos from the darker background. (This can really make colors pop.)

7

Image Info panel

This panel offers the ability to display up to two labels of textual information on the large image pages; see Figure 7–12. These Web gallery titles and captions are *not* necessarily the same as the metadata fields by the same names, though by default that's what they display. Tick the checkboxes to enable or disable Title and Caption text labels. The title is displayed above the photo; the caption below. You can use the dropdown menus to choose what information will be shown for each. Clicking the Edit… selection on this menu opens the Text Template Editor, where you can configure your own titling presets using a wide range of metadata and custom text entries; see Figure 7–13. These work very much like file naming templates, which are explained in Chapter 3.

Output settings panel

The Large Images Quality setting (see Figure 7–14) sets the level of JPG compression for the large images. There is a direct correlation between the Quality setting and the resulting file size. Higher quality = larger files; lower quality = smaller files. For most images you can usually get good quality at settings between 65 and 80, though some images will show unsightly compression artifacts in this range. JPG compression works best with large areas of solid color. Photos with very fine detail will always produce larger file sizes than those with less detail, even at the same Quality setting. Between 80 and 100, every incremental increase starts to significantly increase file size. 85 is usually the practical limit for most Web images.

Figure 7-12

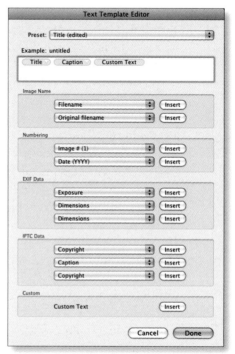

Figure 7-13

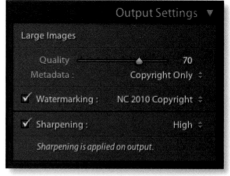

Figure 7-14

The Metadata popup menu (see Figure 7–15) gives you a very basic selection of what metadata to embed within the JPG files. This is independent from any metadata you may also be displaying on the pages; this setting refers specifically to what gets included *in the image files themselves.* "All" will include all metadata you've assigned to the file, including keywords, captions, titles and ratings, etc. "Copyright Only" is just that—everything else will be stripped from the exported image file that ends up in your Web gallery (but, of course, will remain on the original image within the Lightroom catalog).

Figure 7-15

Depending on the amount of metadata you've applied to a file, using Copyright Only can help reduce the size of the resulting files. This can be important in cases where fast loading is a priority over complete metadata, or where there are file size limitations. Unfortunately, Lightroom does not show you what the difference in file size will be without all the metadata; you'd need to compare the file sizes on your hard drive to see where they end up.

Watermarking: you can also apply a watermark to the photos in your Web gallery. Check the box to enable the option, then choose a watermark from the popup menu. Watermarks are covered in detail in Chapter 5.

Finally, to apply output sharpening to the files, tick the Sharpening box and choose a *strength* from the menu. You only have three choices: Low, Standard or High. With these simple controls Lightroom is pretty good at applying the optimal amount of sharpening for the size of the images being output for the gallery. This is especially true if you've done a good job sharpening the images at earlier stages of the workflow. Lightroom applies sharpening as the last step, after rendering the thumbnails and large images at the sizes specified by the Layout Style. I usually use High sharpening.

⌘+N or Ctrl+N
Make a new template

Saving a template

At this point, if you've made changes to the layout that you want to save for later, be sure to either create a new template or update the

Figure 7-16

settings for the current template. To make a new template, click the + button at the right of the Template Browser panel header; see Figure 7–16. Or, to update an existing preset using the current settings, right-click or Ctrl+click on the template and select that option from the popup menu.

7

UPLOADING YOUR WEB GALLERY TO A SERVER

When you've got your gallery set up the way you want, you can use Lightroom to upload the entire gallery to your Web server. Lightroom will render all the files for the gallery and then put them on the server using the account settings and directory locations you specify.

To do this you need to have a Web site/domain already set up, and have FTP access to the Web server. You'll also need to know a few things about the way the files and folders are structured on the server. If you're going to be publishing your own Web galleries to your own hosting account, I strongly recommend that you first understand the basics of Web hosting, hyperlinks and FTP file transfers.

With innumerable variables related to the setup and configuration of Web hosting servers, I can't possibly cover every scenario here. However, there are many settings and procedures that will apply in all cases.

Upload Settings panel

To upload files to a server, you need to first enter the FTP server and Subfolder information in the Upload Settings panel (see Figure 7–17).

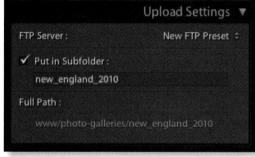

FTP Server

The first and most important
Figure 7-17

configuration settings to make are those for the FTP server. From the popup menu, select Edit… to open the Configure FTP File Transfer window.

In the Configure FTP File Transfer dialog box (see Figure 7–18), enter the server name or IP address, the user name and the password for the FTP account. If you plan to

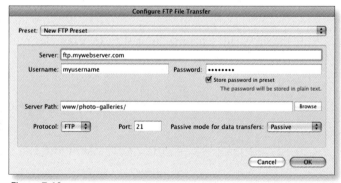

Figure 7-18

save a preset for this server, I recommend you also enable the option to store the password in the preset (unless you have some reason not to). This will simplify the uploading process in future sessions.

If you need to put the files in a folder other than the site root, enter the directory path in the Server Path field. Most often this would be something like /www/, /public_html/ etc. The use of leading and training slashes is important; check your hosting account documentation as necessary.

In most cases you can leave the Protocol, Port, and Passive Mode for Data Transfers fields at their default values.

If you're not sure what to enter for any of the above settings, check your Web hosting account information or ask your Web server administrator.

Before leaving this dialog box, be sure to save this as a new preset. At the top of the window, click the Preset: menu, and select Save Current Settings as New Preset. Be sure to give your preset a meaningful name.

Click OK to apply the FTP settings (or Cancel to leave the dialog box without saving changes).

Next, in the Upload Settings panel, you can choose to put the uploaded files into a subfolder (the default is a folder called "photos"). If you entered a value in the Server Path field the subfolder(s) will be created under that directory (see Figure 7–17).

At the bottom of the Upload Settings panel, the Full Path: text shows the complete directory path where the Web gallery will be uploaded (not including the domain name).

If you're sending someone a link to the gallery, you will need to provide the full URL (Web address) including the domain name and the Full Path shown in Lightroom.

Create multiple subfolders
You can create multiple subfolders by entering their names and directory path into the text field, separated by slashes, for example:
/photos/trips/new_mexico_2009/.

Always use Web-friendly names for directories
When you're creating any folders (and files) for Web use, don't use spaces, punctuation other than hyphens and underscores, or any special characters. Otherwise, Web browsers might not be able to access your pages.

Do a few test runs before sharing the link
It's likely that even with lots of experience under your belt you will occasionally do Web uploads or exports from Lightroom's Web module that, for one reason or another, don't turn out how you wanted. This is normal and should not be feared!

If you're under the gun, like when presenting to a client, it's a good idea to do a few trial runs with any new templates and settings that you haven't used before uploading the final gallery files and sharing the link. Just like in all Web site development, thorough testing is necessary to be sure everything's right before announcing your gallery with the world.

Upload the gallery

When you're done configuring your Web gallery, click the Upload button. Lightroom will generate all the files required for the gallery, including JPG images and HTML pages (and Flash files, if necessary) and will upload them to your Web server in the location specified.

Uploading does not save a local copy to your hard drive. When you use the Web module to upload gallery files directly to your server, no files are stored on your hard drive. If this matters to you, you have two options: 1) use Export instead, and manually upload the files using an FTP program, or 2) after using Lightroom to upload, use the FTP program to download copies to your local disk.

Update your template

All the panel settings—including Upload Settings—will be stored in the template. In the future, you will only need to tweak a few settings to publish new galleries!

Updating pre-existing Web galleries

Each time you upload or export a gallery from Lightroom's Web module, every file must be re-written. You don't have the option to add just a single file, or change one text option, without re-generating the entire gallery. Usually, this is not a problem, as long as you're not in a hurry. Keep in mind that if you make changes to a Web gallery and need to re-upload to your server, the entire gallery will be re-written. If you've made changes to those files outside Lightroom, such as changing CSS files, etc. you will need to be careful with this.

⌘+J or Ctrl+J
Export the Web gallery as files on your hard drive

EXPORTING WEB GALLERIES

You can also export Web galleries from Lightroom even if you don't have a Web hosting account set up. In a way, a Web export is the opposite of Upload: the files are saved to your hard drive but *not* to a Web server. (It's important to understand that exporting a *Web gallery* is different than using the regular Export command to make derivative files, in which only image files are produced.)

Because of the way Lightroom packages all the files within a single, top-level directory, and because all the links to files and pages are relative to one another within that folder, you can do all kinds of useful things with exported Web galleries. For example, you can export a Web gallery today, and then upload it to a server next week. (If you have a dedicated FTP program, this might be the fastest/easiest way to upload Lightroom galleries to your server.)

Lightroom Web galleries also make great *offline* presentations, even without an Internet connection. For example, I've produced some effective disc-based galleries using this method: I make Web galleries and burn them to disc for delivery to clients, galleries and prospective vendors. Simply export the gallery to your desktop, then burn it to a CD or DVD. From the disc, people can then open your gallery index page in the browser on their own computer, and navigate the gallery, just as if it was delivered from a Web server.

To accomplish this, click the Web module's Export button at the bottom of the right panel group (see Figure 7–19). A dialog box appears, asking you to choose the location and name for the new folder that will contain all the gallery files. Enter a name and click Save. Lightroom will generate all the necessary files for the Web gallery you've created,

Figure 7-19

including all the files and subfolders required to run the gallery from within the folder specified, using relative links (see below).

About relative hyperlinks

By default, the links that Lightroom generates are always *relative* to each file. In other words, all the pages in the Web gallery are linked relative to each other. This allows viewing the gallery without an Internet connection, and the presentation looks and works just the same as if it was being accessed from a Web server. This also means that if you change the folders or files after the gallery has been generated, the links will be broken.

Making changes to Web gallery links requires you to either generate a new gallery, or use dedicated Web development software (such as Adobe Dreamweaver) to modify the files.

You can include a link to a standalone Web site from any Lightroom gallery, including those that are disc-based, as long as you use a full URL, including http://.

CHAPTER 8
SLIDESHOW

Making and presenting slideshows

If you want to make quick, easy slideshows that you can present and/or send to other people, Lightroom's Slideshow module often fits the bill. You can create, present and export slideshows with customized designs, transitions and soundtracks. You can play a slideshow from within Lightroom or export it in several formats.

Lightroom 3 offers some significant improvements in the creation of slideshows. That said, Lightroom really can't compete with dedicated slideshow programs. I hope this chapter will show you all that's possible within Lightroom slideshows and help you see where Lightroom's slideshows fit in the larger landscape of on-screen presentation software. Set realistic expectations and I think you'll find you can use Lightroom for most of your slideshows.

Working in Slideshow is similar to working in Web. The Slideshow workflow is:

1. Organize the photos that will go into the slideshow

2. Go to the Slideshow module (and open all the panels)

3. Make sure your photos are showing in the correct order in the Filmstrip

4. Check the options in the Toolbar and change them if necessary

5. Choose a template to start the layout process

6. Customize the slide designs

7. Add music or other audio soundtrack (optional)

8. Preview your slideshow and make any necessary adjustments to settings

9. Play the slideshow in Lightroom or export it to file(s) on disk

ORGANIZE PHOTOS FOR THE SLIDESHOW

In Library, organize photos for your slideshow in Library first, including adding any metadata you want to use in the slideshow, such as titles and captions.

Multi-line captions

In the Library Metadata panel, you can insert line breaks if you want to have multi-line captions.

Slideshow module panels

After switching to the Slideshow module, start your work with all the panels open.

⌘+Return or Ctrl+Enter
Play impromptu slideshow in another module

⌘+Option+3 or Ctrl+Alt+3
Open the Slideshow module

The left panel set contains Preview, Templates and Collections. The right panels contain all the controls for customizing the slideshow; see Figure 8–1.

Figure 8-1

Remember that you can right-click or control+click on a panel header to enable Solo Mode; this is especially useful in Slideshow. As you work top to bottom on the right panels, it's a lot easier to stay focused on the current task if the other panels are closed.

Check the Toolbar and Filmstrip

Make sure the Toolbar is visible (T). Make sure all the photos showing in the Filmstrip are the ones you want to include in the slideshow. If not, on the Toolbar, click the Use: popup menu to change the source of photos to be included (see Figure 8–2). You can click and drag photos in the Filmstrip to change the order. If you have photos showing that you don't want in the slideshow, make a new collection and you can then remove the unwanted photos without affecting your original source.

Figure 8-2

8

Choose a template

Within the Lightroom default installation, there are two sets of Slideshow templates shown in the Template Browser: Lightroom Templates and User Templates. Lightroom comes with several basic (and generally unattractive) templates; you likely won't want to use these just as they are but they provide a good starting point. If you haven't saved any of your own Slideshow templates before, the User Templates set will be empty. Later, when you're done customizing the design, you can save your own templates.

From the Template Browser panel, choose a template to use as the basis for the new slideshow (see Figure 8–3). As you move your cursor over the templates they are shown in the Preview panel above. Click a template to load it. (I'm starting with Default.)

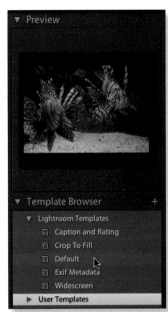

Figure 8-3

CUSTOMIZE THE SLIDESHOW

Customize your slideshow design using the panels on the right side of the screen. I almost always work from top to bottom, but inevitably there will be some going back and forth. If you're not sure how a specific control works, try it! Just keep tweaking the controls until you like the way the slideshow looks. Details for each of the panels are below.

Figure 8-4

⌘+1 or Ctrl+1
Open/close the
Options panel

Options panel

Starting in the Options panel (see Figure 8–4), set how the photos are placed on the slides. Zoom to Fill Frame will enlarge (and most likely crop) the photos to fit within the "live" area of the slide defined by the margins. With Zoom to Fill enabled, you can't control the position of the photo within the live area.

Next, you can add a Stroke Border by ticking its check box. This adds a solid outline around the photo. Set the width of the border using the slider, or by typing in a numeric value. To set the color of the border, click the rectangular swatch to the right of the panel. This opens the color picker (which is explained in detail in Chapter 4).

When you're done making changes in the color picker, click the X in the upper left corner or simply press Return/Enter. If you want to cancel any changes you made in the color picker, press Esc. For more on the color picker, review Chapter 4.

The bottom portion of the Options panel contains the settings for Cast Shadow. These shadows show "behind" the photos, as if the photos were floating in front of the background. You can't apply a color to the Cast Shadows; they're always neutral gray.

Tick the checkbox to enable or disable shadows. Then use the following four settings to customize the shadow:

Opacity: the overall strength of the shadow. 100% opacity will be solid black, and lower opacities will make the shadow lighter and transparent over the background. If you're using a solid color or gradient for the background, the effect of Opacity is not as evident as when using a photo as a background (which we'll discuss in just a bit).

Offset: sets how far away from the edge of the photo the shadow is placed. Larger offsets give the appearance of more depth between the photo and the background.

Radius: defines the softness of the edge of the shadow. A radius of zero will be a totally hard edge. Larger values will apply more feathering of the shadow edge. You'll need to work a bit with the settings for Offset and Radius to get your ideal combination of distance and softness.

Angle: simulates a single light source positioned to illuminate the slide. The circle shows this as if the slide is laying flat and the light is above. You can click and drag inside the circle to position this virtual light source, use the slider or enter numeric value. Like Radius, the effect of the Angle will be more, or less, obvious depending on the Offset.

⌘+2 or Ctrl+2
Open/close the
Layout panel

⌘+Shift+H or
Ctrl+Shift+H
Hide/show the
layout guides

Layout panel

The Layout panel (see Figure 8–5) is where you set the slide margins, which determine the photo's distance from the edges of the slide. You can set different margins for each side, but the same margins are used for all slides.

Tick the checkbox to Show Guides or uncheck the box to hide them. With guides visible, you can set the widths for Left, Right, Top and Bottom using the sliders or by typing in numeric values. Also, when the guides are visible, you can click and drag to position them directly in the preview.

Figure 8-5

8

To quickly apply the same values for all the margins, tick the Link All box. You can tick individual boxes to link the values of specific margins such as top and bottom, etc..

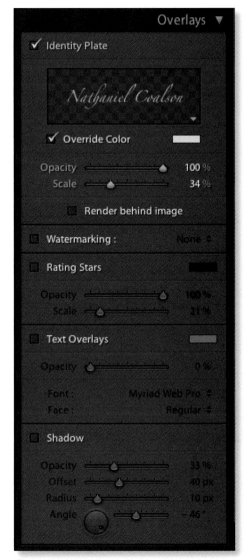

Figure 8-6

⌘+3 or Ctrl+3
Open/close the Overlays panel

Overlays panel

In the Overlays panel, you can configure text and graphical elements that appear on the slides along with the photos; see Figure 8–6. Like the other panels, Overlays is split into distinct sections that control different options.

Identity Plate: as explained in other chapters, Lightroom's identity plates are graphical or text elements that you can create, customize and use in a variety of ways. In Slideshow, identity plates are typically used to "brand" the presentations. As do the other modules, Slideshow allows you to place an optional identity plate on the slideshow. A slide layout can only include one identity plate. (However, you can apply additional text overlays, see next section).

The following example explains how to place your name in text on the slides.

First, check the box to show the identity plate. (When the box is unchecked, the identity plate is inactive and the controls are dimmed.)

The identity plate preview box shows the currently selected identity plate. A checkerboard pattern in the background indicates areas of transparency, where elements "behind" the identity plate will show through. With a text-based identity plate, everything but the letters themselves will be transparent; when you're using a graphical identity plate, areas of transparency will be determined by the image that's loaded.

The default preview is your Main Identity Plate, as configured using the Identity Plate Setup window. If you've made other identity plates, you can click the preview and choose another from the popup menu. If not, click Edit… to make a new one. This opens the Identity Plate Editor, which functions the same in all modules.

At the top of the window, set the radio button to "Use a styled text identity plate". Type your name, studio name, or any text you want in the text area. You can then apply settings for Font, Style, Size and Color. To change the fonts, the text must first be selected. By selecting individual parts of the text, you can style the different parts with multiple fonts, sizes and colors (see Figure 8–7).

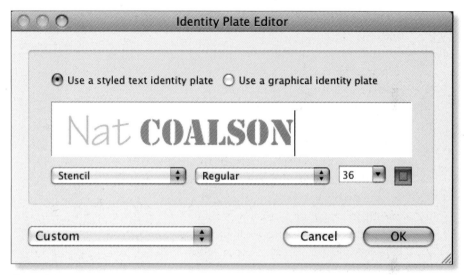

Figure 8-7

After you've styled the identity plate, be sure to save it as a preset for later. Click the dropdown menu at the bottom left of the window (it will say "Custom") and then Save As…. Enter a name and click Save. Click OK to exit and apply the changes.

Design graphical identity plates in Photoshop

For the most control over the appearance of all the identity plates you use in Lightroom, I recommend you design them in Photoshop, save them as PNG files, and then bring them into the Lightroom's Identity Plate Editor. This is explained in detail in Chapter 6.

Back in the Overlays panel, the preview shows your selected identity plate. Below the preview box is an option for Override Color, which as the name implies, will override any colors in the identity plate with a color you set here. Tick the box to enable the function, then click the swatch to the right to open the color picker and set the color.

8

Below Override Color are sliders for Opacity and Size. Opacity sets the level of transparency for the identity plate; at 100% it is solid and totally opaque. At lower levels you can see elements showing through the identity plate. To scale the identity plate, you can drag the size slider or enter a numeric value.

To position the identity plate in the slide layout, just click and drag it to the position you want. Also, when you've clicked to select the identity plate in the layout, you will see control handles appear. Click and drag the handles to scale the identity plate interactively. Rotate the identity plate by selecting it and clicking one of the rotate buttons in the Toolbar; see Figure 8–8.

Figure 8-8

It is possible that a combination of dragging and rotation will place your identity plate off the slide entirely, where you can no longer access it by clicking. If this happens, simply uncheck the box to turn it off, then back on again. It will reappear in the default location at the top left of the slide layout.

At the bottom of the Identity Plate section is an option to Render Behind Image. This can be useful if you want to use a large identity plate as part of the background of the slides. With this option enabled, the identity plate will be placed behind the photos, and in front of the background.

Watermarking: you can also apply a watermark to your slideshow. Check the box to enable it, then choose a watermark from the popup menu. Watermarks are covered in Chapter 5.

⌘+Option+T (Mac only)

To show the Character Palette. Windows also has a Character Map (under Accessories on the Start Menu) from which you can copy and paste characters. You can do all kinds of cool things with type and symbols in watermarks and identity plates.

Rating Stars: enabling this option will display any rating stars on the slides, for photos that have them applied. Click the color swatch to change the color of the stars. New in Lightroom 3, you can also change Opacity and Scale for the Stars.

Text Overlays: check the box to display text overlays on the slides. The checkbox hides or shows *all* text overlays. **However, with an *individual* text overlay selected in the layout preview, the Text Overlays controls affect *only* the selected overlay.**

To make a new text overlay, first make sure the Toolbar is showing (press the T key to hide/show the Toolbar). On the Toolbar, click the ABC button (see Figure 8–9) or use the shortcut. The text entry field becomes active. This allows you to set custom text. Type your text into the box and press Return or Enter when you're done. The new text overlay is inserted at the bottom left corner of the slide, using default values based on your operating system.

Figure 8-9

Or, instead of custom text, click the popup menu text to the custom text field (see Figure 8–10) and choose another kind of text to display. The options contained here represent *tokens,* which are variable placeholders for specific types of metadata. There are options for Equipment, Date, Exposure, Caption etc., all which will use the specific data unique to each photo in the text overlay,

Figure 8-10

so each photo will show different text. This is in contrast to the custom text overlay, which remains the same on *all* slides.

8

If you want to show individual Titles or Captions for the photos, they need to be entered in those corresponding metadata fields first (in the Library module).

Once you've inserted a text overlay, you can click and drag to move and/or resize it with the control handles. You can also use your keyboard arrow keys to nudge overlays in small increments.

Also, when a text overlay (or identity plate) is active, you'll see a small square with a straight line connecting it to the text overlay box (refer back to Figure 8–8). This is an *anchor point* to aid positioning the overlay precisely on the slide. If you click the point and drag it around the slide, you will feel it "snap" to various key positions such as the corners and centers of the slide edges and photos. As you move it, also notice that it becomes attached to different corners of the text overlay.

Once you've snapped the point to a location, you then snap the text overlay to the point, using the straight line as a visual reference. The benefit to this method is that the point always remains snapped to the center or edges of the photo or the slide, independent of the size or position of the text overlay itself. If you need to resize or move a text overlay to a precise position, you'll find that this straight-line, snapping behavior makes it very easy, without the need for rulers or math.

You can also rotate text overlays. With the desired overlay selected, click one of the rotate buttons in the Toolbar.

When you've positioned your text overlay where you want it, use the Text Overlay controls on the panel to change Color, Opacity, Font and Face for the overlay.

Continue making as many text overlays as you need by clicking the ABC button or using the shortcut. To delete an existing text overlay, select it with your mouse and press Delete.

⌘+4 or Ctrl+4
Open/close the
Backdrop panel

Backdrop panel

On the Backdrop panel you can customize the background for the slides. For a solid black background, simply uncheck all the options. Otherwise, use the provided controls (see Figure 8–11) to apply styling for the following:

Figure 8-11

Color Wash: this setting applies a gradient across the background, which smoothly transitions from one color to another.

Click the swatch to open the color picker, then either select a color from the box or click and drag the eyedropper to choose a color from anywhere on your screen. Use the Opacity and Angle controls to fine tune the application of the gradient.

Background Image: here you can select photo in the catalog for the slide background, which then interacts with the other Backdrop design controls. (The background chosen must be in the current catalog.) Click and drag a photo from the Filmstrip to place it into the background. You don't have any control over the scaling or placement of the background photo.

Background Color: this sets a solid color for the background. Click the swatch to open the color picker.

Keep backgrounds simple

Remember that the goal of the presentation is to feature the photos. To that end, keep your backgrounds and other elements simple and clean so they don't distract from the images.

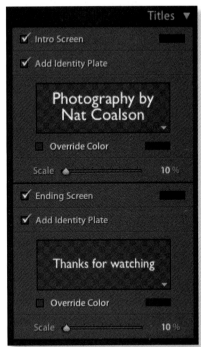

Figure 8-12

⌘+5 or Ctrl+5
Open/close the
Titles panel

Titles panel

The Titles panel (see Figure 8–12) provides options for creating intro and ending screens for your slideshow. The title screens can be made simply of a solid color background or you can use identity plates to apply text or graphics. You could instead design custom images to use as intro and ending screens.

To enable one or both screens, tick the appropriate checkbox(es). You can then apply the settings for each screen independently.

Considering the ability to use straight text and/or graphics files, the options here are endless. The only potential shortcoming to this feature is that you can't independently control the timing of intro and title screens. The intro screen will have the same timing as the rest of the slides, as will the ending.

However, if the slideshow isn't set to automatically repeat, the ending screen will show indefinitely. (I'm hoping future versions of Lightroom will provide more control over title and ending screens, including support for videos and animated text for credits, even if it's just using GIFs).

8

If you want to make identity plates to show textual titles or credits, consider setting up the text in a text editor first, then copy and paste the text into the Identity Plate Editor.

Design title screens and backgrounds in Photoshop

For the most control over the look of your backgrounds, set them up in Photoshop and import them to the catalog as JPGs or TIFs. You can then insert them in the slideshow as slides of their own wherever you like, or drag and drop to apply them as the backgrounds or identity plates for photo slides.

⌘+6 or Ctrl+6
Open/close the
Playback panel

Playback panel

Here, you set the parameters for the playback of the slideshow; see Figure 8–13.

To add audio to the playback, tick the box to enable the Soundtrack. Beginning in Lightroom 3, it is no longer necessary to use an iTunes playlist for this. As a matter of fact, Lightroom no longer supports the use of a playlist at all; you can only assign one audio file to the slideshow. If you need a long soundtrack using multiple songs or audio clips, you will need to edit them all together into one file first. Lightroom can use MP3 or AAC format audio files, but can't work with audio files that are encrypted by digital rights management (DRM) encoding (as the warning icon on the example shows).

Figure 8-13

Click the button labeled Select Music. This opens a dialog box from which you can choose a single audio file from any connected drive.

To the right is a button labeled "Fit to Music". This feature only applies when the Slide Duration checkbox (below) is ticked. This allows you to automatically set the length of the slideshow to match the song duration.

If you want to manually advance the slides during playback, leave the Slide Duration box unchecked. Otherwise, to have the slides advance automatically, tick the Slide Duration checkbox. Using the Slides value, you can then manually set the amount of time that each slide will be displayed, or click the Fit to Music button above and the timing will be calculated automatically.

8

The Fades setting determines the blend between outgoing and incoming slides. Fades won't show when manually advancing the slideshow.

The fade Color can also be set here, which will blend the selected color with the photos being faded together, as well as transitions to and from the intro and ending screens. This can help make your slide transitions appear smooth.

If you're not using Fit to Music, you can set the Slide and Fades timing however you wish. If you are using Fit to Music, the Fades setting has a direct relationship to the Slide setting. Lowering one value will increase the other in order to produce equal spacing for all slides.

Ticking the Random Order checkbox will show all the slides randomly. If you enable repeat, the random order will apply during each loop, so it's possible that the same photo will be shown twice in a row. If you're presenting photos from a group of people, Random Order might be a good idea as it doesn't show any preference. But if you're just showing your own work, or have a specific sequence to use, you'll probably want to leave this unchecked.

Finally, the Repeat checkbox determines whether the slideshow will automatically loop to the beginning and play again after reaching the last slide or the ending screen. You don't have the option to set a specific number of loops. If Repeat is enabled, you must stop the slideshow manually by pressing the Esc key.

Save a new template
After you've designed a slideshow you like, be sure to save it as a template. Click the + button on the Template Browser panel header and give the template a meaningful name.

Update a template
To save changes you've made to an existing template, right-click or Ctrl+Click on the template, and from the popup menu, choose Update with Current Settings. (You can't update Lightroom's built-in templates this way.)

Option+Return or Alt+Enter
Preview the slideshow

PREVIEW THE SLIDESHOW
You can see how the slideshow will look by previewing it in the main content area. This is essentially the same as playing the slideshow, but it doesn't blackout or fill the screen while playing. In most cases, while you're previewing the slideshow this way, you can also make adjustments to settings and the changes are applied—in real time—as the preview continues.

To start previewing the slideshow, click the Preview button at the bottom of the right panel, or the arrow button on the toolbar.

8

To exit the preview, press the Stop button in the Toolbar (see Figure 8–14) or press Esc.

Figure 8-14

Color spaces and previews

Lightroom slideshows (and slideshow previews) use the Adobe RGB (1998) color space to render the files to screen. For this reason, in very rare cases, your photos might look different in the slideshow than they do in the other modules. Adobe RGB is a larger color space than sRGB (which is used for the Web module) but smaller than ProPhoto, which is used for high quality previews in Develop. Usually, only some colors will be affected—those with extreme saturation in certain hues like pure blues, reds and oranges. In most cases, this shouldn't cause a problem. I just wanted you to be aware of the reasons, if this should occur.

PRESENTING OR EXPORTING THE SLIDESHOW

When you've finished designing your slideshow, you have four presentation options:

Return or Enter
Play the slideshow

1. Play the slideshow in Lightroom. Click the play button at the bottom of the right panel, or use the shortcut. This blacks out the display, starts the slideshow immediately and shows all the slides full screen. You can pause the slideshow by pressing the space bar. To stop the slideshow, press Esc.

Space bar
Pause the slideshow (press again to resume)

Apply attributes while the slideshow plays

To apply attributes while a slideshow is playing, you can use the keyboard shortcuts for ratings (0-5), flags (P, X, U) and color labels (6-9) .

Esc
Stop the slideshow

Play the slideshow on a second display

If you have a secondary display connected to your computer, you can play the slideshow there. In the Slideshow module, under the Window→Secondary Display menu, choose the option for Slideshow, or press ⌘+Option+Shift+Enter or Ctrl+Alt+Shift+Enter.

Playback problems

If the slideshow stops playing, shows blank slides, or jumps back to the first slide at the wrong time, it's likely because large previews haven't been rendered for those photos. Lightroom 3 offers a new feature to Prepare Previews in Advance, which you enable by checking the box at the bottom of the Playback panel.

⌘+J or Ctrl+J
Export the
slideshow as
a PDF

⌘+Option+J
or Ctrl+Alt+J
Export the
slideshow as a
video file

⌘+Shift+J or
Ctrl+Shift+J
Export the
slideshow as
JPG files

2. Export the slideshow as a PDF file. Click the "Export PDF" button at the bottom of the left panel set. A dialog box appears, providing options for the exported file; see Figure 8–15. If you want Adobe Acrobat and Acrobat Reader to auto-play the slideshow, and show it full-screen, you must enable the option for "Automatically show full screen" (or you can change these kinds of settings by editing the PDF with the full version of Acrobat). The PDF file will not contain a Soundtrack.

Figure 8-15

3. Export the slideshow as a movie file. A single mp4 movie file (H.264) will be created containing the entire slideshow with all title screens, slides, and transitions. If a music file was selected, it will be included as well. (However, if the music track is longer than the slideshow, it will fade out and the movie will end after the last slide.) The Save dialog box allows you to specify the location to save the new movie file and provides a menu to select the size of the video; see Figure 8–16. These movies can be shared online or optimized for mobile devices.

Figure 8-16

4. Export the slideshow as a set of JPG files. Select the menu command Slideshow➔Export JPEG Slideshow, or use the shortcut. Each slide will be saved as a single JPG file. Title and ending screens are not created. Output sharpening is not an option. The Save dialog box provides controls for the size and compression level of the files; see Figure 8–17.

Figure 8-17

CHAPTER 9
ADVANCED TECHNIQUES

9

Welcome to the next level

In the previous chapters, we've covered the basics of all the great things you can do with your photos in Lightroom. I think by now you've seen that, in most cases, you can do everything you want with your photos, entirely from within Lightroom, using a repeatable set of workflow procedures.

Now's the time to take it a few steps further. There will eventually be situations that fall outside the norm, in which you need more than just the basics of Lightroom. This chapter provides detailed instructions on numerous ways that you can leverage the strengths of Lightroom when you want to also use other software for processing your photos or have unique logistical requirements.

Publish services

Lightroom 3's new Publish Services panel, accessed from the Library module (see Figure 9–1), provides one-click—or even automatic—exporting to local hard disks and online photo sharing services such as Flickr.

Figure 9-1

Publish services keep track of versions of photos, when they were published, and what's been modified since the last publication. Publishing photos provides essentially the same functionality as exporting, but with ties to collections of images and automation, making it very easy to keep your exported files always updated to the latest version.

Publish services function similarly to collections and smart collections (and can even import settings from smart collections) with additional export capabilities. You can drag and drop photos to your saved services, or set them up to use dynamic criteria such as keywords, attributes or any other metadata. A published source can also be designated as the Target Collection (see Chapter 3 for more on Target Collections.)

By default, Lightroom 3 comes with publish services for Hard Drive and Flickr, listed in the panel at the lower left. You can also add publish services for other export plug-ins (such as SmugMug, which is described in the export plug-ins section later in this chapter).

It's expected that, over time, many more publish services will be added. For one, it's my hope that publish services will become part of the mechanism by which Lightroom eventually offers book printing directly from within your catalog. Cool stuff!

The Publish Services panel functions somewhat like the Volume Browser in the Folders panel: as you set up new publishing presets, they are stored under the appropriate Service.

Publish services need to be configured before they can be used. When initially configuring a publish service, it doesn't matter if you have any photos selected; you'll add them to the service later.

EXAMPLE: PUBLISH TO HARD DRIVE

Following are instructions for setting up a publish service to automatically export JPG files to a folder on your desktop:

Click the **Set Up...** button on the Hard Drive publish service; see Figure 9–1. This opens the Lightroom Publishing Manager (see Figure 9–2), which contains essentially the same controls as the Export screen (covered in Chapter 5). In the Publishing Manager window, we'll configure the settings for this Service.

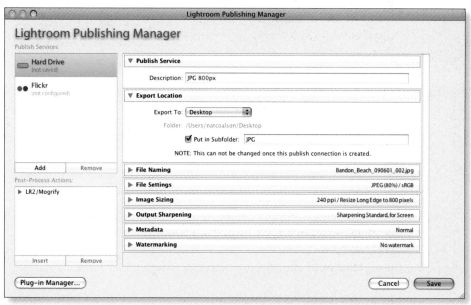

Figure 9-2

Publish Service

Description: enter a name for the service, like "JPG 800px".

Export Location

Export To: choose a destination folder from the popup menu. This is the master folder for this published Hard Drive service; all folders created in this service will be subfolders of this. In this example, I selected Desktop.

Put in Subfolder: tick the checkbox and type in the name to create a subfolder called JPG.

File Naming

Rename To: Optionally, select a new file naming template, or type in a Custom Name. (File naming is discussed in detail in Chapter 3.) The example name shown will be based on the active file selected in Library. If no photo is selected, Lightroom will use the example name IMG_0001. For this example, you can use whatever name you like.

File Settings

Format: choose JPG from the popup menu

Color space: use SRGB for this example

Quality: set to 80

Limit File Size To: leave unchecked

Include video files: leave unchecked

Image Sizing

Resize to Fit: check the box, and from the popup menu select Long Edge.

Below, type in 800 and make sure the menu is set to pixels.

(The other settings in this panel won't matter for this example.)

Output Sharpening

Check the box to sharpen for Screen at Standard amount.

Metadata

Leave at Normal settings (both boxes unchecked).

Watermarking

If you've set up a custom watermark, you can apply it here if you like. See Chapter 5 for more details on watermarking. (Doesn't matter for the example.)

Before we leave the Publishing Manager, note the Add button at middle left of the window. You can add more instances of the main publishing services in order to organize them in different ways. We'll come back to this in a bit.

Click the **Save** button to save the publish service.

Back in the Publish Services panel, take a look at what's happened. The Hard Drive service now shows the name you added in the Publishing Manager (you can go back and change this name later if you like). Below the service is a Published Folder; see Figure 9–3 . Lightroom has established a dynamic

Figure 9-3

link to a new folder on your desktop. Check your desktop to confirm the folder has been created, and notice that it's empty. This is because, although we've established the connection and the export parameters, we haven't yet *published* any photos to the folder.

Load any folder or collection source in your catalog. Select a few photos, and drag and drop them onto the new publish service. Note that the name now shows the number of photos in the published folder.

Next, to publish the photos to the folder, click the Publish button (or Publish Selected) or right-click or Ctrl+click on the

Figure 9-4

published folder in the list (see Figure 9–4) and from the popup menu select **Publish Now.** While Lightroom is publishing the photos, notice that the main preview updates to show what's been published and what's still waiting to be done; see Figure 9–5.

When the process is finished, go back out to your desktop and look in the folder to confirm that, in fact, your photos are now saved there. Good?

Now, to see the real advantage of publish services: make a change to one or several of the photos you're viewing

Figure 9-5

9

in the preview. For this example, I just pressed V to convert to black and white; see Figure 9–6. The main preview now shows that I have photos waiting to be re-published. Again, right-click or Ctrl+click on the published folder in the list, and select Publish Now. Lightroom re-exports the modified photos to the same folder, using the same settings.

Figure 9-6

If you're asking "why would I do this instead of regular exports?" consider these points:

1. Publish services show you photos that you've exported and which have since been updated in Lightroom. Published photos are automatically separated out in the preview area so you know what's been changed.

2. In a regular export, if there are file conflicts, you'll need to specifically allow Lightroom to overwrite those files. But when you re-publish, the files are automatically rewritten to update to the current version.

3. Publish services combine the advantages of collections and export presets. You can set up any number of publish services to handle groups of images you're using for any specific purpose.

These factors are especially important if you're continually distributing files to other people, such as clients or family members. However, publishing to your own hard drive is just the beginning. For example, you could use publish services to sync files between multiple computers on a network. Think about the possibilities!

Another example: if you have an iPhone or other smartphone (or even an iPad), you probably have some of your favorite photos stored there. I know many photographers who use their iPhone as a portable, electronic portfolio. You can use Lightroom's publish services to very effectively sync your favorite photos in your Lightroom catalog with your mobile device. Simply set up a hard drive publish service to sync Lightroom with a folder that is also set to sync with your phone. Publish (or re-publish) the photos to the folder, then sync the phone with your computer.

As powerful as publishing to a hard drive is, the true power of publish services is their ability to help you publish to remote servers and Web services, making it easy to keep your photo collections up-to-date in those environments, even as you make changes to them in your Lightroom catalog. It used to be difficult to manage versions of photos and collections between your local computer, Lightroom catalog and a server, etc. But now, with Lightroom's ability to connect to network drives or Web servers, the functionality of publish services can eliminate the bottlenecks and allow you easily to keep your Web galleries or other image collections in sync with your Lightroom catalog.

EXAMPLE: PUBLISH TO FLICKR

Let's look at an example using Flickr (you'll need a Flickr account for this); see Figure 9–7 on the next page for the example settings described below:

1. Click the Set Up… button on the Flickr publish service.

2. In the Publishing Manager, click to select the Flickr service in the list.

3. As with the Hard Drive service we just looked at, work down the right side of the window to configure the service.

4. Give your Flickr publish service a useful name.

5. You'll need to log into your account; click the button at right. This will take you to the Flickr site for authorization. When you're done there, come back to the Lightroom Publishing Manager.

9

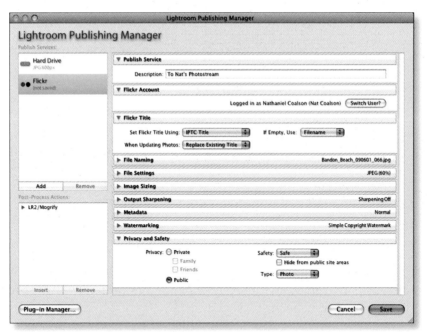

Figure 9-7

6. Work through the rest of the file settings, same as you would for any export.

7. There's a group of settings for Flickr title with enhanced support for titling the photos as they're sent to the Flickr Web site, and at the bottom of the window, the Privacy and Safety section provides controls specific to the Flickr service.

8. When you're done with the settings, click Save.

9. Back in the Library, add photos to your published folder by dragging and dropping.

10. Then right-click or Ctrl+click on the new service and choose Publish from the popup menu.

Viola! Lightroom uploads the photos to your Flickr photostream. Go to the Flickr site to see the new photos; you can then add them to Flickr sets and/or make any other necessary changes within the Flickr configuration.

Flickr comments
With a FlickrPro account, visitor comments on your photos are automatically shown in the Comments field on the right panel in Lightroom's Library module.

MORE PUBLISH SERVICE SETTINGS

There are a couple of menus containing additional options for creating and modifying publish services.

The + button

Click the button on the right side of the Publish Service panel header.

The first item is a link to open the Publishing Manager. Below that are listed any services you've set up. You can also change the sort order and turn on/off the service icons.

Right-click or Ctrl+click

…on a publish service in the panel. A popup menu opens to provide the following options:

Edit Settings: opens the Lightroom Publishing Manager with the current service loaded so you can make changes.

Rename Publish Service: opens a dialog box to rename the service.

Delete Publish Service:: will remove the service after you confirm in the resulting dialog box.

Create Published Folder: allows you to make a new published folder (like a distinct collection) using the same settings as the main service. Note that the name of the published folder cannot contain spaces.

Create Published Smart Folder: provides controls like smart collections (see Chapter 3) to add a smart folder to the publish service.

Create Published Folder Set: allows you to group publish folders into sets. After making one here, you can drag and drop to nest publish folders under sets, from which you could publish one or all of the folders in the set.

Create another Publish Service via [publish service name]: makes a new service with initial settings copied from an existing service.

Changing published folders

Right-click or Ctrl+click on a published item in the panel, a popup menu opens with some of the above options, plus the following:

Set as Target Collection: sets that folder as the Target Collection (see chapter 3).

Rename: change the name of the published folder.

9

Delete: remove the published folder from the service.

Publish Now: updates all items in the folder according to the settings saved in the publish service.

Mark to Republish: indicates that all items in the published folder need to be re-published; this could be done manually or when initiating a publish update from the parent service.

Go to Published Folder: in the case of Hard Drive services, this will show the folder in Finder or Explorer.

Import Smart Collection Settings: allows you to import settings from a smart collection (see Chapter 3) as the criteria for a smart publish folder.

Lightroom integration with other programs

In most cases, Lightroom plays nicely with other image editing programs. The important thing to keep in mind is that Lightroom's metadata (including adjustments) will typically need to be preserved when going back and forth between Lightroom and another application.

For example, if you have a photo in your Lightroom catalog, and then make changes to it using Adobe Camera Raw or Bridge, Lightroom will not automatically reflect the updates. As described in Chapters 3 and 4, Lightroom offers the ability to read and write metadata to and from the catalog, but this is something you must do manually. Lightroom will let you know about metadata status conflicts and you can decide whether to read in the updated metadata from the file on disk, or overwrite it with the metadata from the Lightroom catalog.

Lightroom's use of industry-standard XMP and IPTC metadata ensures that other software can recognize that information and will show the same data as Lightroom.

EXTERNAL EDITORS

In addition to reading and writing metadata between applications, there will also be situations in which you have processed as far as you can in Lightroom and want to continue working with the photo in another program. Below are a few typical scenarios where you will want to take photos out of Lightroom and into other software:

- **HDR (High Dynamic Range) imaging:** you can use Photoshop or other software such as Photomatix to blend exposures for HDR. To do it in

Photoshop CS5, use the menu command in Lightroom: Photo→Edit In...
→Merge to HDR PRO in Photoshop.

- **Panoramas:** from Lightroom, you can use Photoshop or other software to stitch exposures for panoramas. To do it in Photoshop, use the menu command in Lightroom: Photo→Edit In...→Merge to Panorama in Photoshop.

- **Placing multiple images in a Photoshop (TIF) file as layers:** Photo→Edit In...→Open as Layers in Photoshop.

- **Advanced noise reduction:** if you specify a standalone noise reduction program as an external editor (see below) Lightroom will hand off files for processing in that program.

External editor preferences

In Preferences, you can specify other programs to use as *external editors* for Lightroom; see Figure 9–8. If you have one or more versions of Photoshop installed on your computer, the most recent version will be selected as the primary external editor by default (and you can't change this). But you can set any other program as the secondary external editor, and can save presets for as many as you need.

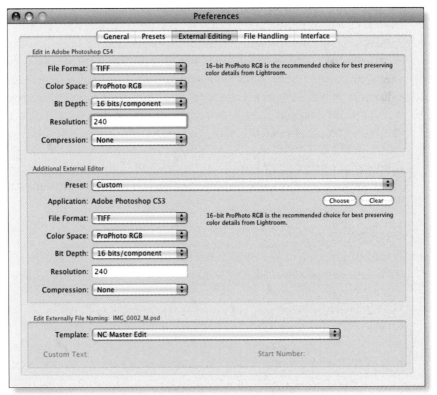

Figure 9-8

9

When you use the Edit In… command, Lightroom lists all the external editors you have configured. Select one from the menu, and Lightroom will provide options for rendering the file. Click Edit, and Lightroom will hand off the file to the other program using the settings you specified.

Some programs offer different methods of integrating with Lightroom. For example, when you install Photomatix for Lightroom, you access it from within the File menu.

File Settings

Lightroom's External Editing Preferences allow you to specify the settings for the files that will be created when Lightroom hands off a file to another program. The main considerations are File Format, Color Space, Bit Depth and Resolution. In most cases, you will also have the option to change these settings during an Edit In session.

I recommend always using TIF for the file format here. For color space, use Adobe RGB (1998) for the most flexibility, or ProPhoto to preserve the most color data from the original capture.

Don't use PSD

From this point forward, I recommend that you don't use PSD files for any of your layered Photoshop work. Use TIF instead. It provides all the same capabilities as PSD (layers, type, alpha channels, etc.), with a distinct advantage: TIF offers much more long-term viability than PSD. The TIF format is an open source, industry standard. It's much more likely that software many years in the future will be able to read TIF files than PSD. PSD is proprietary, and in my opinion, outdated, with a number of programmatic disadvantages to TIF.

Color consistency

For the most predictable results, be sure that your Photoshop Color Settings are set to use the same Working Space as you set in Lightroom's External Editing preferences.

Bit depth

Whenever possible, I recommend working in 16-bit. More bits means more data is used to describe the values of the pixels. A 16-bit image provides much more "headroom" for processing than does an 8-bit image; the data can be manipulated further before the appearance of the image starts to degrade. An 8-bit file uses 256 levels of brightness per color channel; a 16-bit file uses 65,536 levels. 16-bit allows smoother transitions between colors and reduces the appearance of *posterization* where areas of color become solid and transitions become hard-edged.

ROUNDTRIP EDITING WITH PHOTOSHOP

⌘+E or Ctrl+E
Edit a photo in
Photoshop (or the
primary external
editor)

⌘+Option+E or
Ctrl+Alt+E
Edit the photo
in the secondary
external editor

As much as Lightroom is capable of, there will be times when you've got to take a file into Photoshop to finish your work. One common example is when you need to combine multiple captures. This is called *compositing*—you're making a *composite* image from multiple original photos. Compositing can be done manually, such as stacking multiple layers with masks in Photoshop, or automatically, such as with HDR tone mapping or stitching panoramas. The outcome of all of these processes is a final, composite image.

Another example is heavy retouching, which also could reasonably be considered compositing. If you need to replace a large or complex section of a photo, you'll likely need more retouching power than Lightroom can provide.

Or, many photographers like to apply elaborate special effects, like watercolor painting, charcoal, etc., which can be done in Photoshop.

Also, there are advanced sharpening and noise reduction packages available that go far beyond what Lightroom can do in these areas, and are often implemented as Photoshop plug-ins.

Another case where you might want to use Photoshop is *soft-proofing*. Photoshop can simulate, on-screen, the appearance of an image printed on a certain printer and paper combination. You can then make Photoshop adjustments to get the image to look as much like your reference image as possible. Lightroom currently doesn't provide soft-proofing.

Prepping files for printing at an outside vendor, such as an offset print shop, can also require Photoshop, especially if it's a CMYK process. Lightroom does not support editing files in CMYK color mode—any adjustments made to CMYK files in the catalog are done using Lightroom's internal RGB space, and you can't export CMYK files from Lightroom.

Edit in Photoshop

With one or more photos selected in Library Grid or the Filmstrip in any module choose the Photo menu➜Edit In… command, or use the shortcut or contextual menu.

Depending on the version of Photoshop being used and type of original, one of two things will happen:

For DNG and camera raw files and virtual copies, Lightroom will render the file and open it into Photoshop memory. Note that a file on disk has not yet been created; the image data has simply been opened as a new file in Photoshop.

9

For all other file types, Lightroom opens a dialog box offering the following options (see Figure 9–9):

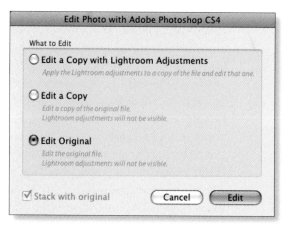

- **Edit a copy with Lightroom adjustments:** instructs Lightroom to render a copy file to disk, including all the currently active Lightroom adjustments, and open that image into Photoshop;

Figure 9-9

- **Edit a copy:** same as above (creates a new file on disk), but Lightroom adjustments will be ignored. The resulting copy is then opened in Photoshop; and

- **Edit original:** opens the original file, ignoring Lightroom adjustments.

In Photoshop (or other external editor) do your necessary work, and when you're done, Save the file in that application. Lightroom will automatically update the catalog to include the new file. (If you don't save from the other program, no file will be created on disk.)

Opening multiple photos as Photoshop Layers

With multiple photos selected in Lightroom, use Photo menu➔Edit In…➔Open as Layers in Photoshop. Each photo will be opened as a new layer, all in the same file.

Open as Photoshop Smart Objects

Using Smart Objects helps keep your Lightroom edits to originals in-sync with copies edited in Photoshop. If you open photos from Lightroom into Photoshop as Smart Objects, any future changes you make to those images in Lightroom will automatically be updated in the Photoshop file the next time it's opened. To open a photo/photos in Photoshop as a smart object, go to Photo menu➔Edit In…➔Open as Smart Object in Photoshop.

Differences and similarities to export

Whereas an export operation generates new files and saves them to disk (or burns to CD/DVD, etc.), the Edit in… commands rely more on computer memory (RAM) to maintain an active, "dynamic" link between image files from the Lightroom catalog being edited in Photoshop. For more about exporting, see Chapter 5.

You may need the latest version of Photoshop for full functionality with Lightroom

If you have photos selected in Lightroom and the above described options are grayed out, it's because you don't have a recent enough version of Photoshop. You'd need to upgrade for full interoperability between Lightroom and Photoshop. During a roundtrip editing session, you may also see Lightroom dialog boxes warning you that you should update Adobe Camera Raw or Photoshop. You have two choices: Render using Lightroom, or Open Anyway. I haven't seen a difference in results using either option, but depending on the software versions involved (as well as the camera used to make the capture) there may be variability in quality.

Export post-processing

You can apply post-processing actions in the Export window (see Figure 9–10). These can be Photoshop actions saved as droplets, or in many cases, actual standalone programs on your computer.

In these cases, Lightroom will fully complete all its processing, then hand off the file to the specified application or script. For example, if you run a

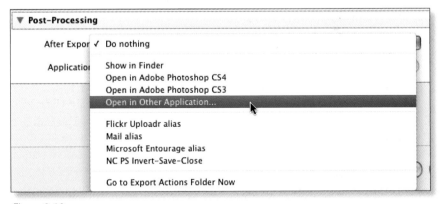

Figure 9-10

Photoshop action on the exported files, all the steps in that action—and any resulting changes to the files—will be performed *after* Lightroom's color space conversion, resizing, sharpening, watermarking, etc. Keep this in mind when you're planning the export workflow; it has a significant effect on how your steps should be arranged when post-processing is involved.

9

After Export

Select an item from this menu to either open the selected application or run the actions contained in a Photoshop droplet or script upon completion of Lightroom's export. Some example uses of After Export menu items:

- Running Photoshop actions contained in droplets, such as applying noise reduction, advanced sharpening routines, etc.;

- Sending photos in email or transferring by FTP;

- Uploading to photo sharing Web sites; or

- Opening the files in another program.

If the derivative files are added to the catalog during the export, any changes applied during post-processing will also be automatically shown on the files in the catalog.

How to add your own Export Actions

You can add Photoshop droplets, scripts and shortcuts to other software programs to the After Export menu. Any item that can be executed by opening a photo (or batch of photos) can be added as an Export Action.

How to do it: from the popup menu, select "Go to Export Actions Folder Now". This will take you to the Export Actions folder within the Lightroom presets folder on your computer. (The Lightroom presets folder contains subfolders for all the methods for extending Lightroom.) Place your droplets or shortcuts in the Export Actions folder and they will be added to the After Export menu. In some cases you'll need to restart Lightroom to see the new actions listed.

EXPORT PLUG-INS

Lightroom Export Plug-ins are standalone scripts that independent developers have created for specialized post-processing outside of Lightroom. You can find and download Lightroom plug-ins from the Web. Some examples of popular plug-ins currently available are:

- **LR/Mogrify by Timothy Armes:** performs a wide range of very useful image modification functions, including highly customizable watermarking and graphical overlays, borders, resizing and sharpening.

- **LR/Enfuse by Timothy Armes:** a very capable HDR processor for Lightroom.

- **Web photo sharing plug-ins:** for SmugMug, Picasa, Flickr, Zenfolio, Photoshelter and more by Jeffrey Friedl.

- **Lightroom Export Plug-in to Photomatix Pro:** for owners of Photomatix HDR software, this plug-in streamlines the interaction between Lightroom and Photomatix. If you like to make HDR images, I highly recommended Photomatix.

- **DxO Optix Pro:** specialized software offering advanced lens corrections and much more.

- **Export to Facebook** and other social networking sites.

Adobe's Web site offers the Plug-in Exchange, where you can find many of these plug-ins and others. The easy way to get there is from the Plug-in Manager, under Lightroom's File menu, where there's a link to the Plug-in Exchange at the bottom right; see Figure 9–11.

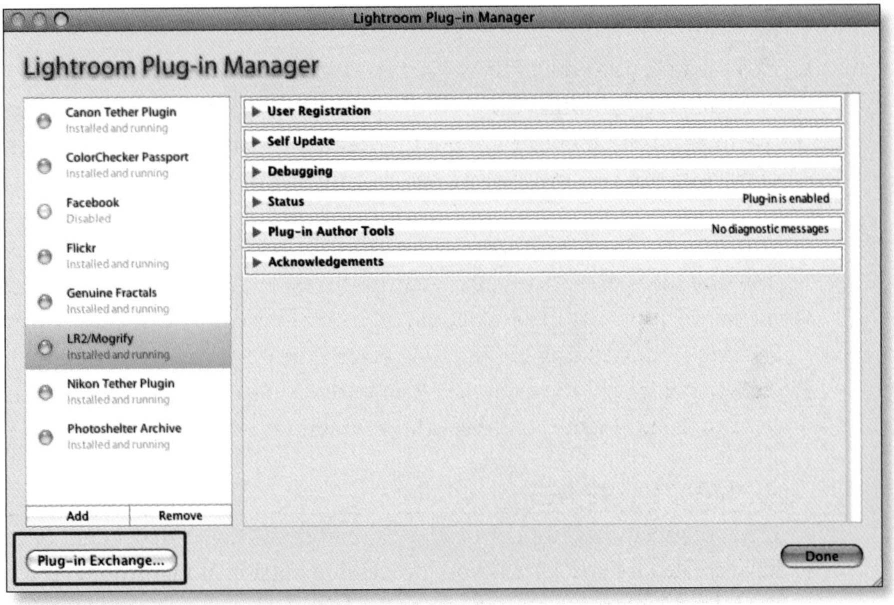

Figure 9-11

Also, Google "Lightroom plug-ins" or "Lightroom Export plug-ins" to find others online. Most plug-ins are very inexpensive; many are free.

After you download the plug-in files, there are several ways they may be installed. Some come with their own installer. For others, if you copy them to the Lightroom/Modules folder, they will appear in the Plug-In Manager (see Figure 9–11) the next time Lightroom is started. Or, for some plug-ins the Add button

9

allows you to install them from any folder location (but they have to stay in that location to remain accessible).

Always consult the installation instructions that comes with the plug-in. Once the plug-ins are installed, each will offer different settings and controls within the Export screen.

To remove a plug-in setting from the Plug-in Manager list, select it and click the Remove button; see Figure 9–12.

Export plug-in example: SmugMug
SmugMug.com is a very popular Web service that's made a name for itself hosting photographer's Web galleries and full-blown Web sites.

Jeffrey Friedl developed a Lightroom export plug-in that allows you to export photos directly from Lightroom into your SmugMug account. This plug-in is simply

Figure 9-12

astounding in its breadth and depth of functionality. It's a prime example of how far modern digital image processing and distribution has come in a few short years. (Even if you don't use SmugMug, you might want to install this plug-in just to see what's possible.)

To get the full effect, obviously, the first step will be to establish a SmugMug account. Then download the Lightroom export plug-in from http://regex.info/blog/lightroom-goodies/smugmug. Follow the installation instructions provided on the Web page where you downloaded the plug-in.

Once successfully installed, the SmugMug export plug-in provides additional options in the Export dialog box.

At the top of the window, in the Export To: menu, select SmugMug. The plug-in options become available.

Enter your SmugMug nickname and password and log in.

Under Export location, choose whether to save in a temporary location (files won't be saved on your hard drive after upload) or choose a folder to save the files locally in addition to uploading to the SmugMug site.

Set the rest of the options for the exported files as you normally would: File Naming, File Settings, Image Sizing, Output Sharpening, Metadata and Watermarking.

SmugMug: Tools: in this section, the plug-in provides an impressive range of controls for creating and managing categories, galleries and metadata on the SmugMug site; see Figure 9–13.

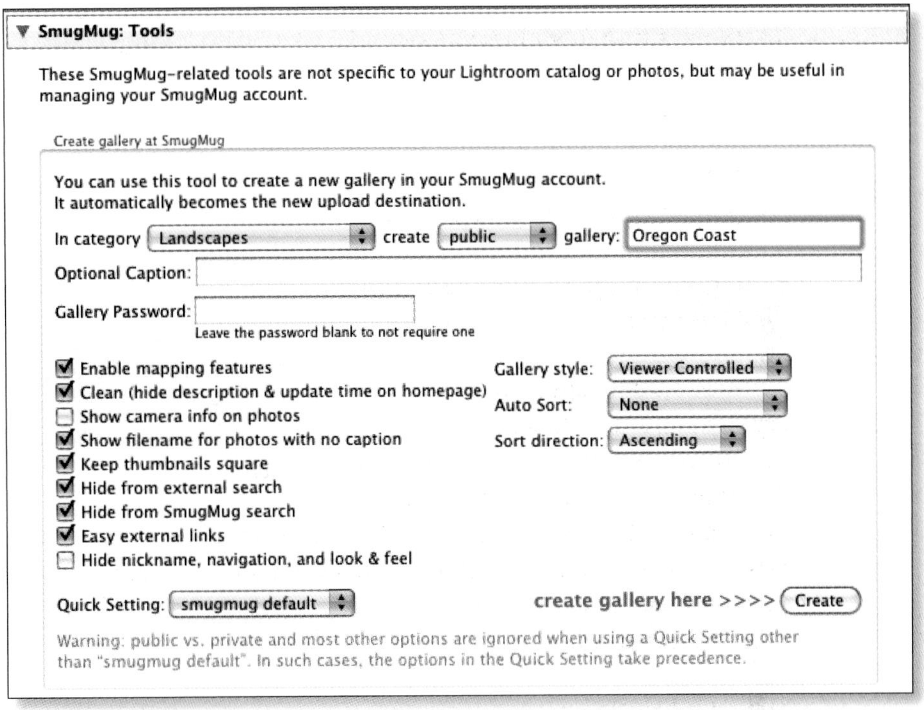

▼ SmugMug: Tools

These SmugMug-related tools are not specific to your Lightroom catalog or photos, but may be useful in managing your SmugMug account.

Create gallery at SmugMug

You can use this tool to create a new gallery in your SmugMug account. It automatically becomes the new upload destination.

In category [Landscapes ◆] create [public ◆] gallery: [Oregon Coast]

Optional Caption: [ ]

Gallery Password: [ ]
Leave the password blank to not require one

☑ Enable mapping features
☑ Clean (hide description & update time on homepage)
☐ Show camera info on photos
☑ Show filename for photos with no caption
☑ Keep thumbnails square
☑ Hide from external search
☑ Hide from SmugMug search
☑ Easy external links
☐ Hide nickname, navigation, and look & feel

Gallery style: [Viewer Controlled ◆]
Auto Sort: [None ◆]
Sort direction: [Ascending ◆]

Quick Setting: [smugmug default ◆]   create gallery here >>>> (Create)

Warning: public vs. private and most other options are ignored when using a Quick Setting other than "smugmug default". In such cases, the options in the Quick Setting take precedence.

Figure 9-13

SmugMug: Upload Destination: based on the categories and galleries you have set up in your SmugMug account, in this section you determine where the new photo(s) will be placed within your galleries.

SmugMug: Metadata Management: copies keywords, titles, captions, etc. from the Lightroom.

Develop Snapshots: creates a Lightroom Snapshot in the Develop module. This is handy if you're using Snapshots to produce multiple versions (which I generally don't recommend). Otherwise, leave these checkboxes off.

Twitter: as the text states, you can have the plug-in post a Twitter tweet when the upload is done. You'll have to authenticate on Twitter, then set basic options back in the plug-in. Also includes geotagging. Tweet, tweet… sweet!

9

SmugMug Export Plugin Info: shows info for the currently installed version of the plug-in, plus some links for more info.

By no means is SmugMug the only option for sharing (and selling!) your photos online. Whatever hosting service you prefer, when Web services can integrate this well with desktop software, the potential is significant.

This is just one example of how Lightroom plug-ins can empower and enable your workflow. If you're using a Web service or a print lab, another imaging program, or any other systems to which you want to send files from Lightroom for any reason, find out about the availability of Lightroom plug-ins. If you're like me, you'll be at least pleasantly surprised—and maybe excited—about all the new possibilities!

Using Lightroom with multiple computers

Lightroom 3 does not offer support for opening catalogs over a network. If you need to work with a catalog on multiple computers, your best option is to use a portable external drive and simply connect the drive to different computers as needed. In this case, to make things easier you'll probably want to include both the catalog file(s) and the image files on the same drive.

If you're moving the drive between Mac and Windows machines you'll need to use special procedures due to the difference in file systems support on the two platforms. Either format the drive as FAT32 prior to loading your files (which imposes limitations on file size that could affect the Lightroom catalog and previews package), or use specialized utility software (available for both Mac and Windows) that allows reading volumes formatted with non-native file systems.

When you're using multiple installations of Lightroom to work with catalogs on different machines, make sure all installations of Lightroom are running the same version.

MOVING PRESETS AND PROFILES BETWEEN MACHINES

You'll also need to be sure that your presets and profiles (especially camera and lens correction profiles) are the same on all affected machines. You can easily copy the contents of your Lightroom presets and profiles folder from one machine to another; the challenge may be keeping them in sync, for which there is no automated method.

The easiest way to do this is to right-click or Ctrl+click on a preset and choose Show in Finder or Show in Explorer to find the presets folder. You can then copy the preset(s) or entire folders to the same place on the other computer.

The default locations of camera and lens profiles are as follows:

Mac os x: Macintosh HD /Library/Application Support/Adobe/CameraRaw/CameraProfiles

Windows 2000/XP: C:\Documents and Settings\All Users\Application Data\Adobe\CameraRaw\CameraProfiles

Windows Vista and 7: C:\ProgramData\Adobe\CameraRaw\CameraProfiles

Custom camera profiles under Windows 7 are stored in c:\Users\username\AppData\Roaming\Adobe\CameraRaw\CameraProfiles. Custom lens profiles are in the same location, just under LensProfiles.

Working with multiple catalogs

For most photographers using Lightroom, working with one main catalog will be best. But there will inevitably be cases where using multiple catalogs can help.

Consider that through the import and synchronize processes, a single Lightroom catalog "knows" about certain photos and the work you've done to them; if you import pictures into one catalog, and later work on them in a different catalog, whatever you did in the previous catalog will not be visible in the latter catalog unless you sync data between the catalogs.

For this reason, I think using multiple catalogs should only be a consideration when you've really got a handle on the database concepts of Lightroom. From that foundation, you'll find all kinds of ways to use multiple catalogs to empower your workflow.

Import from catalog on network

Although Lightroom currently can't directly open a catalog over a network, you CAN import from a catalog on a network drive! If you're in a workgroup environment, with multiple people needing to access the same data, you can set up a system using publish services and import from catalog to make sure everybody's in sync.

About catalog locations and naming

Lightroom can open and work with a catalog in a location on any local drive. Also, you can use any name for a Lightroom catalog. (Obviously, you wouldn't want to have multiple catalogs with the same name… that's a recipe for disaster.)

9

Use meaningful names for catalogs

If you use multiple catalogs, name each one for its specific purpose and keep the names simple and functional. For example, if you're shooting a wedding, name the catalog for the client; if you're on a trip, name it for the trip, etc.

Use care when renaming existing catalogs

The catalog and the preview package have a symbiotic relationship; the locations of the preview files are stored in the catalog. If you rename the catalog (or its preview package) in Finder or Explorer, Lightroom won't be able to match them up and will need to rebuild the previews for all the photos in the catalog. Of course, this isn't always necessarily a problem, and in some cases may actually be desirable. You can rename any catalog file in Finder or Explorer, but plan to allow Lightroom to rebuild previews afterward.

Always know the name and location of the catalog you're using

Many photographers have had big problems unknowingly using more than one catalog! As you can imagine, this can result in significant confusion and frustration. The easiest way to ensure that you're in the catalog that you intend is to check the name of the catalog, which is located in the window title bar in Lightroom's standard window mode. You can also view the name and location of the current catalog in the Catalog Settings dialog box (accessed from the Lightroom menu on Mac os x or the Edit menu on Windows).

Setting the Default Catalog

The default catalog that loads when Lightroom launches is set in the main Lightroom Preferences. You can also hold the Option or Alt key when launching Lightroom to change the catalog that will be loaded.

EXPORT AS CATALOG

You can export one or multiple photos as a new catalog. To export individual images into a new catalog, they

Figure 9-14

must first be selected. Then, from the File menu, choose Export as Catalog. Also, if you press Option or Alt, you'll see the standard Import and Export buttons (bottom left, Library) change to Import Catalog and Export Catalog; see Figure 9–14.

In the resulting dialog box you must type a name for the new catalog. A folder will be created using that name. Inside the folder will be the catalog and preview package, using the same base name. In the Export as Catalog window you also have the following options:

Export selected photos only: when this is checked, only selected photos will be exported to the new catalog. Otherwise, all photos from the currently selected source will go into the new catalog. A text display above the checkboxes indicates this.

Export negative files: in this case, "negative" simply means the image files on disk. When this is checked, Lightroom will make copies of the files and the new catalog will link to those files, not the originals. If this is left unchecked, the new catalog will remain linked to the original files on disk.

Include available previews: when this option is checked, Lightroom will also copy the previews from the old preview package into the new one.

You can also export entire collections and folders as catalogs. Right-click or Ctrl+click the folder or collection and from the popup menu select "Export [folder or collection] as catalog". For the export, you will have the same options described above.

Export catalogs to share them

Exporting catalogs is a great way to share work between different people, multiple computers, etc.

IMPORT FROM CATALOG

The Import from Catalog command is an essential technique for transferring Lightroom edits between catalogs. In particular, the workflow described in the next section, for working with Lightroom while on the road, relies on the capability to work in one or more temporary catalogs, and then merge that data into your main catalog later. (There's currently no way to "synchronize" two Lightroom catalogs.)

Maybe most importantly, when you do an Import from Catalog, any folders, collections, virtual copies and filter settings in the imported catalog will also be transferred along with the photos. This means that you can work in any catalog for any purpose, using all of Lightroom's functions, and can later merge all that data into another catalog.

To import data from another catalog, either choose the command from under the File menu, or press the Option or Alt key and the regular Import button (bottom left, Library) changes to say Import Catalog.

When you initiate this process, the first dialog box displayed is asking you to choose a catalog. Navigate through the directory structure to select the catalog from which you'll be importing and click the Choose button. (Yes, you can import from a Lightroom 2 catalog into a Lightroom 3 catalog.)

The resulting dialog box is very similar to Lightroom's old Import screen. (It's expected that the Import from Catalog window will be updated to look more like the Lightroom 3 Import window in future releases.) You can resize/maximize this window to show more of its contents.

9

Just like a regular import, you have options for which files will be imported, how the files will be handled, and what to do about any existing files in the current catalog.

If necessary, choose from the folder list at the top left to check or uncheck folders for the import. With image thumbnails showing (click "Show Preview" at bottom left) you can also check or uncheck individual photos.

Below, under File Handling, choose whether to have Lightroom copy the files to a new location (if it's on another hard drive), or Add new photos to catalog without moving. If you're using the import from catalog process to merge files into your main catalog from another drive, you'll likely want to have Lightroom do the file copies for you, too.

In the last section, Changed Existing Photos, Lightroom will indicate photos that exist in both catalogs but have different settings applied. If none are found, this option is disabled. If Lightroom detects photos with the same names in both catalogs, but different versions, you have the choice of keeping the version in your open catalog or using the one that's coming in from the imported catalog. In the latter case, there's a check box to Preserve Old Settings as a Virtual Copy, which is a good idea if you're not certain which is the correct version.

When you're ready, click the Import button and the process begins. You'll be taken to the Library module and see the new photos as they are added to the catalog, just as with a regular import.

Merging multiple catalogs into one

If you've been working in multiple catalogs and want to combine them, you can use Import from Catalog to merge them all into one.

Duplicate collection names

One thing to watch out for when you're importing photos from one catalog into another: if collections with the same name exist in both catalog, the photos being imported will be merged into the collection with the same name in your main catalog. Depending on how you've set up collection and sets, this could produce an unintended outcome. If you have collections with the same name in both catalogs, and you *don't* want the photos to be merged in that collection, you'll need to change the name of the collection in one or the other catalog before doing the import. See Chapter 3 for more about collections.

Workflow: On the Road

When I am shooting on the road, I always start a new (temporary) Lightroom catalog on my laptop for each trip. During the trip, each shooting day I download/

import new photos into the trip catalog, convert to DNGs, add all my custom metadata (copyright, contact info, keywords etc.). I also apply my custom Develop defaults during import (most important is Camera Calibration). Immediately after importing, converting, keywording etc. I save the metadata out from Lightroom into the DNG files. This ensures that the edits stick, and using DNG avoids the need for sidecar files. The files are backed up immediately to an external hard drive or USB flash drive.

During the trip I will also do some quick edits using ratings to start identifying selects. Obvious rejects are sometimes deleted, but only if I am completely sure about it. While editing, I also save metadata after changes to ratings or keywords, so I come home with files that are already processed through my workflow.

At home, depending on the number of files involved, I either connect my laptop to my studio computer over the network, or connect my external backup drive directly to my main machine. In my main, ("master") Lightroom library I use "Import from Catalog" to copy the files to my main working drives and import them into the main catalog.

When this is done, I sync my master photo drive to a duplicate hard disk, then I delete everything from my laptop and traveling backup drive so they're ready for the next trip.

STEP-BY-STEP WORKFLOW FOR ROAD TRIPS

Following is the set of procedures I use when out shooting on location, and download using a laptop computer. Depending on your own computer hardware and software setup, you can follow this workflow verbatim, or use it as a basis for developing your own methods. In any event, the basic steps remain the same.

Overview of steps

1. On my laptop, I create a new, empty Lightroom catalog for each trip.

2. While on the road, I import all new captures into the trip catalog.

3. After returning home, I import the photos (and accumulated metadata) from the trip catalog into the main, "master" catalog.

4. After confirming the import and making backups, I delete all the image files and temporary trip catalog from the laptop, which is then ready for the next trip.

9

Before the trip

1. On the laptop, launch Lightroom and select File→New Catalog.

2. The dialog box that appears is asking you to give the catalog a name. This will also be the name given to the folder containing the catalog and preview files.

   Using your standard naming convention, give the catalog a name, as you would a folder. For example, Tucson_1005. Do not specify a file extension here.

3. Save the new catalog in a place you can easily find. Always using the same location, such as your Desktop or Pictures folder, makes this easier.

4. Clicking Save will create a new folder, with the specified name, on the desktop. Inside that folder will be the new Lightroom catalog with the same base file name.

During the trip

1. Always verify you're working in the correct catalog.

2. Import images from memory card(s) into the trip catalog using the same methods and settings you would at home.

3. As necessary, create subfolders for individual days or locations. Just be sure that all the image files/folders are put in the main trip folder.

4. Verify your imports, making sure that all the desired files have been imported/converted, etc.

5. You can process your files as you see fit during the trip. Remember to save out your metadata as you work (see Chapters 3 and 4 for more about this).

6. While on the road, make regular backups of your trip folder onto a portable hard drive or flash drive. You can do this with drag-and-drop or with dedicated software. Just be sure your backups all remain current during the trip.

7. Continually, after backing up your image files and confirming their integrity, reformat your card in the camera before each shooting session.

Back home after the trip

1. Be sure that the trip catalog on the laptop is fully up-to-date and backed up onto the portable hard drive. Also, whether you're using camera raw files or DNG, make sure all metadata has been saved to disk.

2. Prepare to transfer/import the files to your main computer in one of two ways:

    a. Connect the external, portable hard drive to the computer; or

    b. Connect your laptop to the other computer over a network.

    (Using the backup drive is usually faster and easier; just make sure it's identical to the working files on your laptop's internal drive.)

3. From within your main catalog, select File➔Import from Catalog. Navigate to the trip catalog folder, select the .lrcat file, and click Choose (or double-click it) to select it as the import source.

    In the Import from Catalog dialog box:

4. Enable Previews to see the image thumbnails (optional).

5. File Handling: Select "Copy new photos to new location and import" Since you're having Lightroom perform the copy for you, in Copy to: select "Choose"; navigate to your main photo drive and select the parent folder that the trip folders will be placed into.

6. Click "Import".

7. After the import has completed, locate the new folders/photos in the Folders panel. (If you had collections in the trip catalog, those will be imported as well.) Confirm the names and locations of the folders and the number of photos is consistent with the original trip files. If anything is out of place, you can rename folders and/or drag and drop to rearrange them (see Chapter 3) or perform additional imports.

8. Synchronize the backups for your main photo library.

9. Wipe all temporary catalogs, files and folders for the trip from your laptop and portable drive.

9

Appendix

From anywhere in Lightroom:

G	Library Grid
E	Library Loupe
D	Develop Loupe
R	Develop Crop
Tab	Hide/show side panels
Shift+Tab	Hide/show all panels
Right-click or Ctrl+click	Open contextual menu
T	Hide/show Toolbar
L	Cycle Lights Out
Numbers 1-5	Apply star rating
X	Apply reject flag
B	Add to/remove from Target Collection
⌘+B or Ctrl+B	Go to Target Collection
Delete	Remove photo or virtual copy
Return or Enter	Finish typing into a text field
Esc	Close a text field, import screen color picker, etc. without saving
⌘+Z or Ctrl+Z	Undo
⌘+Option+Left Arrow or Ctrl+Alt+Left Arrow	Go back
⌘+Option+Right Arrow or Ctrl+Alt+Right Arrow	Go forward
⌘+Shift+I or Ctrl+Shift+I	Import
⌘+Shift+E or Ctrl+Shift+E	Export
⌘+' or Ctrl+'	Create virtual copy
⌘+= or Ctrl+=	Zoom in
⌘+- or Ctrl+-	Zoom out
⌘+[or Ctrl+[	Rotate left
⌘+] or Ctrl+]	Rotate right
⌘+E or Ctrl+E	Edit selected photo in Photoshop (or other primary external editor)
⌘+R or Ctrl+R	Show selected file(s) in Finder or Explorer

⌘+Shift+S or Ctrl+Shift+S	Synchronize selected photos
V	Apply Black & White color treatment
⌘+, or Ctrl+,	Open Lightroom Preferences

In Library:

Arrows	Move between photos
Shift+Arrows	Select contiguous photos
⌘+A or Ctrl+A	Select All
⌘+D or Ctrl+D	Select None
⌘+G or Ctrl+G	Stack selected photos
⌘+Shift+G or Ctrl+Shift+G	Unstack selected photos
C	Compare two images
N	Compare multiple images
\	Hide/show Filter Bar
⌘+L or Ctrl+L	Enable/disable filters
⌘+N or Ctrl+N	New collection
⌘+Shift+N or Ctrl+Shift+N	New folder

In Develop:

W	White balance selector
A	Constrain aspect ratio
Q	Spot Removal
M	Graduated filter
K	Local adjustment brush
[	Smaller brush
]	Larger brush
Option or Alt	Erase from brush mask
H	Hide/show tool overlay
Y	Show Before/After
\	Toggle Before/After in main preview

FROM LIGHTROOM® 3: STREAMLINING YOUR DIGITAL PHOTOGRAPHY PROCESS BY NAT COALSON